AMERICAN LITERARY HUMOR DURING THE GREAT DEPRESSION

AMERICAN LITERARY HUMOR DURING THE GREAT DEPRESSION

Robert A. Gates

Contributions to the Study of American Literature, Number 5

Greenwood Press
Westport, Connecticut • London

Library of Congress Cataloging-in-Publication Data

Gates, Robert Allan.
   American literary humor during the Great Depression / Robert A.
Gates.
      p.   cm.—(Contributions to the study of American literature,
   ISSN 1092–6356 ; no. 5)
   Includes bibliographical references (p.   ) and index.
   ISBN 0–313–31036–X (alk. paper)
   1. American literature—20th century—History and criticism.
   2. American wit and humor—History and criticism.   3. Depressions in
   literature.   I. Title.   II. Series.
   PS438.G37   1999
   817′.5209358—dc21   99–20129

British Library Cataloguing in Publication Data is available.

Library of Congress Catalog Card Number: 99–20129
ISBN: 0–313–31036–X
ISSN: 1092–6356

First published in 1999

Greenwood Press, 88 Post Road West, Westport, CT 06881
An imprint of Greenwood Publishing Group, Inc.
www.greenwood.com

Printed in the United States of America

The paper used in this book complies with the
Permanent Paper Standard issued by the National
Information Standards Organization (Z39.48–1984).

10 9 8 7 6 5 4 3 2 1

*For my parents
and all those who lived
through the Great Depression*

Contents

Preface

Probably no other event of modern history, except that of war, has been so closely documented or discussed as the Great Depression. Not only a period of great economic upheaval, the Depression transformed and shaped the destinies of countless millions of people worldwide, created tyrants and heroes, and forever changed our perception of what modern government should be. It is easy for the contemporary student of American history to glibly dismiss the events of tragic human proportions while pursuing the statistical facts of that decade. And the facts do, indeed, speak for themselves: 25 percent of America's labor force unemployed, close to two hundred thousand children abandoned and homeless, and over seven hundred thousand vagrants "riding the rails" in search of a job or a home. But while pursuing these facts, while calculating and statistically arranging them into neat comprehensible columns that are easily digested, we lose sight of the indelible human tragedy that was occurring and shaping forever our views of ourselves as Americans and as human beings.

When President-elect Roosevelt delivered his famous inaugural address at the onset of the 1930s and warned the nation that it had nothing to fear but fear itself, he fully realized the enormity of the task of revitalizing the American economy. The struggle was only half financial. Far more ominous was a creeping paralysis of will and spirit that had sapped the American people of their belief in themselves as decent, hardworking individuals. A population that had been raised in the stern traditions of free enterprise and rugged individualism, so popular during the twenties, now found itself in the thirties at a loss to explain its tragic surroundings and personal failures. Men and women, who had worked hard and saved for the future of their children, awoke to a New World, where their property and possessions were suddenly gone and no one was to blame for it but themselves, or so they thought.

In the midst of the growing national dilemma, the American writer found himself in something of a quandary. During the twenties, novelists and poets had been content to adopt an iconoclastic attitude toward the nation and its institutions. In an age of general prosperity, it was acceptable to cast stones at some of the golden idols. If Sinclair Lewis attacked the shallow business practices of realtors in *Babbitt* or e. e. cummings found much to criticize about society in general in "pity this busy monster, mamunkind," it ruffled few feathers in a society that was more intent on stock prices than social mores. But by the thirties, things had drastically changed for the American writer. Popular writers of the twenties, such as Hemingway and Fitzgerald, found themselves gradually eclipsed by a new generation of literati that espoused proletarian ideals of socialist reform and economic change. Albeit the new order relied heavily on the sarcasm and criticism of the previous decade of writers, and the targets of writers such as Louis Adamic and Howard Fast were not too distinguishable from those who had come before them, but what did change was the general tone of the works, which became increasingly more strident and even aggressive in their attempts to achieve the higher ideals of social manipulation. A lot was lost in the process.

Significance became the catchword for the writer of the thirties, and at times it fell out of step with the objectives of the Roosevelt administration itself. For many writers, the "fear" that Roosevelt was attempting to dissolve was something rather to be maintained, for without it would grow a complaisance toward and acceptance of an insufficient and imperfect world. Proletarian literature rarely concluded with the strikers triumphant and management defeated. The "cause," as it was seen, was more important than a quick victory; the struggle was a constant against overwhelming odds. Thus the writer of the thirties found himself adopting a tone and establishing themes that had propelled the Romantic writers of a century earlier.

Such themes had long since been popular in both American and European literature. In the midst of a cruel and insensitive world generally addicted to the luxuries of modern technology and Western civilization, the protagonist stood alone, at home more with the untamed and unexplored world of nature and the primitive than the world of modern man. In this environment, the Romantic hero was essentially a doomed man, unable to achieve his objectives. The battle may rage on interminably, but the forces of evil, the power of wealth and position remained intact. Thus we find the strains of *Werther* reverberating throughout the lines in *Of Mice and Men*.

Yet despite its potential and proven formula for success, much of Depression literature has faded into oblivion. To this day, it remains largely untouched in anthologies of American literature. During the turbulent years of McCarthyism, the "profound sentiments" of Depression writers were labeled the vituperation of "hacks" bent upon a political agenda, largely communist and definitely subversive. In the years that followed, the intense, almost humorless, themes of much Depression literature did little to perpetuate it. In short, it became boring and dated, largely hysterical, and out of touch with a resilient America.

Literary humor of the same decade is a different matter. Although its concerns and sometimes its themes sprang from the same sources that fed Depression literature in general, it rarely proselytized, intending instead to approach the issues obliquely and often with more effect. The terrific growth of humor during the thirties has been well documented. Comedians such as W. C. Fields, Burns and Allen, Jack Benny, and the Marx Brothers were among the greats that entertained thousands on the radio and in the cinema. Their popularity was largely based on humor's unique ability to allow the audience a means by which it could defuse the anxieties plaguing it. Literary humor was especially prone to do this because it did not rely on the alternative avenue of escapism frequently found on the screen or on the radio. The literary humorist had to address his audience more on a one-to-one basis that precluded disingenuousness and show. The message always had to be clear and direct because it had to be truthful and from the heart.

The themes of the humorists of the thirties were as varied as the events of that decade, and in the writings of Robert Benchley, Ogden Nash, E. B. White, James Thurber, Damon Runyon, and many others, the major social concerns underline the comic relief. Even the sanctuary of the Algonquin Club was not sufficient insulation against the cold chill of the Depression, and the scalding prose of Dorothy Parker is tempered by Depression realities. Many of the humorists' observations focus directly on the times, but frequently, too, they proved to be remarkably prophetic of the times to come and foreshadowings of the concerns of future generations. Some of Benchley's perceptive comments on Japanese-American attitudes predate similar issues in any modern American newspaper of the 1990s. In fact, there are few issues of the 1930s that have not again surfaced as major concerns for the 1990s. Once again the American writer or, specifically, the

American humorist finds himself or herself doing battle with the issues of a former generation. Homelessness, unemployment, world crises, a growing national debt, an increasing separation between the nation's poor and rich, and the role of government in attempting to solve these and other issues have again resurfaced to confront the contemporary American writer. As is often the case, the writer need only turn to the past to find the answer for the future, and the answer, as was true in the past, often lies with the resilience of humor.

AMERICAN LITERARY HUMOR
DURING THE
GREAT DEPRESSION

CHAPTER 1

The Crisis

Despite the financial emergency created by the stock market collapse in 1929, the full effects of the Depression would not be felt until well into the 1930s. By this time, close to a third of the nation had undergone the devastating psychological dilemma of long-term unemployment. If the crisis at hand had been limited only to an economist's drawing board, the recovery would have been a lot sooner. Even as the newly elected Roosevelt administration assumed office, the economy had begun to show signs of recovery. But the mood of the nation had not, and fear and concern for the future of the nation still gripped at the hearts and minds of most Americans. It was this "fear" that Roosevelt immediately addressed in his inaugural speech when he warned us that it, more than anything else, was at the center of America's paralysis of soul and spirit.

For Roosevelt, the solution lay in a myriad of programs and agencies, such as the WPA, whose sole intent was to restore in part or in full a sense of dignity and self-worth among those who had suffered most by the Depression—the long-term unemployed. The government, along with many in the business sector who had hoisted up high the blue eagle of the National Recovery Act, attempted to "do our part" in turning about the prevailing doldrums of psychological despair. But the success or failure of these programs can only be measured in the long run or, as the cliché goes, according to the test of time. Admirable as the Recovery Act was, many historians would later claim that the Depression was killed only by the onset of World War II and the full employment it brought. In retrospect, one may well wonder if such assumptions are too glib, too closely affiliated with economic statistics and political ideologies. For many, the Depression did not end with the coming of the Roosevelt administration or, for that matter, World War II. For many who lived through those years and are still alive, the Depression has never ended. The psychological scars went too deep to easily heal over and be forgotten in prosperous times.

An excellent study about the psychological effects of the Great Depression has noted that a clearly defined pattern of behavior set in gradually among the unemployed both in the United States and abroad as the crisis took on global proportions. Studies made in the 1930s revealed that the unemployed gradually evolved through various psychological stages as they readjusted to their inability to find work. During the first two stages, labeled *momentum stability* and *unstable equilibrium*, the unemployed continued to search for work, sometimes at a feverish pace, with some concern but remaining strong in their conviction that work would be found eventually. Then followed the stages of *disorganization* and *experimental readjustment*, where the unemployed person became increasingly disenchanted by his inability to find work, suffered from a loss of self-esteem, and began to neglect his health and appearance. In the last stage, *permanent readjustment*, the desire to look for work ceased; the unemployed withdrew from society in general, stopped looking ahead or making plans, and accepted unemployment as natural and inevitable. By the mid-1930s, millions of Americans had bottomed out on the last stage and could not foresee a time when their lives would change for the better. Nor did the coming of prosperity revive the former spirit or rekindle a feeling of self-worth. Unemployment was not merely a financial embarrassment; for many it was a state of mind. As one person observed at the time: "You fell into the habit of slouching, of putting your hands into your pockets and keeping them there; of glancing at people furtively, ashamed of your secret, until you fancied that everybody eyed you with suspicion" (Shannon, 110–11). Social workers in American employment agencies often noted in their reports the general indifference, lethargy, submission, and apathy of the long-term unemployed.

The road to recovery was definitely arduous, probably (in light of the psychological scars) impossible. But humor, for many, offered an alternative, if not a temporary cure, for the "creeping paralysis" of will. While Roosevelt strove to restructure America's economic platform, writers such as Benchley, Parker, Thurber, and White busied themselves with the restructuring of America's psychological platform, and their tool was humor. Many presented in their poems, plays, and essays a platform not too different from that of the Roosevelt administration. Robert Benchley was one who even captured the President-elect's confidence of tone.

Benchley already had a well-established reputation in humor at the time of the stock market crash. He had been composing humorous pieces since his collegiate days at Harvard, had published numerous sketches in magazines, and had created his famous "poor boob" persona for a series of home-life pieces published in *Collier's*. By 1930, he had published three major collections of humorous essays, *Of All Things* (1921), *Love Conquers All* (1922), and *The Early Worm* (1927). All three were generally collections of numerous humorous essays he had previously published in various magazines. By the midthirties, he devoted more of his time and talents to the more financially lucrative movie industry, only occasionally taking up the pen for a humorous sketch of the changing times, a trend not uncommon for most writers during those financially difficult times.

Ironically, the "poor boob" persona created in the twenties was more in step with the following decade than the one for which it was intended. Benchley viewed the Depression as a series of deterministic events over which the common man, or Roosevelt's forgotten man, had little control. Buffeted and knocked about by economic forces and governmental policies that are difficult to understand, Benchley's poor boob can do little else than accept his fate and hope for the best in times to come. But, for Benchley, within this powerlessness lies the intrinsic strength of the American people and especially the common, forgotten man. Unable to shape his destiny, he nevertheless exerts a control over it via his passivity and compliance. In his flexibility lies his strength to change and adapt and become a permanent fixture in the American panorama. Thus, weakness becomes power, and ignorance in turn wisdom. Benchley's poor boob would therefore become the quintessential exponent of a decade where traditional values and conceptions of normalcy would be radically altered.

In "How I Learned Tennis" (*From Bed to Worse*), Benchley points out that there is more than one way to master the game of tennis. Others may practice difficult and complicated techniques, but, for Benchley, success can be as easily achieved by exhibiting one's incompetence on the court. In so doing, any opponent, no matter how skilled at the game, is rendered helpless. "He sometimes would even give me the game by default and retire to the side-lines in hysteria." Benchley concludes, "So I cultivated this knack of mine, and to it I lay what success I have had in the game to date. Naturally, I prefer singles to doubles, as a partner does not always think it so funny" (209).

In another essay from the same source, Benchley notes that people who are best suited to weather crises are generally oblivious to the cataclysms and turmoil going on around them. In "Johnny-on-the-Spot," he points out how it is impossible to pick up a photograph of any major event in the history of modern man and not find somewhere amidst the general turmoil and chaos, an individual, usually wearing a bowler hat, who is either reading a paper or smiling into the face of the camera as though nothing at all is going on around him.

> Revolutionary disturbances are particularly subject to this blasé treatment on the part of bystanders. Photographs which have come up from Cuba lately, and even those of the wildest days in Russia during the Rein of Terror—photographs taken at the risk of the lives of the photographers themselves—all show, somewhere in their composition, an area of complete calm in which at least one man is looking at his watch or picking his teeth. (256)

Thus, concludes Benchley, such behavior leads to a "calm, well-ordered existence, with practically no nerve strain" (257). As long as one does not get hit by a stray bullet and takes care of his kidneys, he should live to a ripe old age. "Dynasties may fall, cities may collapse, and the world be brought down about our ears, but, unless something hits us squarely in the back, we are sitting pretty" (259). Thus, again does power spring from helplessness or more likely in the above case, ignorance.

Two years later in 1936, Benchley would again comment on the general mental paralysis caused by the Depression and offer a solution in his essay "Lucky World" from *My Ten Years in a Quandary*. Characteristically upbeat, he notes that things could be a lot worse in the world. The rising tide of fascism in Europe and the advances made by the Japanese Empire in the Pacific must have given Benchley pause to contemplate the comparative prosperity and security most Americans enjoyed despite the economic reversals of the last eight years. Given the accident-prone nature of most of mankind, it is a miracle, he ponders, that most people are able to survive as long as they do. Looking out onto a busy Manhattan street at noontime, he wonders how most of the cars below are successfully navigated throughout the city's busy corridors without incident: "The next time you are up in a tall building looking for a place to jump from, just take a peek over at a couple of busy traffic intersections below. Then figure out how many of those drivers should be at large on the street at all, much less at the wheel of an automobile. Then make your jump" (142). Nor is this the only instance of man's instinctive ability to stay put on the earth: "Look at the people in the Congress, or the Chamber of Deputies," Benchley concludes, "the only logical ending to it all is the world is headed for *dementia praecox*. . . . yet automobiles dodge each other as if by magic . . . and only occasionally does hell break loose entirely. It's a pretty lucky old world we live in, when you consider the possibilities" (144).

Benchley's sentiments were not by any means unique among the literary humorists of the Depression. Ogden Nash would pen a bittersweet poem similar in content to Benchley's "Lucky World" in which a man on the eve of his 28th birthday celebrates his good fortune to be "young and healthy and alive" and for not having experienced numerous disasters such as being "run over by the Lexington Avenue Express or gored by runaway steers" or, for that matter:

> For never having written a best-seller, only to be
>   wounded by the critics;
> For never having gotten impeached for making millions
>   in dirty politics;
> For never having made any enemies by getting ahead too
>   speedily;
> For not finding the world at my feet while still as
>   young as Lindbergh or Gertrude Ederle;
> For not having tried to impress my girl but being
>   naturaler with her and naturaler;
> So that now instead of having to marry and all that I
>   can continue to be a careless baturaler; (Smith and Eberstadt, 6–7)

All things considered, he concludes, he, too, is quite lucky.

But in "Kindly Unhitch That Star, Buddy," Nash also presents the limitations of optimism and self-worth which all too often are created at the expense of the feelings of others and to the benefit of one's own vanity:

> In short, the world is filled with people trying to
>   achieve success,
> And half of them think they'll get it by saying No and
>   half of them by saying Yes,
> And if all the ones who say No said Yes, and vice
>   versa, such is the fate of humanity that ninety-
>   nine percent of them still wouldn't be any better
>   off than they were before,
> Which perhaps is just as well because if everybody was
>   a success nobody could be contemptuous of anybody
>   else and everybody would start in all over again

trying to be a bigger success than everybody else
so they would have somebody to be contemptuous of
and so on forevermore,
Because when people start hitching their wagons to a
    star,
That's the way they are. (71)

The limitations of optimism created a dilemma for most of the humorists of the Depression, primarily because they were seen as the end result of deterministic forces. Evil, whether in the form of natural catastrophes such as the terrible dust storms in the midwest or man-created wars and civil strife, had an inviolate endurance. Clarence Day's "The Rabbits Conquer Fear" in *After All* questions the validity of blind optimism. A group of rabbits that have recently learned to read English find a popular book entitled *Inspirational Talks* which inspires them to adopt the credo that fear is one's greatest enemy. In a parody of President Roosevelt's inaugural address, a preacher rabbit exhorts his audience to ignore fear because it alone is the "Ghost that knocks the Cup of Success from your lips, just when you are about to drink. It is Fear that unstrings your nerves, and pours its Senile Impotence into your heart. If you are afraid of anything," he concludes his harangue, "walk right up to it!" A young, easily impressionable rabbit queries if it is safe even to walk up to a very large dog. "The rabbit preacher stood as tall as he could stretch, and his round pink eyes glowed. 'Yes!' he shouted." A member of the older generation pipes in at this moment to conclude that nothing is bad when you get to know it: "I have seen a lot of troubles in my day . . . and most of them never happened" (45–47). Embolden by such optimistic thinking, the young rabbit is last seen blithely heading down the road toward a dog kennel, repeating over and over, "Drag the Dreaded Thing out into the Light" (48). Needless to say, we know where his blind optimism will lead him.

If political ideologies were creating roadblocks on the road to recovery for some writers, for others, such as Dorothy Parker, the problem lay more in the false sentimentality that permeated much of the decade and was primarily apparent in the movies of the day. In one of her stories, "Sentiment," from *Here Lies*, a passionate and overly sentimental girl who has recently broken up with her boyfriend rides aimlessly in the backseat of a taxi through the streets of New York City. Her intention is to run away from her problems, but she cannot, simply because her sentimental side prevents her from doing so. She repeatedly imagines seeing her former lover on each sidewalk she passes, at each intersection, and each time the taxi makes a turn. Her increasingly sentimental thoughts of the past drive her further and further into depression. She soon realizes that it was just this very aspect of her personality that drove her lover away: "This is the sort of thing he hated so in me. I know what he would say. 'Oh, for heaven's sake!' he would say. 'Can't you stop that fool sentimentalizing? Why do you have to do it? Why do you *want* to do it?' " (333). When her taxi takes a sudden turn down one block, she is thrown into a paroxysm of fear, certain she is on the street where they used to live. She buries herself deep into the upholstery of the backseat and keeps her eyes closed, but she is plagued by the memory of the shops and buildings along the way where they had spent so much time together: "Though I had no eyes, my heart would tell me this street, out of all streets. I know it as I know my hands, as I know my face. Oh, why can't I be let to die as we pass through?" (337). But her heart has lied to her and her mind has deceived her, for at the end of the ordeal she discovers the truth—it was the wrong street after all.

Sentiment was not, however, without its supporters among a number of Depression humorists, principally Alexander Woollcott and Damon Runyon. For Woollcott, sentiment offered the average American a sense of belonging to a past that was more appealing and a definitely more stable universe governed by a caring God. In a charming little story from his 1934 work *While Rome Burns* entitled "Reunion in Paris," he describes how a close friend, Anne Parrish, while visiting Paris one summer, chanced to find in one of the dozens of bookstalls along the Seine a little English book for children that she had often read as a child. Indeed, it not only turns out to be the same edition but the actual book she owned when she was growing up in Colorado many years ago. Woollcott confesses that when he first heard the story he "walked down the street in quite a glow, for all the world as if I had just found a tidy sum on the pavement" (61). What particularly inspires Woollcott is the hidden significance of the tale, namely, that it carries with it "the reassuring intimation that this is, after all, an ordered universe, that there is, after all, a design to our existence" (61).

For Damon Runyon's characters, chance and sentiment are equally important. In one short story, "Tobias the Terrible" in *Money from Home*, a milquetoast Tobias Tweeney from Erasmus, Pennsylvania, gets the girl of his dreams by steadfastly holding onto his sentimental convictions while making the most of his fate. Befriended by a streetwise denizen of the New York night scene who takes pity on him after overhearing him crying to himself in Mindy's restaurant on Broadway, Tobias soon finds himself in the company of a group of ne'er-do-wells who, during a police raid, hastily hide their guns on him. When the police arrest Tobias for having concealed weapons, he makes the headlines as Tobias the Terrible and finally attracts the eye of his girl. Although his case is dismissed because the judge can clearly discern that Tobias is no criminal, the publicity surrounding the trial so pleases Tobias's girlfriend that she falls hopelessly in love with him because he now has finally become a "big gunman" who can go around "talking up to politicians and policemen, and maybe looking picturesque and romantic like Edward G. Robinson, or James Cagney or even George Raft" (330). He returns to his hometown, a hero, and is elected constable because a fellow with such a reputation is bound to keep wrongdoers away from Erasmus. By holding on to his sentiments, Tobias gets more than he had ever dreamed of originally.

Optimism, however, has its limitations for most of the Depression humorists, including Runyon. In another story, "The Lemon Drop Kid," a cheap hustler stumbles onto some good fortune but is unable to appreciate it because his sweetheart dies at the end. We last see him laughing at his fate with a "laughter" the story's narrator describes as being a terrifying, bittersweet, hollow type of laughter.

This "laughter of despair" became a trademark for many of the Depression writers, but one in particular dominated the field—Donald Robert Perry Marquis, or as he was more commonly known, Don Marquis, the creator of Archy the literary cockroach and Mehitabel the cat.

Don Marquis was as much a chronicler of the twenties as he was of the thirties. A newspaperman by trade and a humorist by inclination, during the twenties he created the characters of Archy, a spunky cockroach, and Mehitabel, a soporific but resilient cat, whose lives and times would evolve into a series of brilliantly perceptive and iconoclastic poems penned by Marquis well into the thirties. The dual tone of optimism and defeat found throughout these poems was, in many respects, a grim parody of his own troubled life, but, in so being, also became a reflection of the troubled thirties as well. A heavy drinker and a chain smoker, success and fame always eluded Marquis, despite the friendly criticism and applause much of his work received during his lifetime. At the time of his death, his reputation as a writer in no way rivaled those of equally gifted writers such as Benchley and Thurber. After his death in 1937, Marquis's reputation was boosted in part by an anthology of his works compiled by his close friend and fellow humorist, Christopher Morley. During the 1950s, E. B. White and Bernard DeVoto wrote favorably of his work, and in 1962, Edward Anthony published a lengthy biography, *O Rare Don Marquis*. Despite these and other accolades, Marquis still remains largely unknown to the majority of the American reading public, fulfilling Marquis's own prediction that he would be remembered at best as the creator of "a cockroach character."

Part of the reason for Marquis's ambivalent reputation stems from the fact that much of his work on his masterpieces about Archy and Mehitabel is and was, freely by his own admission, hack work. Throughout much of his creative years, Marquis was plagued by severe financial difficulties largely brought on by his selfless care of two indigent and often belligerent sisters. Besides his publications, he tried to garner more income by working for the great movie houses in Hollywood but found the task less than gratifying and often demeaning. A series of personal problems began with the death of his son, Robert, in 1921, at the age of five. His first wife, Reina, died suddenly two years later. Then ten years following the death of his son, his daughter Barbara died at the age of thirteen. The combination of financial stress and personal tragedy increasingly influenced his poems about Archy and Mehitabel until their fatalism and depressive moods would become one with their creator's own worldview. The irony lay in the fact that while working through this catharsis, Marquis had simultaneously laid the foundation for one of the most representative pieces of Depression literary humor, culminating in his last two collections on the famous duo: *archys life of mehitabel* (1933) and *archy does his part* (1935).

Hope and despair run concomitantly throughout these two anthologies. At the beginning of *archys life of mehitabel* (the punctuation and capitals characteristically left out because Archy's tiny legs couldn't reach the keys on the typewriter), Archy points out that Mehitabel is to be the subject of his "literary work of some importance," in that she is an astonishing resilient cat who, despite the fact that she has seen better days and has "drunk cream at fourteen / cents the half pint / in her time and now she / is thankful for a / stray fish head from a / garbage cart" she, nevertheless, remains "cheerful under it all toujours / gai is ever her word / toujours gai kiddo . . . wotto hell / luck may change" (170). Like her creator, Mehitabel is determined not to accept her present state as final. Keep up the spirit and the battle is half won is her motto, in accord with the tone of much of the Depression literature, humorous or serious, at the time.

In the later, more grim, *archy does his part*, her condition has significantly worsened, but she has learned to live with adversity, accepting a kernel of satisfaction out of the suffering. The times have not improved for Mehitabel. In fact they have gotten a lot worse, as they had for Don Marquis and thousands of others by 1935. Good times were not immediately forthcoming, and one had to learn to live and find pleasure with a lot less: "good times and bad times / recoveries and depressions / wotthehell do i care / as somethings doing / when i lived on salmon / and oysters stewed in cream / i wasnt always happy / when i dug my scoffins / out of frozen garbage heaps / i wasnt always sad / economic problems / never tell the story / as far as im concerned" (445).

The optimism of Mehitabel offers little consolation for her sidekick, Archy, who, like many of his contemporaries, including his creator, finds the paralysis of will so pervasive during the thirties that even the simplest of tasks that were taken for granted during prosperous times have now become insurmountable. Even the alcoholics in Pennsylvania Station are unable to perform their prime duty—falling down! The observant cockroach laments one derelict's persistent failure despite an obvious perseverance to succeed, a perseverance hindered by an escalator: "he could not fall down as / fast as it / carried him up again but / he was game he kept on / trying he was / stubborn about it / evidently it was part of / his tradition habit and / training always to fall down / stairs when intoxicated and / he did not intend to / be defeated this time i / watched him for an hour / and moved sadly away" (230). For Don Marquis, the world of the Depression has shifted reality and locked it into a new status quo whereby the formerly successful find it as hard to rise as the successful bum finds it to fall. Determination is not enough in this scenario: the moving escalator, fate or bad luck, or whatever it is, keeps getting in the way, thwarting our best intentions.

In a world where the best intentions of men or cockroaches are constantly facing brick walls, the avenues of escape or reform are few. Archy may be proud of the fact that he and his kind have been on the earth for millions of years and have weathered many a storm and reversal of fortune, but it seems to him that the best way out of the current mess is to kill oneself or, as he says, "end it all." Reincarnation, he feels, might offer some chance for a new start and a more promising future. But even this agenda presents obstacles. After all, if bums cannot fall down the elevator stairs at Penn Station, can a cockroach devise an effective means of suicide? He presents his dilemma to his boss: "well boss you would / be surprised to find / out how hard it is for a / cockroach to commit suicide unless / you have been one / and tried it of course i / could let mehitabel the / cat damage me and die that / way but all my finer sensibilities / revolt at the idea i jumped out / the fourth story window and / a wind caught me and blew / me into the eighth story i / tried to hang myself with a / thread and i am so light i / just swung back and forth and / didnt even choke myself shooting / is out of the question and poison / is not within / my reach i might drown myself / in the ink well but if / you ever got a mouthful of it you / would know it was a / thing no refined person could go / on with boss i am going to / end it all before long and i / want to go easy have you / any suggestion yours / for transmigration" (251–52).

In a later poem, Archy begins to reevaluate his condition. Suicide may not be the best way out of his problems because if reincarnation exists, he will merely find himself again born into a world of chaos and ever worsening paralysis and despair. In the end, he comes to the conclusion that the only way things are going to change for the better on earth is for there to be a complete change in the dominant species. As long as the human race remains, war and disease, famine and pestilence, political chaos and economic upheavals will remain a part of life. In *archy does his part*, he overhears the beginnings of an underground revolution directed against the human race by the insects of the world in "what the ants are saying," Marquis's final and darkest entry:

> men talk of money and industry
> of hard times and recoveries
> of finance and economies
> but the ants wait and the scorpions wait
> for while men talk they are making deserts all the time
> getting the world ready for the conquering ant
> drought and erosion and desert
> because men cannot learn (477)

For Marquis, man's incapacity to peacefully coexist with his surroundings prevents any chance for reform or recovery. The specter of greed that now prostrates the world on the eve of a second great war is, for him, also the catalyst of the Great Depression. Recovery becomes impossible and hopelessly optimistic.

Archy's prophetic insight into this dilemma called "man" would resound well into the twentieth century until his sentiments now have become the platform upon which preaches many a modern-day Jeremiah of ecological doom. Between the lines can be seen the first flowering of the seeds of concern now echoed by such groups as Greenpeace. One may well ask if Archy was right. Will man ever change intrinsically? Is all "reform" merely cosmetic?

For Marquis and many of the other humorists of the thirties, the problems of the Depression grew increasingly transcendent by the end of the decade. The reason for this lay in the growing world crisis of war or impending war. Rumblings in fascist Germany and Spain and the advances of Japanese marines in China were increasingly becoming the staples of the daily news. No sooner had the American people reasonably survived the stormy seas of economic chaos of the early thirties, than they found their eyes affixed on another menacing wave of international Armageddon.

For one humorist, E. B. White, the growing complexity of the times was reason enough to seek out an alternative form of existence. By 1938, White, who had spent a good part of his creative years in or around New York City writing for *The New Yorker*, found the allure of a farm in Maine too great to be ignored. His move, however, was not so much a retreat as it was an attempt to sort out the complexities of his own personal life, as well as those of the world. A collection of essays and philosophical observations, both humorous and somber, would result from this move; they appeared as a collection in *One Man's Meat* in 1941.

White, like Marquis, viewed the Depression as more of a psychological than economic crisis. As such, his writings, like those of Marquis, tend to reflect more on reform from within man's soul than within the institutions he creates. Many of White's essays in *The New Yorker* during the thirties often revolve around two major areas of concern: man's isolated self and the mental paralysis created by fear.

In an essay titled "Fitting In," White attacks the notion that man is capable of easily adapting to any environment no matter how extraordinary it may be. In a thinly veiled attack on the social philosophers of his day, White presents his argument along the lines of modern architecture which steadfastly refuses to conform to the form and function of the human race. "Must the next generation," he asks, "be as structurally inefficient, as architecturally inappropriate, as the present?" Cannot the environment be created to suit the man than the other way around? Architecture is not the only issue here. White's concern lies more with man's way of envisioning reform as something that can be neatly packaged and legislated and forced upon whole generations, present and future. How lasting can the reform be if man himself has not changed? So he concludes: "It often seems to us that the only people who really fit into the modern picture are certain department-store dummies and occasionally a pattern figure in a fashion magazine. The rest of us definitely don't belong" (Dale, 167).

At the onset of the Depression, White's pessimism focused more than once on the fundamental psychological impasse created by fear. In one such essay from *The New Yorker* titled "Hunger," a man comments on his friend's startling loss of weight only to find out that fear, not illness, has a grip on his friend's stomach—the fear of all food. He refuses a cup of coffee after reading an article about how the beans are processed with rancid oil. Orange marmalade contains traces of bilgewater, and pork has worms. What formerly was mere curiosity has now turned into phobia:

> At meals I began to see not the food that was actually before me—I'd
> see it in its earlier stages: oysters lying at the mouths of typhoid rivers,

oranges impregnated by the citrus fly, gin made from hospital alcohol, watercress in drainage ditches, bottled cherries dipped in aniline dyes, marshmallows made of rotten eggs, parsley vines covered with green caterpillars, grapes sprayed with arsenate of lead. I used to spend hours in my kitchenette testing cans of foodstuffs to see if the cans sat flat. If a can doesn't sit flat, it has an air bubble in it, and its contents kill you after a few hours of agony. (Dale, 107)

At the end of his narration, he faints from exhaustion brought on by starvation. When his listener offers him at least a glass of water for revival, he pushes it away. The reservoirs are too low, and it's undrinkable!

Fear as the single most dominant trait of Americans during the Great Depression is repeated again and again in White's essays in *The New Yorker*. "Crossing the Street" and "Visiting Motorists" are two good examples. In the former, published in 1932, White sees fear lurking behind the simplest of the New Yorker's eccentricities. They have the unique habit of always glancing both ways before proceeding to cross the quietest of city streets, even if it is a one-way street. Furthermore, they invariably "cast one small, quick, furtive look in the opposite direction—from which no cars could possibly come." It is this final quick glance, White concludes, that underlines man's uncertainty with his environment and his belief that he can never be completely optimistic about his life no matter how well regulated and ordered it may appear. When he least expects it, "something big and red and awful will come tearing through town going the wrong way on the one-ways, mowing down all the faithful and the meek. Even if it's only a fire engine" (Dale, 196).

In "Visiting Motorists," White carries his argument one step further. The unpredictability of the driving habits of the average New Yorker can, with time, become strangely predictable. In the city, reverse logic seems to frequently apply, and, as such, we grow used to it. But just when we have become certain of the uncertainty, another obstacle presents itself to us, another hurdle to surmount, and that is the driving habits of the uninitiated, specifically the suburbanite who comes into town on the weekends either to shop or see a show. These people create new problems for the natives, because tourists invariably respond rationally to the irrational. They are governed by a different type of fear:

The minute a red light shows, they stop dead, imperiling everybody behind. The instant a taxi seems about to sideswipe them, they swerve desperately over and sideswipe somebody else, usually us. When they are confronted by a mass of pedestrians at the crossing, instead of

charging boldly in and scattering them in the orthodox manner by sheer
bluster (which is the only way), they creep timidly up blowing their
horns, which lulls the pedestrians and ties up everything. (Dale, 196)

The only thing the native urbanite can do when he encounters such people,
White concludes, is to hold fast to his irrationality and "nudge them frequently on the bumper and chivvy them about" (196).

Man's ability to "overreason" his environment until he can no longer
function effectively in it surfaces again in "Security." By 1938, White, along
with many of the other humorists of the Great Depression, began to examine
the events of the decade in retrospect. The Roosevelt administration was
nearing the completion of its first term, and many programs for the rehabili-
tation of the nation had been put in motion. But White, while willing to con-
cede that some badly needed changes in governmental policy had been
effective, is not completely convinced that any long-lasting changes have
occurred. The reason for this, he feels, lies, as already noted in the above essays, in entrenched, unremitting fear. Such fear had become seemingly permanent and impervious to reform. Furthermore, it had grown more
disturbing by the end of the decade, afflicting both the young and old alike.
If the youth of the nation were to be seriously considered as the hope for the
future, something had gone wrong along the road toward progress.

In "Security," White brings together all his observations on the above. A
nation largely tempered or at least sobered by the unpredictable events of
the early thirties now found itself by the end of the decade at odds with two
irreconcilables—a desire for security and "the yearning for dizzy release"
(Dale, 13). White's insight comes from observing passersby while riding
high above in a precarious gondola of a Ferris wheel at a local fair. Looking
down on a cautious friend, "even his hat was insured," White finds himself
uniquely alive and free. Later he is distressed by a cluster of mild-
mannered, pale men gathering outside a tattoo parlor "asking glumly for the
sort of indelible ignominy that was once reserved for prisoners and beef cat-
tle," having their social security numbers stenciled to their forearms. "I
hope," he sadly notes, "the art which produced the bird's eye view of Syd-
ney will not be forever lost in the routine business of putting serial numbers
on people who are worried about growing old" (14).

Farming has evidently changed his perspective of life. After losing some
chickens to disease and a marauding weasel, he realizes that there can be no
trust in security. Although he resolves to "make the best of it," he is saddened by a report he read the other day regarding a meeting of young people
where "security" became "a dominant note in the resolutions that were
passed" (16). In the past, youth was generally equated with adventure, ro-

mance, and daring-do. But now, White sadly feels, "they are holding out their arm for the branding iron, surrendering their free selves to an illusive certainty"—a certainty that translates into good paying jobs, that makes few demands on one's mind or creativity. Girls fly planes, he continues, not so much for the spirit of adventure, but more to snag and marry "an Eastern branch manager en route to his branch through the sky" (17).

As for White, his thirty-six pullets, he notes, are ready for the laying house. But all the security-minded federal pamphleteers say he must "culle" or purge them "rigidly." Throwing caution to the wind, he prefers to run his farm on his own terms: "Those that like to lay eggs can do that; the others can sit around the groaning board, singing and whoring" (17).

In "Clear Days," White confronts a cult of security that had recently resulted in the ignominious peace at Munich. While the negotiations over the division of Europe dragged on, White was busy replacing the roof on his barn: "One's perspective at that altitude, is unusually good. Who has the longer view of things, anyway, a prime minister in a closet or a man on a barn roof?" (Dale, 20). The peace to be gained from such negotiations is for White, "the ugliest peace the earth has ever received for a Christmas present" (20).

Part of the problem with modern man's quest for security and concomitant desire to become insulated from the rigors of existence is attributable to a growing dependence, as White sees it, on modern technology. For many, it represented man's hope for the future, a plan that would be abundantly clear at the World's Fair at Flushing Meadow in 1939. Technology offered the masses a fail-safe escape from the Depression, an alternative program to take up where political aspirations had been less than fruitful. Here at last was a future that only the most resolutely pessimistic could fail to appreciate. Nevertheless, White has his reservations. Television, he claims in his essay "Removal" from *The New Yorker,* "is going to be the test of the modern world," where modern man "shall discover either a new and unbearable disturbance of the general peace or a saving radiance in the sky. We shall stand or fall by television—of that I am quite sure" (Dale, 2).

White admires certain advances in technology, such as the radio during the 1920s and the beginnings of television at the end of the 1930s, and how they basically offer man a means by which he can distill the events of the world in the comfort of his living room. But this too has a price. "Together with the tabs, the mags, and the movies," the new technology, he claims, "will insist that we forget the primary and the near in favor of the secondary and the remote." A world of illusion can never adequately replace a world of substance, and even more ominous, a world of illusion might become tomorrow's world of reality: "A door closing, heard over the air; a face con-torted, seen in a panel of light—these will emerge as the real and the true; and when we bang the door of our own cell or look into another's face the impression will be of mere artifice" (3). Such a new world would create more problems than it solves. The yellow brick pathway is not leading Dorothy to the resolution of her problems in that famous Depression film. Instead it is leading her to bitter disappointment.

Similarly, White perceives the modern age of television to be little more than a sleight of hand, special effects created by the new wizards of Holly-wood, equally unsatisfying: "When I was a child people simply looked about them and were moderately happy; today they peer beyond the seven seas, bury themselves waist deep in tidings, and by and large what they see and hear makes them unutterably sad" (3). Unhappy too will be the purvey-ors of the new enlightenment. White's research into the field indicates that its performers will be required to wear electrical shockers from which their thoughts, gestures, and expressions will be cued by a higher authority: "Ac-tor Smoothjowl will wince slightly at the little pain, and appear suddenly to all the people" (4).

A close friend of White's, James Thurber, had already crafted a similarly pessimistic outlook in his humor, but unlike his contemporaries it tends to be a bit more internal and psychological in focus. Although other literary humorists echo foreign rumblings, the family house often borders Thur-ber's panorama with subtle dialogues between men and women and even humans and animals dealing with this age of Depression.

For Thurber, it is an age that has forgotten how to laugh or laugh properly, a point made in one of his stories from *The Middle-Aged Man on the Flying Trapeze* titled "The Funniest Man You Ever Saw."

"The Funniest Man You Ever Saw" details the "humorous" antics of a fellow named Jack Klohman who has a small but devoted following. Our narrator happens to listen in on one conversation the devotees are having re-garding their idol but strangely cannot share their enthusiasm because, quite frankly, the man's jokes are not in any way funny. As the story unfolds, it be-comes obvious that Klohman is nothing more than a bore who employs thoroughly tired jokes as a means of becoming the center of attention. Ironi-cally, he has been successful, in his own small way. The "funniest" man is not really funny, but in 1935, at the very depths of the Great Depression, he has become a big "hit." People will now laugh at *anything*, no matter how tired and stale it is. Inspired by a professional comedian's gag to come out on stage with nothing more than a horse's harness and the line, "I've either lost a horse or found a piece of rope," Klohman reduces his sidekicks to tears with such antics as ripping out a bathroom fixture ("I've either lost a bathroom or found a faucet") and part of a church ("I've either lost a church or found a chancel rail") (154).

Another tactic of his is to take things out of his pockets or off a table and claim that he has just invented them. As one of his followers notes: "He always takes something that's been invented for *years*, say like a lead pencil or something, and goes into this long story about how he thought it up one night. I remember he did it with about twenty different things" (156). They all agree that it must have been as "funny as the dickens."

A new routine of his, however, is claimed to be the best—fake card tricks. He solemnly cuts a deck and engages in a lot of fancy handwork, only to do nothing at all. "Does he do imitations?" inquires our listener. "Does he do *imitations!*" his fans bellow, and with this our story ends (158). Thurber's tale is not simply an insight into party clowns; it is an indictment of the troubled times where a sense of proportion is sadly lacking.

In another story titled "One Is a Wanderer," Thurber presents us with an even darker side of the Great Depression—loneliness. Mr. Kirk, at the age of forty-one, finds himself at more than just the crossroads of his life; he is encountering the mixed feelings and attendant confusion of what is commonly termed the "midlife crisis." The crisis for Mr. Kirk is more a reflection of the world he is living in than his own life or, for that matter, Thurber's own mental anxiety and bouts with depression. Wandering the streets of the city, like any of the countless thousands who were unemployed or dispossessed by the Depression, Kirk finds himself the habitué of late-night bars, conversing with bartenders, hotel clerks, and taximen whose solicitousness is not genuine and whose concerns are strictly personal. Mr. Kirk wonders if he would be welcome in the company of any of his married friends, but dismisses the idea of joining any of them for the evening because, as he sees it, he would only be a "wet blanket" tossed into their conjugal happiness. Friends have advised him to "get married and shut up," but he never will, he realizes, because he has always been too much of an "analyzer" and a "rememberer," two characteristics that dominated much of the politics and social thought of the midthirties. So in the end, Mr. Kirk is not a story of an unhappy man in the city. Nor is it a reflection of any personal dilemma for Thurber. It is a document, instead, of the decade and the sense of futility that often underlay even the most frantic efforts for recovery.

Thurber's "The Secret Life of Walter Mitty" emphasizes again this sense of futility, but with the difference that it has now found its only expression in escapism. Walter Mitty has often been viewed as Thurber's ultimate exponent of the cliché of the hen-pecked husband. But Mitty's persecution lies mostly outside the influence of his exasperatingly bossy wife. A parking lot attendant intrudes into Mitty's fantasy world when Mitty almost hits another car in the lot. A couple of women reduce him to utter mortification when they laugh over his audible self-reminder to get some "puppy biscuits." Not only has his wife reduced this poor man to the ineffectual daydreaming fool he is, but a world of seemingly otherwise "with it" people sneer at his daily mistakes, forcing him to visualize his life and masculinity in romantic illusions—as a commander of a ship in distress, a brilliant surgeon, a fire-eating lawyer, an airplane ace, and last, and most significantly, as a man about to be executed with his back up against a wall. Thurber's Mitty is a man who has obviously seen too many movies, and, in his world, the illusion has finally succeeded in pushing out the reality and pushing him up against a mental obstacle he can never scale. As such, he becomes an excellent example of the dilemma E. B. White had predicted the previous year in the essay, "The World of Tomorrow," and a sad reminder that even by 1939 the Depression was far from over in the minds of the American people. The economy might have been on the mend, but the memory of those who had suffered through those times was still confused and despondent.

One writer who, as early as 1933, had anticipated the long, enduring effects of the great Depression on the American psyche was Nathanael West in the novel titled *Miss Lonelyhearts*. West's dark brand of humor in this and most of his other works was more in sympathy with the themes and situations found in Thurber's stories than with the works of other Depression humorists such as Benchley and even Don Marquis. One reason for this affinity of spirit between the two men is probably attributable to their both having suffered considerable psychological and physical torment even before the Depression years. For Thurber, it was the onset of blindness in his one good eye; the other eye had been damaged during a childhood accident. For West, it was a painful self-consciousness and anxious childhood that had forced him to change his name from the overtly Jewish Weinstein to the more Anglicized West and habitually to avoid most Jewish religious, cultural, and social associations.

During the thirties, West participated in "popular front" activities and met a wide variety of people from all walks of life and professions, including a reporter for the *Brooklyn Eagle* who was the editor of the lovelorn column. She showed West some of the letters she received on a weekly basis for her column, signed by such names as "Broad Shoulders," from which West would draw a nameless race of disillusioned city dwellers in *Miss Lonelyhearts*.

The New York of West's novel not only serves as the physical backdrop for his chief character, Miss Lonelyhearts, a reporter whose real name we never discover, but also serves in West's dark panorama of the Depression as a city of stone, imprisoning forever its inhabitants within their unrequited dreams. Their dreams are many and varied. At a local bar, frequented by our columnist, the dreams are evident in the patrons' self-images, how they dress and present themselves to the world. In many ways, they are a reflection of the cries for help Miss Lonelyhearts reads every day at his job. Here at the bar, he realizes, are those who, like his correspondents, live by the advertisements of the modern world, who wish to be engineers and wear leather puttees, who want to live the life of an artist or writer, who want to develop a grip that will impress the boss, or who long to "cushion Raoul's head on their swollen breasts" (22).

Striking a tone similar to that found later in E. B. White, Hollywood is criticized and condemned as the primary culprit, for instead of pulling the American people out of the Depression, it has made it even worse by creating in the populace a craving for a world that few if any can ever enjoy. The radio and the newspapers too have joined in on this "betrayal" of the human spirit, which for Miss Lonelyhearts is the worst because it plays upon the imagination of people seeking salvation from the brutalities of everyday existence.

> He saw a man who appeared to be on the verge of death stagger into a movie theatre that was showing a picture called *Blond Beauty*. He saw a ragged woman with an enormous goiter pick a love story magazine out of a garbage can and seem very excited by her find. (39)

For West, the limitations of reform lie primarily in man's pursuit of false dreams, as well as the failure of the human heart to genuinely reform. Nowhere is this more apparent than in the character of Miss Lonelyhearts, who seeks his own particular brand of salvation among the suffering in the city. In former times, he and his friends believed in ideals such as "literature. . . . Beauty and in personal expression as an absolute end" (14). But the Depression has evaporated these beliefs and has replaced them with a coarse cynicism that grows increasingly impervious to human suffering.

Miss Lonelyhearts tries to rejuvenate the past by living out, as he calls it, the "Christ dream," but even this dream is another illusion caught within the grip of hypocrisy. At times he feels "conscious of two rhythms that were slowly becoming one. When they became one, his identification with God was complete. His heart was the one heart, the heart of God. And his brain was likewise God" (57). But in this attempt he loses sight of his own humanity, assuming, as he calls it, the posture of a rock: "calm and solid," able to "withstand any test" (52). Compassion became an alien emotion in the thirties because the Depression taught us to effectively turn our backs on the suffering around us. It is our means of survival, of maintaining our sanity amidst the increasing suffering and hopelessness of mankind. Christ could forgive His tormentors, but He was not like ordinary men who are unable to sympathize with their fellow men, except maybe, through personal experience. Like an experienced nurse, he has learned to look upon intense grief with increasingly distant feelings. He must do this or be destroyed by the grief.

But the dark side to this is a final retreat into sadism. Miss Lonelyhearts assaults an elderly homeless man in a public toilet in an attempt to strike back at all his suffering correspondents he has tried but failed to help: "He was twisting the arm of all the sick and miserable, broken and betrayed, inarticulate and impotent. He was twisting the arm of Desperate, Brokenhearted, Sick-of-it-all Disillusioned-with-tubercular-husband" (18). Thus in the end, the "compassion" of the thirties evolved into a mockery of mankind's finer instincts and virtues. It became an indictment of the human heart itself. As one contemporary critic perceptively noted: "The entire jumble of modern society, bankrupt not only in cash but more tragically in emotion, is depicted here like a life-sized engraving narrowed down to the head of a pin" (Light, 111).

Although Miss Lonelyhearts escapes into a world of quasi-religious fanaticism, the average route open to the everyday American was more often found in the local movie house in the form of the weekly newsreels. In an age before television, the movie newsreel became a window to the world for most Americans. But that world was not always the real world. The average newsreel, although for the most part objective and truthful in its content, was not without segments that were created largely for the amusement of the audience. The topics were extremely varied and largely minor in content, detailing anything from strange and highly unlikely inventions to housewives forcing their husbands to sleep in doghouses. Such stuff was bound to cause some chuckles within the audience, but did people actually begin to accept this as the new reality? Was it becoming a new avenue of escape for Depression-worn audiences?

Benchley's "Fiction Stranger than Truth" in *From Bed to Worse* implies that the gullibility of the American public is endemic. "Is truth stranger than Fiction?" he asks. "Of course, in order to settle it, one must know just how strange Fiction is," he continues in this lighthearted spoof of the contemporary newsreel. For example, there is the case of a Philadelphia man who, while milking his cows one day, happened to lean his head against the belly of one and overhear an animated conversation "carried on in low tones." The subject of the quarrel, it seems, involved a woman, "as usual" (185). Upon having the cow butchered and opened up, two small men emerge still arguing about a woman. "The men were released on bail," Benchley concludes, "and the milkman went home, still puzzling" (185).

Another story involves the strange case of James Gargey of Pennsylvania who "surprised himself in the act of tearing off steps from a house he had just robbed." Evidently trying to "cover his tracks and make it look like an inside job," he is startled by his alter ego, which serves equally as the chief of police:

> Confronted by the necessity for making an arrest and escaping, he went to a neighboring saloon (one of the saloons which did come back, in spite of the slogan "The Saloon Must Not come Back") and treated himself to a series of concoctions invented by the bartender in an off moment when he was working on a new drink for the "Miss Pennsylvania" prize. Following these, our hero swung on himself, landing a neat left to the eye, and then, wrenching himself out of his grasp, ran pell-mell down the street and hid in a Chinese laundry until the affair had blown over. A rookie policeman brought food to his superior while he was in hiding. (186–87)

"These little incidents in real life," Benchley concludes, "are . . . as strange as anything in fiction, or, in case you think of them as fiction, as strange as anything in real life. The point is that they are pretty darned strange" (186–87). The other point is that they are similar to the stories found in many of the newsreels of the time, and it is this point that becomes the foundation of Benchley's satire.

Besides the bizarre, another means of escape from the trials and tribulations of the Great Depression is presented in Clarence Day's extremely popular novel of the decade, *Life with Father*. Day's humor relies on the past for its effect, or, in other words, it presents the reader with a bygone era where life was more regimented and definitely less confusing. In an age where each new year presented another list of governmental agendas and policy decisions to the American public and where no one could be absolutely certain what the future might hold, Day's novel opens the door into the "good old days" at the turn of the century where the sun seemed to never set and tranquillity reigned supreme. Of course, Day's novel is not as simplistic as contemporary critics envisioned it, and despite its being quickly snatched up and reprocessed into an equally popular film of the thirties, the novel displays underlying currents of cynicism that are more than evident if one is willing to read between the lines of its heart-warming sentimentality.

At a time when many fathers found themselves dispossessed of their traditional "rights" within the family unit as the principal breadwinner and voice of authority, Day's novel must have stroked many a bruised ego because its protagonist is a strict authoritarian who rules his domestic brood absolutely. It is probably pointless to speculate whether such families have ever existed except in the imagination of the most inveterate male chauvinist, and Day's treatment is obviously but gently sarcastic. Nevertheless, for the Depression reader its appeal was probably more in the form of mental escape into an illusionary time of tranquillity and stability than as a satire of sexual attitudes and mores.

In fact, the father in our novel is an exemplary form of escape artist, for he adamantly refuses to accept the unpleasant realities around him. This becomes quite clear in one chapter titled "Father Is Firm with His Ailments." Illness, he claims, is not the result of germs but weak character, the result of a person giving in to the prevailing medical gossip of the day:

> All this talk about germs, he said, was merely newfangled nonsense. He said that when he was a boy there had been no germs that he knew of. Perhaps invisible insects existed, but what of it? He was as healthy as they were. "If any damned germs want to have a try at me," he said, "bring 'em on." (62)

Later, when he actually falls ill with pneumonia, he becomes slightly alarmed that God could do this to him. But in the end he recovers, firm in his belief that most ailments are the result of mass hysteria guided by greedy physicians. "You can trust people to get any ailment whatever that's fashionable," he informs his wife. "They hear of a lot of other people having it, and the first thing you know they get scared and think they have it themselves. Then they go to bed, and send for the doctor. The doctor! All poppycock" (67). The Roosevelt administration would have applauded these sentiments, at least in part, for did it not prescribe the elimination of fear as the best first step in recovering from the sick economy of the Great Depression?

Like Clarence Day, Christopher Morley offers a solution to the Great Depression in a novel detailing the life of one individual. But unlike Day, Morley's approach concentrates on the present and not the past. Unlike the theoreticians that proposed various schemes, economic and otherwise, that focused on the necessity for change either within the American system or among its people, Morley finds a solution by celebrating the average and ordinary and believing that they alone offer a stability that will enable modern man to get through the troubled times. The work that would present these fundamental views was his novel titled *Human Being*, published in 1932.

Unlike his previous works that had often been characterized as "whimsical," *Human Being* presents a tone that is more somber and discerning. In short, Morley's purpose is to create a work that will be warm and humorous without being overtly sentimental, that would attempt, as he described it, to "catch a human being in the very act of being human, and to set it down without chemical preservatives" (Wallach, 57). It would be a book about American life, specifically the life of a "traveling salesman. . . . A long book, full of the egregious humors of American life; a very plain and unembroidered book; to be written . . . like a translation from the Russian, so that none of its merit would depend on mere 'style' or verbal charm; but lucid; strongly *narrative*; a merry, droll, candid book, with its deeper pathos well concealed. A book *humorous* in the true sense" (57).

As early as 1920, Morley planned to write a novel of perception, consisting of what he called a series of "stories revolving about the character of one man, who never appears, but is the motif of the whole, showing his personality from different angles, and leaving the reader to make up his mind as to his man's nature" (57). The end result was a plot based on the efforts of Lawrence Hubbard, a retired accountant of a publishing firm, who decides to compose a biography of a deceased, former employee named Richard Roe. In the course of his research, Hubbard discovers a rich panorama of events and personality in an otherwise ordinary, "forgotten" man. He also becomes increasingly involved with the friends and associates, including a mistress, Minnie Hutzler, with whom he eventually falls in love. As Morley described the completed work: "This is not only the biography of Richard Roe but a biography of that biography" (57).

As such, it seems to have been Morley's intent to reach out and document the existence of all the nameless and forgotten people who were trying their best to weather the economic upheaval at hand. Such people would never be featured in the newspapers or newsreels of the day, but instead could be seen on any street in any American city, trying to make a living for themselves and their families, commuting daily between their homes and their jobs—surviving. Such people remain forever unknown to the world outside their immediate families and friends, except for a brief mention in some obituary column at the back end of a daily newspaper. Beyond this, it is as though they had never lived at all. Thus, the idea for the novel presented itself to Morley when he chanced to read an obituary about a man dying from heart failure while commuting on the Hoboken ferry: "And I began to think about the middle-class man, the inarticulate and frustrated little man. Then I began to think about the people who might have known him, and of some of them talking about him and it was as though I were sitting in a dark theatre, with the characters coming out onto the stage" (58).

The fact that Hubbard and Roe are affiliated with a publishing house is too largely based on Morley's own experience with the publishing firm of Doubleday, where he had spent a good part of his early career and had developed a deeply rooted respect for his associates who, although not necessarily literary men, represented an integral part in the creation and maintenance of authors and the literary establishment. "The clippings and memorabilia which hardheaded citizens carry in their wallets," Morley would later observe about his associates, "are often important" (60).

It is this sense of urgency for the commonplace that sets the tone for the novel *Human Being*. In chapter 1, Hubbard presents us with the primary motivation behind his task—the fact that life is short and we die before we have sufficiently understood each other or ourselves. Man's achievement is not displayed in his accumulated possessions or accomplished deeds, but more in the innermost feelings of his heart. It is Hubbard's task to unlock these feelings in at least one human being and, by doing so, discover his own feelings and beliefs before it is too late. "I look back with a miserable sense of frustration," Hubbard admits, "when I realize that I once sat at a table with Richard Roe himself and guessed so little. If I had known then what I do now, how I should have longed to tell him that I also understand. But to know what we need to know, at the moment when we need to know it, is few men's privilege. He was gone almost before I knew he was there. There are many like that. To all such I would like to dedicate my record" (8).

What we eventually learn about Roe, and mankind in general, is that our identities are primarily the result of the countless interactions we have with other people on a daily basis. Therefore, a man is not known by his possessions, but by the people he has touched, the lives he has shaped, and the memories he leaves behind. It is from the intangible that the tangible is created, and Hubbard starts his study of Roe by listing all the dead man's friends and associates: "Unaware how much work there was to be done, Hubbard stood off and contemplated the shelves thoughtfully. What strange wraiths of that obscure and vanished life would come drifting into the several compartments?" (20). The traditional manner of evaluating a man's memory by the wealth he has accumulated is of little significance in Morley's Depression America. That which will endure into the future is the memory of the man and not his empire. Even the dispossessed can have their fair share of immortality.

Roe is such a man. He is a man touched by a speech in Congress he hears from the Visitor's Gallery despite its being "some deplorable rhodomontade with a ludicrous Star-Spangled peroration" (13). In his own modest way, he loves his country and is a well-meaning patriot, undoubtedly fooled, like many, by the glitter of Washington politics. But his most endearing trait is his willingness to see the bright side to life and laugh, as he does one beautiful day, for the mere pleasure of doing so. His mirth catches the eye of a passerby who finds it infectious and ends up shaking Roe's hand simply because Richard is the first person he has seen smiling that day. Thus, for Morley, the ultimate way to deal with the crisis known as the Great Depression is to live life as best as one can and to remember to smile for the simple pleasures of life that come our way.

As we have seen, the alternatives for dealing with the Great Depression varied greatly among the humorists of the decade. From Benchley's confused bungler to Parker's misguided sentimentalist, from Thurber's dreamer to Day's traditionalist, the Depression was an event that denied easy resolutions conceived by the politicians in Congress. All that could be done, at most, was to plant the seeds of alternate strategies. Only time would prove whether they would eventually bear fruit and prosper. And as time has shown, many did.

CHAPTER 2

Men and Women—
Love and Marriage

Throughout most of the nineteenth century and the first few decades of the twentieth century, the "paterfamilias," as it would later be referred to in studies of the American family, would be the dominant social form of the traditional family unit. Although some of its characteristics evolved or were modified during the course of a century, one fundamental trait remained intact and essential to its continuance—the presence of a strong father figure. The father of this type of family was distinguishable by three attributes—remoteness, sovereignty, and benevolence. The mother figure, although essential and usually dominant in the traditional roles of married women, vis-à-vis the raising of the children and tending to the daily demands of the household, was primarily delegated to the vague land of nonexistence whenever the "important" issues of the children's education or finances were set into motion.

The remoteness of the Victorian father stemmed largely from the pressing duties of an active business life filled with social responsibilities. Children were often sent away at an early age to boarding schools where semesters were long and vacations short. The reason for this was that it was customary, and it tended to reinforce the father as a distant, if not unapproachable, figure with his children. Wives too often had to carry out the functions of their daily lives with little communication or dialogue with their husbands who were preoccupied with more "important" activities.

Sovereignty as the second characteristic of the Victorian father referred to his absolute authority in any decision-making process. Like an emperor, the Victorian patriarch could delegate his power to his wife, amply and freely at times, but he could just as easily recall it. Wives and daughters were expected to subordinate themselves to the master of the household and, by doing so, won universal praise and respect. As the head of the household, the wife could easily command considerable authority over family matters, but she was never to forget from whence her authority originated.

Benevolence too was a trait of the Victorian dad, but here there could and frequently did exist exceptions to the rule. Governed primarily by remoteness and sovereignty, the Victorian father was hard pressed to display the more gentle aspect of benevolence, which could just as easily turn into malevolence. One Victorian woman, responding to the query as to why she invariably indulged her malevolent husband's temperament, replied that it was easier to give into his will than to put up with "long days of unbroken sulkiness which hang like a pall over the house" (Wohl, 67). For children, the father could often become an object of terror, either real or imagined. The Victorian father might often be physically absent, but he was always a mental presence. Wives, although maybe less terrified by the presence of their lords and masters, nevertheless could not fail to neglect their duty to the sole breadwinner of the family (59–78).

By the 1920s, the traditional role of the Victorian father had been largely altered by the changing social climate created by World War I. During the war, large numbers of women had found employment in wartime industries while their husbands were fighting overseas in Europe. With the war's conclusion, many women continued to work in the factories, enjoying the freedom and independence they had gained. Such independence brought with it considerable social change, as was evident in the increasing suffrage movement which finally gained for women the right to vote by 1919. Although the man of the 1920s did not have the absolute authority of his Victorian predecessor, he was still perceived as the principal influence in a family's financial success or failure. The man of the house, although he could no longer command authority simply for being the father, was still firmly atop the economic pedestal in the domestic environment.

All this was to change with the onset of the Great Depression. Probably no other institution was more affected by the economically depressed times than the family unit. Some of the changes were obvious and immediate. One was the decline in marriages. Young people who had recently lost jobs and were unable to find another, recent graduates of high schools and colleges who were becoming accustomed to waiting on long unemployment lines, and even those few young people who had the skills or education to find a good position—all were unsettled and disturbed by a future that offered little promise for raising a family. Even more alarming were the frequent accounts in the newspapers detailing the rapid decline of the family unit in general.

In Chicago parks as early as 1931, unemployed and homeless women, many abandoned by their husbands, huddled for warmth in makeshift hovels dubbed "Hoovervilles." The presence of men in such places was to be expected given the unemployment figures, but the rise within the female population created considerable alarm. The *New York Times* reported the concern of Mrs. Conkey, commissioner of Public Welfare, that by the end of the next winter of 1932 the situation would be very critical because existing welfare housing could only accommodate one hundred women (Shannon, 14–15). Equally alarming was the increasing number of homeless children, abandoned by their parents. As one florid article noted:

> A youth shivers all night in a gondola. Next day he falls asleep on a hillside and sleeps the sleep of exhaustion until dusk. On awakening he is hungry, but where can he get food? The bread lines are closed. The police have, in one of their weekly raids, cleaned out the jungles. At none of the customary places are there friends or food. The youth can beg on the streets, walking miles perhaps before he gets a nickel. A boy can steal, but the chances are that he will be caught. A girl can offer her body, but as likely as not she will find nobody in the market with desire and a dime. The usual course is to remain hungry until breakfast at a mission for a boy, or until breakfast can be begged by a girl. If the boy is very hungry, he may glom a grub from garbage cans. (Shannon, 62)

What these and other reports had failed to note was the preexisting situation that had generated so many homeless women and children: the collapse of the traditional American family due to the breakdown of the unemployed husband's status within that environment.

Although unemployment did not automatically result in the collapse of a family, it nevertheless put the unit under unnatural stress. In many cases, husbands and wives switched roles with wives now assuming a dominant position. In the typical family of the 1930s, husbands largely achieved and maintained their status by being the principal wage earner. When they lost their jobs or had to assume another position that paid less, their standing in the family slipped. Some wives found an opportunity to release pent-up hostilities, blame their husbands for unemployment, nag, withdraw customary services, and otherwise find fault with his behavior. This in turn often made husbands increasingly bitter and morose, further precipitating accusations of habitual laziness and neglect of duties. Even in cases where the wife was supportive and sympathetic to her husband's condition, a majority of men still blamed themselves for their unemployment and experienced a sense of worthlessness.

Being at home with more time on his hands tended to make the unemployed man restless and bored. His children might become increasingly cavalier in their attitudes toward him because in their eyes he was no longer a distant and unapproachable figure. Further compounding the problem was the fact that in an age where men's and women's roles were still fairly distinct, the unemployed man found his masculinity compromised by having to assume what had traditionally been considered women's tasks, such as shopping, cooking, or light housekeeping. With more and more women able to find low-paying jobs that their more skilled husbands could not, men had no alternative but to help with the housework. Many men did, and according to a study made by the International Institute of Social Research, did so as a way of maintaining the love and respect of their wives. Others, however, did not—becoming instead sullen and lethargic and never completely recovering from the changes created by the Great Depression. Further compounding this problem was the growing independence of women since the war. Sociologists saw in the new liberalism a trend toward promiscuity and sexually aggressive behavior, traditionally considered the domain of bachelors. The times were certainly changing (Komarovsky, 66–83).

These changes were not unnoticed by the major writers and humorists of the decade. Throughout the twenties and thirties, Benchley's humorous essays in *The New Yorker* continued to evolve the persona of the "little man" at odds with a perplexing and increasingly female-dominated world. Benchley's sentiments would be drawn out further in the cartoons of Peter Arno, who sketched the breakdown of mechanical things—trains, planes, ships, and taxicabs—none of which could be understood or effectively controlled by the contemporary "little man," and William Steig, who produced cartoons of "Mittesque" fantasies, one of which was aptly entitled "Dreams of Glory."

One did not have to confine himself to the pages of *The New Yorker* to see evidence of the growing concern. In the cinema, Charlie Chaplin and W. C. Fields would turn the "little man" into an easily recognized persona. Dale Carnegie would convert thousands in a series of radio broadcasts called "Getting Ahead," espousing self-reliance and ego boosting. These broadcasts together with his immensely successful bible, *How to Win Friends and Influence People*, would make Carnegie one of the richest men in America by 1936.

The Depression's social novelists composed a distinctive genre dealing almost exclusively with the "little man." Their principal characters were generally unknown, unheroic little people who came to difficulty because of social or economic circumstances beyond their control. Thus, parallels were established between the great social novelists of the twenties and thirties, such as John Dos Passos, James T. Farrell, Josephine Herbst, John Steinbeck, and Erskine Caldwell and the major literary humorists of the Depression era, such as Thurber and Benchley.

None of these writers viewed the little man as being incapable of escaping from his dilemmas despite his utter passivity when confronted by the superior forces around him, be they social, economic, domestic, or political. Steinbeck believed in the "phalanx theory" where individualism is unknown. The individual "little man" is like a cell—part of the larger body (society) and is important only insofar as he lends to the whole. Likewise, the whole has an existence—a temperament—all its own that the individual cannot control but from which he derives his true strength.

For Farrell, the blame for man's "littleness" stemmed from the capitalistic system in which he lived. Even if the "little man" experienced a reversal of fortune and became successful or powerful, his success was marred by an intrinsic evil within the system he could not control. In short, everyone was little in Farrell's universe, whether they were out of work or not. For the humorists, such as Benchley or Thurber, there was only one way out—humor.

The majority of Benchley's essays dealing with the little man appeared in two collections published during the thirties—*From Bed to Worse* (1934) and *My Ten Years in a Quandary, and How They Grew* (1936). Throughout these essays the modern man is examined in light of a variety of subjects, such as the physical world, society, nature, marriage and the family, love, and personal health. In all, the modern man is a powerless drifter on the stream of life. Without an oar, he can merely hope for the better but often ends up with the worst. The species of "Pater Familias," he notes in one essay, "The Vanishing Father," from *From Bed to Worse*, is all but extinct in the modern age. "He was one of the bulldog breed, whose word was law, and when he rumbled into breakfast all the boys and girls, to say nothing of Mumsie, threw themselves up against the wall and saluted" (111). In its place is a new class of fathers "turned yellow as a class." "They are lucky if they get what the rest of the family gets to eat and, as for personality, they might as well be the man who holds the tray for a magician" (111). Not only is the modern man afraid of authority, he is afraid of his own sexuality to such an extent, concludes Benchley, that he has seen one father "hurriedly slip a cigar into his son's mouth at the approach of friends, hoping that they will think he is out with a midget business acquaintance" (113).

If the Depression sapped the modern man of his ability to command respect within his own family, it also made him uncertain and fearful of his command in other areas—especially the physical world. Benchley's modern man is frequently troubled by the simplest of modern contrivances, further enhancing his loss of self-respect and the respect of those around him. In "Rapping the Wrapper," he is at odds with an obstinate foil wrapper on a roll of mints. No matter how hard he tries, the ends refuse to unravel, remaining perfectly "air-tight, water-tight, and germ proof" (46). Finally, in petulant desperation he dashes the roll to the sidewalk, "as a child does a torpedo," only for the ends to remain as "tightly clamped down as they had been when they left the foundry" (49).

In "An Old Problem Revived," the issue at hand is the difficulty in extracting paper towels from washroom dispensaries: "Your hands are wet, you take hold of the two ends of the towel to pull it down, and all that you have are two little corners of wet paper stuck between your thumbs and forefingers" (63). Confronted with this situation, the modern man is reduced to a state of utter abject helplessness. Some, Benchley notes, stand there for hours waiting for someone to take the bits of paper off their hands; others resign themselves to fate and wait there, brooding, until the paper dries and falls from their hands on its own.

Continued efforts, however, to extract another towel from the dispenser can only lead to further embarrassment and humiliation. Such an act requires courage, Benchley concludes, a courage most men do not have even though he does admire the man "who can go through with it" (65).

> Stronger men than I am, however, tell me that the way to get rid of the towel corners is to snap the fingers vigorously as if to an inaudible "ha-cha!" thereby disengaging the paper and freeing the fingers for a fresh attack on the towel. Or, for the less spectacular-minded, the fingers may be scraped against the wall of the wash-room in a quiet and dignified manner, with the same result. All that is needed, in any event, is a little initiative and get-up-and-go. (65)

Courage is also needed in the other daily routines of life, especially at breakfast time.

At this time, coordination, dexterity, and digestion must blend in synchronous harmony if one is to get through one's cereal and simultaneously read the morning paper, as he notes in "Read and Eat" from *My Ten Years in a Quandary.* According to Benchley, to be able to do both bespeaks a man of affairs, "none of which attributes I seem to possess. . . . I long ago abandoned the attempt to look like a man of affairs. I even find it difficult, some mornings, to look like a man" (116).

The problem lies principally with coordination. The modern man may wish to keep abreast of the times and issues of his day, but his physical awkwardness prevents him from doing so.

> In the first place, I can't seem to get the newspaper fixed right, even in one of those racks which super-service hotels sometimes provide for the purpose. One corner gets into the butter, another into the marmalade, and, even if I do manage to fold it so that certain headlines are visible, they are either on stories that I don't want to read or I have to unfold the whole thing again in a minute or two in order to keep on reading. (116)

Meanwhile his toast becomes cold and tasteless or he upsets the cream and coffee. Sometimes, while leaning over to read the article better, his lapel "rests neatly in the egg" (117). In short, there are undoubtedly others who are more dexterous, but our author is not one of them. He prefers to stick to one task at a time. "Of course, there are mornings," he concludes, "when I don't want any breakfast. Then I catch up with my reading" (119).

Further compounding his difficulty with the physical world around him is his inability to get things started. A paralysis of the will affects our modern man; he needs the will of a leader but can only play the part of a follower, as Benchley observes in "The Ice-Breaker": "I could probably build a bridge or erect a skyscraper—or even teach a parrot to roll over—if someone would get the job started for me, but I know perfectly well that, if I were handling any one of these enterprises I would spend the first day gazing into space, trying to figure out how to begin" (158). Fortunately, he concludes, no one is about to ask him to do any of the above because he is now in his midforties.

The natural world is equally intimidating for the modern man. Birds may be traditionally viewed as objects of grace and beauty, but for Benchley in "Down with Pigeons" in *From Bed to Worse*, they, and especially pigeons, have a darker side to their nature:

> I am awakened every morning by a low gargling sound which turns out to be the result of one, or two, or three pigeons walking in at my window and sneering at me. Granted that I am a fit subject for sneering as I lie there, possibly with one shoe on or an unattractive expression on my face, but there is something more than just a passing criticism in these

birds making remarks about me. They have some ugly scheme on foot
against me, and I know it. Sooner or later it will come out, and then I
can sue. (276)

His problem with pigeons has occurred throughout his life. They pestered
him when he was in college; while on vacation in Italy, they ganged up on
him in Venice on St. Mark's Piazza. Now, years later, he is determined to
fight them on their own ground: "I have worked up a noise which I can make
in my throat which is just as unpleasant sounding as theirs" (281). But, alas,
he fears in the end that the pigeons will win the contest.

In another essay from *My Ten Years in a Quandary* titled "Help," he is
confronted with a bird whose strategy is to "shatter my nerves during the
night and then attack me in my weakened condition in the daytime" (69).
This bird is no pigeon. It has a diversified repertoire of "*vox humana*" numbers. "Sometimes he giggles. Sometimes he simply says, in a low voice,
'Wait till I get you outside.' " (70). By the end of the essay, the bird has so
broken Benchley's morale that he contemplates the need for a police escort,
"or has a taxpayer no rights?" (71).

The modern man's inability to assert himself in either the physical or
natural world around him is further compounded by his failure to function
effectively in society as well. In "Filling That Hiatus" from *From Bed to
Worse*, Benchley notes that there is one small detail that to his knowledge
has never been mentioned in the etiquette books, namely, what to do "during
those little intervals when you find that both your right-hand and your left-
hand partner are busily engaged in conversation with somebody else."

> You have perhaps turned from what you felt to be a fascinating conver-
> sation (on your part) with your right-hand partner, turned only to snap
> away a rose bug which has charged on your butter from the table deco-
> rations or to refuse a helping of salad descending on you from the left,
> and when you turn back to your partner to continue your monologue,
> you find that she is already vivaciously engaged on the other side, a
> shift made with suspicious alacrity, when you come to think it over. So
> you wheel about to your left, only to find yourself confronted by the
> clasp of a necklace and an expanse of sun-browned back. This leaves
> you looking more or less straight in front of you, with a roll in your
> hand and not very much to do with your face. (36)

To save it, Benchley continues, you may "make believe that you are talking
to the person opposite, making little conversational faces and sounds into
thin air, nodding your head 'Yes' or 'No,' and laughing politely every now

and again, perhaps even continuing the talk from which you had been cut off, just as if someone were still listening to you" (37–38). One can also play with the nuts in front of one's plate, "arranging them on the tablecloth in fancy patterns with simulated intensity which will make it look as if you were performing for someone's benefit" (39). However, because both these approaches will undoubtedly result in either the guest being viewed as seriously unstable by the hostess or ignored altogether, it is best, Benchley concludes, simply to go home.

The social insecurity of the modern man and his fear of rejection surface in many of Benchley's Depression sketches. In "Toddling Along," from *My Ten Years in a Quandary,* he becomes a reluctant party guest, fearful of having to go home alone: "Other people are able to guess they'll be toddling along. One by one, and two by two, and sometimes in great groups, I watch them toddle along, until I am left, with possibly just my host to keep me company. Sometimes even my host asks me if I mind if *he* toddles along to bed. When this happens, I am pretty quick to take the hint" (24). In "Haircut Please," he has become obsessively fearful of standing out while entering barbershops: "I stand and look inside, hoping that all the chairs are occupied. If they are not, I sometimes wait until they are. Then I go on my way with an easy conscience" (289). Such fears and abnormal preoccupations become the mainstay of much of Depression humor. It is, after all, an age of fear.

For married couples, there are other fears, such as the fear of commitment. Economic issues aside, marriages seem to be failing for far less serious matters than infidelity and physical abuse. In *From Bed to Worse*, Benchley presents a humorous panorama that's not too far from the truth. One man divorces his wife for "standing in front of the mirror just when he got to tying his tie." In another, a wife sues, claiming her husband never gets up from the floor. The husband registers a countersuit, protesting the wife's refusal to get down on the floor with him. In still another, an Arizona woman files for divorce despite the fact she isn't married! "I must have been drunk when I did it," she giggles (119). For Benchley, such examples are all part of "Divorce in the U.S."

Such carelessness is a reflection of the decade's confusion concerning love in general and an obsession with being politically correct—an observation he makes clear in "Love Among the Thinkers." For Benchley, young couples who cannot talk "Values and Gestalt Psychology, while necking is going on" might as well resign themselves to "picking the threads" off their sleeves for the rest of their lives. Social philosophy has supplanted romance—as one hypothetical conversation between sweethearts would lead us to believe:

"It's funny our not having met like this before," said Ann, without turning her head. "Woman is Man's logical mate."

"Aren't you being just a little old-fashioned?" asked Theodore.

Ann winced. "Old-fashioned" was a hard word.

"I have seen nothing in Krafft-Ebing to make me think differently," she said, laying her head ever so lightly back on his shoulder. Her hair had the odor of sweet-grass baskets.

"Since the Twelfth Century we have seen Woman come on apace," said Theodore, pressing his lips into its soft fragrance. "And yet hormones are hormones, just as ballots are ballots. You can't evade the issue by calling on Krafft-Ebing." (192–93)

The romance continues with other references to Martin Luther, the Pleistocene Age, the Reformation, and Cro-Magnon Man, but in the end Ann does lay her head on Theodore's chest, which is not like the "weak chest of professor Dinwiddie, nor the pudgy chest of Robert Paster, nor the barrel chest of Dr. Wormser, nor any of the other chests which Ann Vickers, in her search for social justice and prison reform, had encountered as a part of her laboratory work" (195).

Once married, the modern man faces additional problems. One is the difficulty of assuming the liberal attributes of an up-to-date husband and father who is supposed to be aware of the everyday details of child-rearing and family psychology. Unlike the fathers of old, the modern dad is not expected to have nothing to do with the children, and, according to Benchley in "Child Holding," from *My Ten Years in a Quandary*, is frequently called upon to perform tasks that make him look ridiculous, much to the delight of his more experienced wife and other members of the female population. Thus, the paterfamilia father is transformed into a modern-day wimp every time he takes an infant into his hands.

No male relative, in his right mind, ever takes a baby to hold of his own free will. The very thought of dropping it, a thought which is always present, is enough to reduce all his vital organs to gelatin. Some female always suggests it. "Let Joe hold him for a minute. Hold him, Joe!"

So, Joe, sweating profusely, picks the infant up and becomes a figure of fun. "Look at how Joe's holding him, Bessie! Like he has a golf bag!" "Poor kid, put him down, Joe!" "Look out, Joe—you'll strangle him!" Lynching is in the air. (198)

The modern man has become so helpless and dominated by his wife that the best way for him to remove a baby from a crib, concludes Benchley, is to crawl into the crib with the child, and then "call for someone else to come and lift both father and child from the crib at once" (200).

Nor is the modern-day father in his new humbled condition prepared to deal with the demands of his children as they mature. Whereas in the previous century, dads could thoroughly dismiss their sons and daughters until they had matured enough to be classified as young adults, the modern man is expected to be psychologically proficient enough to enter into their private worlds with aplomb—a task traditionally that of the mother. In "The Children's Hour" from *My Ten Years in a Quandary*, Benchley is unnerved by youth and especially its playing habits during vacation time.

> I base my apprehension on nothing more definite than the fact that they are always coming in and going out of the house, without any apparent reason. When they are indoors, they sit for a while without doing anything much. Then they suddenly decide to go out again for a while. Then they come in again. In and out—in and out. (165)

He wishes they would let him into their world, but they won't, and it foreshadows, he feels, something sinister, possibly a revolution! At any rate, he hopes that if they do start something, they do it before he is too old to run.

The impotency of the general male population is, for Benchley, symptomatic of the times. It is an age that champions strength and resolution only to realize in the end that such characteristics are the illusions of inflated egos. Benchley finds himself in step with the thirties because he has never possessed an ego sufficient to deflate. Since childhood, he has inevitably been the victim of a mocking universe, or, as he notes in "My Achilles Heel" in *From Bed to Worse*, the occasional stray snowball, which just as inevitably seems to strike him on the side of his neck or behind his right ear. With time, he has become so conditioned as to now expect the impact anytime he chances upon a snowball fight: "When I enter a block in which boys are throwing snowballs, that same old instinctive hunching up of the right shoulder overtakes me. The boys may be on my left, but the missile comes from the right, by whatever devious ways a snowball may come at its command" (115).

Consequently, he finds safety in retreating to his own apartment, an inveterate couch potato, with no desire for outdoor activities. In "Calorie Spending" (*From Bed to Worse*), we find him concluding he is more a "calorie hoarder" than a spender. Now, at middle age, he derives pleasure from far less strenuous activities, such as "lifting off a milk-bottle cap with some small pointed instrument like a pin or an awl, especially if it resists just a bit around the edges and does not end up splashing into the milk" (135). Included also is eating a lobster, opening a pack of cream cheese, reading the Sunday newspaper "before it has been torn apart by the women of the family. . . . whitewashing a good board fence, applying lather with a shaving brush, snapping the clasps on a well-filled suitcase and puncturing a cellophane top to a bottle" (136–37). Benchley's Depression man finds contentment in limiting his expectations of pleasure within an increasingly limited world, a victory of sorts.

Alongside Benchley, James Thurber contributed to the growing preoccupation with the modern man, specifically the married man, when he consolidated his views in one major work of 1935, *The Middle-Aged Man on the Flying Trapeze*. Unlike Benchley, however, Thurber prefers not to concentrate on the modern man's interrelationships with the physical, natural, and social worlds around him. For Thurber, the world is primarily domestic and dominated by women who enjoy their superiority over their spouses.

One way they are superior is verbally. Unlike the paterfamilias of the past, where the woman rarely spoke unless spoken to, the modern woman is determined to exert herself to the fullest. A winsome woman may not be able to match the physical strength of her husband, but she can make him look quite foolish through her command of the English language. In "The State of Bontana," mixed couples are playing a game called Oral Categories where they have to guess a word based on a letter and a hint. The women outshine their husbands in one game after another, much to their delight and their husbands' dismay. A good example, Thurber notes, are his friends the Almonds:

> Almond has as fine a mind and as wide a general knowledge as any man I know, but he invariably becomes mind-tied when Oral Categories is started. If you took R and then said "Name a flower" he would be unable, for some strange reason, to think of Rose. He just sits there, staring at the floor, a heavy, angry look on his face. I daresay the machinery of his mentality is too complex for him to turn out instantly an obvious and meager little word. But he is sensitive and easily annoyed. The game has got to him. He worries about it, hates it, but comes back to it the way an unlucky player comes back to the roulette table. (51–52)

Of course his wife, Grace, takes great delight in her superiority and enjoys "railing" at him during games, calling attention to his stupidity, and belittling him before the other guests. Another unhappy husband, Garrison, likes to retreat to a corner and read a book, but his wife invariably drags him back to the game with a "rasping voice," exclaiming, "Now you're *not* going to *sit* there and *read* all evening!" Of course he returns to the contest with about the same confidence "Jeffries came into the ring with Jack Johnson, if you happen to remember," Thurber observes (52).

In "The Curb in the Sky" a husband is slowly driven to madness by a wife who demonstrates her superiority by perpetually ending his sentences:

> Dorothy would let Charlie get almost to the climax of some interesting account of a happening and then, like a tackler from behind, throw him just as he was about to cross the goal-line. There is nothing in life more shocking to the nerves and to the mind than this. Some husbands will sit back amiably—almost it seems, proudly—when their wives interrupt, and let them go on with the story, but these are beaten husbands. Charlie did not become beaten. But his wife's tackles knocked the wind out of him, and he began to realize that he would have to do something. (77)

What Charlie does is retreat to a world of dreams, for it is the only canvas his wife can't anticipate. His favorite tale is about a flight to the moon in a ship constructed of telephone wires. Unfortunately, his "retreat" becomes permanent as he falls victim to monomania and has to be confined to a mental hospital. Even here, however, the poor man is unable to find peace because now his wife concludes even his favorite dreams! Our narrator last sees him, pale and wan, while his wife, radiant and happy, corrects the ending of one of his stories: "Charlie sighed and turned slightly in his bed and looked at me. Dorothy looked at me, too, with her pretty smile. 'He always gets that story wrong,' she said" (80).

Women in Thurber's world are also beginning to invade the traditional bastions of male dominance. One in particular is the world of cars. In "Mr. Pendly and the Poindexter," a mild-mannered husband has resigned himself to being driven around town by his wife. At times he fantasizes about descending in an autogyro on some garden party she is attending, making a fine landing, leaping out, shouting "Hahya Bee!" and zooming off with her in the machine. But in reality, he knows very little about such things, and when he goes shopping for a new car with his wife, she is the one who does all the talking with the salesman-mechanic. All Mr. Pendly can do is keep out of the way while she discusses the intricacies of grinding valves, relining brakes, and putting in a new battery. When the conversation turns to vacuum pumps, Mr. Pendly jumps to the conclusion that they are talking about something "you can buy and put in the back seat, like a fire-extinguisher," and suggests they pick one up at an appliance shop. (59) For a moment his wife and the mechanic give him a confused look, only to ignore what he has said and again continue their discussion, this time on tires.

In a similar story, "Smashup," a Tommy Trinway finds it impossible to learn how to drive the car "his wife picked out for him to buy" (194). His wife drives aggressively but always in command of the road, "with keen concentration, quick reflexes, and evident enjoyment" (196). He finds it all very depressing. Then one day, while driving the car in the city (his wife having sprained her wrist), he narrowly avoids hitting an old woman crossing the street against the light. He momentarily blanks out but is revived by a policeman patting him on the back and calling out to the pedestrian: "You're lucky, lady. . . .You can thank your stars that fella can drive like that. You wanta stay on the sidewalk when you see that red light. This street ain't no playgrounds" (199). Tommy's ego is momentarily bolstered by this incident, but when he and his wife arrive home, she deflates it by pointing out that the only reason the accident was not severe was because *she* had the presence of mind to apply the emergency brake at a critical moment: "You'd have hit that pillar sure, and killed both of us" (200).

Thurber's men, however, are sometimes resourceful—in eccentric ways. This is especially evident in "The Private Life of Mr. Bidwell." Mrs. Bidwell is being driven to distraction by her husband's incomprehensible behavior. A rather shy, retiring type of individual, Mr. Bidwell prefers at times to keep a low profile which, unfortunately, excites his wife's curiosity. It is during such times she becomes convinced he is "up to something." One evening while she is reading a book, she becomes intuitively aware that he is not inhaling and exhaling normally. When she questions this, he simply responds: "I was just holding my breath" (69). She tells him to stop it, but a week later at a party he does it again:

> Mrs. Bidwell . . . suddenly turned around as if she had been summoned. In a chair in a far corner of the room, Mr. Bidwell was holding his breath. His chest was expanded, his chin drawn in; there was a strange stare in his eyes, and his face was slightly empurpled. Mrs. Bidwell moved into the line of his vision and gave him a sharp, penetrating look. He deflated slowly and looked away. (71)

Later, while his wife is driving him home, he protests, "I wasn't hurting anybody" (71). But this doesn't impress his wife who complains that he looked perfectly silly: "What do you suppose people thought—you sitting there all swelled up, with your eyes popping out?" (71). Unable to assert his independence in this matter, he retreats, cautiously keeping outside the reach of his wife's criticisms. For one month he doesn't do anything to annoy her other than leaving his razor on the dressing table and failing to turn off the hall light before going to bed. But at another party, she senses again something peculiar, and under the third degree he admits to multiplying numbers in his head. In the end, she leaves him, which is what he wanted all along. He is last seen walking along a country road with his eyes shut, trying to see how many steps he can take without opening his eyes!

The impotency of the modern man has evidently reduced him to the status of a child, and it is no oversight that the Bidwells and Trinways of Thurber's world are treated like children by their wives. In one story, "Back to the Grades," the narrator actually returns to grade school and discovers it to be a mixed blessing. He is partially motivated by his failure to understand "taxation, gas-meter readings, endowment or straight-pay insurance policies, compound or simple interest, time tables, bank balances, and electric-light bills," along with his wife's suggestion that he ought to "go back to fifth grade" (116).

In accord, he moves back with his parents and enrolls at the local elementary school where he is again subjected to improbable mathematical homework assignments which he works out with his dad at night. Unfortunately, it turns out that his dad has been trying to figure out the same material since he too was a child. His mother forces awful tasting medicine down his throat when he claims to have a stomachache and cannot go to school one day, and, in the end, he gets thrown out of class for pulling the hair of a bright female student. However, when the teacher, Miss Malloy, hits him across the hand with a ruler for being naughty, he does get the chance to take it away from her, put her over his knee, and spank her. His analyst claims that being able to return to school and spank your teacher is excellent therapy, but our narrator claims he has yet to see any benefits.

For some of the men in Thurber's world, fate steps in and allows them to escape their present conditions, but not always for the better. A good example is the "Remarkable Case of Mr. Bruhl." Mr. Bruhl is the mild-mannered and very nondescript treasurer of the Maskonsett Syrup & Fondant Company, Inc., who has the unfortunate luck of being the double of a Mr. Clinigan, a notorious mobster who has rival gangs out to murder him. At first, Mr. Bruhl is terrified that he is going to be mistaken for the mobster and be accidentally gunned down. But as the story progresses, he becomes increasingly more and more like his double until he even assumes his mannerisms.

> He talked out of the corner of his mouth, his eyes grew shifty. He looked more and more like Shoescar Clinigan. He snarled at his wife. Once he called her "Babe," and he had never called her anything but Minny. He kissed her in a strange, new way, acting rough, almost brutal. At the office he was mean and overbearing. He used peculiar lan-

> guage. One night when the Bruhls had friends in for bridge—old Mr.
> Creegan and his wife—Bruhl suddenly appeared from upstairs with a
> pair of scarlet pajamas on, smoking a cigarette, and gripping his re-
> volver. After a few loud and incoherent remarks of a boastful nature, he
> let fly at a clock on the mantel, and hit it squarely in the middle. (171)

By the end of the story, he thoroughly assumes the identity of the gangster
and is actually gunned down. When the police question him as to who did it,
he refuses to talk. "They never talk," says one of the cops. "Hearing this, Mr.
Bruhl smiled, a pleased smile, and closed his eyes" (173).

Another one of Thurber's modern men maintains his identity as a man by
becoming something of a "wild card" in the story "Everything Is Wild." His
name is Mr. Brush and he is very unpleasant. He grumbles with the garage
man in his apartment house; he dislikes foreigners no matter how friendly;
he detests most parties and the people he meets there, and he hates most
games—except poker. While at a party with his wife's friends, he gets the
chance to name the game when it is his turn to deal the cards. The game he
wants to play is called Soap-in-Your-Eye or, he claims, as they call it out
West, Kick-in-the-Pants. Nobody has heard about it and with good reason.
It is his own invention and has rules that are incomprehensible and inconsis-
tent to everyone except its inventor! In the end, he pulls in all the chips. On
the way home, he is delighted by his coup despite his wife's disapproval.
She thinks he is a "terrible man," but he has a jolly good time—being mean!

Unlike Benchley and Thurber, E. B. White approached the male-female
dominance issue another way. For White, weakness can be translated into
strength if it is part of an evolutionary process whereby survival is granted
not to the most masculine but rather to the most philosophical of men.
White's retreat to the country from the hectic atmosphere of New York City
became the source of a series of reflective, humorous essays collectively
published in *One Man's Meat* (1938). In them, he frequently refers to his
own life, whether past or present, as a guide to how man may accept the
present and prepare for the future because, by this time, the growing rise of
fascism abroad was beginning to preoccupy the American mind more than
the Great Depression. Amidst a world filled with seemingly powerful and
invincible men or supermen, as some may have called them, White would
side more with the temporal failures of life and like Milton recall that "they
also serve who only stand and wait."

In "The Summer Catarrh," he discovers a comforting parallel between
his life and that of the eminent American statesman, Daniel Webster. They
are both victims of ragweed and the other various airborne irritants that precipitate itchy eyes, clogged sinuses, and a general feeling of malaise. Web-

ster, however, was not affected until he had reached the age of fifty, whereas White has been suffering since he was six.

As a youngster, White first discovered that he was different from the other boys when he went for summer drives in his father's surrey:

> I noticed that every time I rode behind a horse my nose began to run and my eyes grew unbearably itchy. I told my father that it was the smell of the horse that did this thing to me. Father was skeptical. It was a considerable drain on his finances to support a horse at all, and it was going a little far to ask him to believe that the animal had a baleful effect on any member of the family. Nevertheless he was impressed—I looked so queer and I sneezed with such arresting rapidity. (7)

Webster too faced a harsh realization in that his aspirations for the presidency would be forever thwarted by a "runny nose [that] bore a predictable relationship to the Gregorian calendar." (7). Vilified by his friends for betraying the cause of humanity and freedom, what, White asks, could these detractors know of the man scourged by an allergic body?

> Across the long span of the years I feel an extraordinary kinship with this aging statesman, this massive victim of pollinosis whose declining days sanctioned the sort of compromise that is born of local irritation. There is a fraternity of those who have been tried beyond endurance. I am closer to Daniel Webster, almost, than to my own flesh. (8)

Thus, from the weakness comes strength and an ability to endure the hardships to which the flesh is heir. And as Webster found the need to accept compromise—the Compromise of 1850—so, too, does our author with the freshly cut grass in his backyard. To be hindered by an allergy, White feels, allows for a "special identification with life's high mystery which in some measure indemnifies us for the violence and humiliation of our cosmic distress and which makes up for the unfulfillment of our most cherished dreams" (10).

Weakness as inner strength again becomes an issue in the essay titled "Clear Days," where White finds himself at odds with the local gentry for failing to "do something" about "his" deer.

> "You goin' to get your deer?" I am asked by every man I meet—and they all wait for an answer. My deer-slaying program is a matter of considerable local import, much to my surprise. It is plain that I now reside in a friendly community of killers, and that until I open fire myself they cannot call me brother. (Dale, 19)

But the truth, he confesses, is that he finds it impossible to give the venture serious thought. He has fired a rifle once or twice in his youth, but most of his shots have been directed at mechanical ducks in the penny arcades along Sixth Avenue.

While White was making the best of the current situation, Clarence Day was fondly reminiscing about an earlier time where the paterfamilias ruled supreme. *Life with Father* became one of the most popular novels of the thirties and was soon grabbed up by the Hollywood studios eager for a sentimental success. Actually, the original movie version starring Irene Dunne and William Powell was a derivative of a popular stage play, which in turn had been derived from the book. Its success not only was immediate but understandable; all three versions struck a responsive chord in the American soul which was eager to recall an age where society and life in general were understandable or, at least, predictable. Whether Day is advocating a return to a world of fixed, almost impenetrable, values or whether the American public actually thought that such an age could ever exist again is moot. In all likelihood, it was probably just pleasant to dream, for a moment, of a time that could only exist in the imagination.

It is hard to say whether men dreamed a bit more about this world than did the women in the audience. The world as Day's "Father" sees it is quite clear—men are strong and women weak. Furthermore, men are always right and need to be placed on a pedestal within their families. Thus, when Mother becomes ill in the chapter "Father Is Firm with His Ailments," Father becomes "lumpy with gloom," not having his wife about to "laugh at or quarrel with" (64).

In the world of finances, women are more prone to spend on impulse and fail to consider the long-range effects of their decisions. Father finds charge accounts a serious temptation for his wife: "They were no temptation to him. He knew that the bill would arrive on the first of the month and that in a few days he would pay it" (111). Mother, however, is of a different persuasion: "When she bought something and charged it, the first of the next month seemed far away, and she hoped that perhaps Father wouldn't mind—he might be nice about it for once. Her desire for the thing was strong at that moment, the penalty was remote, and she fell" (111). She is woefully ignorant of the daily household finances. Every now and then she feels sorry for Father's attempt to establish a sense of order:

> She put down all sorts of little expenses, on backs of envelopes or on half-sheets of letter paper of different sizes, and she gave these to Father with many interlineations and much scratching out of other memoranda, and with mystifying omissions. (112)

Father, of course, can never establish order from this "feminine chaos," but when he gets angry or critical, his wife relies on the status quo: "She had to do the mending and marketing and take care of the children, and she told Father she had no time to learn to be a bookkeeper too" (112).

Secure in their separate worlds, Father and Mother become the rockbed of matrimonial solidity. The thought of either suing for divorce or being unfaithful to their partner is incomprehensible. Mother is too dependent on her spouse for support. As for Father, his egocentric perception of the world precludes any infidelity whatsoever.

> He thought of his marriage as one of those things that were settled. If any woman had really tried to capture him, she would have had a hard time. He was fully occupied with his business and his friends at the club, and he was so completely wrapped up in Mother that she was the one his eye followed. He liked to have a pretty woman next to him, as he liked a cigar or a flower, but if either a flower or a cigar had made demands on him, he would have been most disturbed. (175)

Even if it never really existed, such stability remained an ideal that Depression audiences could easily appreciate in their troubled times.

Among the American humorists of the Great Depression, Dorothy Parker adopted a different approach in her analysis of men-women relationships. Subtle changes had occurred, and, for Parker, the best way to explore these changes was through a series of one-sided dialogues, often from the woman's point of view, as is seen in *Here Lies*. Parker is rarely obvious in her approach, preferring instead to tease the reader into imagining the thoughts between couples who are largely preoccupied with themselves. This is not to say that her narrators are intrinsically selfish and self-centered. Their preoccupation stems more from a terrible sense of loneliness and a fear of abandonment. The narrators in many of Parker's stories are usually sympathetic figures who, if anything, have forgotten how to love, or probably have never really experienced it. As such, they become pathetic creatures, the psychological cripples of an economically declining age, unloved and loveless. A paralysis of the spirit has set in.

A large part of the paralysis is evident in the characters' inability to effectively communicate with one another. It is very evident in their one-sided conversations, one of which appears in "Just a Little One." The story is replete with the clichés of conventional courtship. A boy and a girl are out on a date and have stopped in at a local bar to have "just a little one." It is obvious from the girl's tone that she is very interested in her companion, Fred. She talks gaily about the decor and her love for animals: "Don't let me take any horses home with me. It doesn't matter so much about stray dogs and kittens, but elevator boys get awfully stuffy when you try to bring in a horse" (122–23). A shift in tone occurs, however, when her boyfriend happens to mention that he has been out previously with another girl, Edith. Our narrator becomes "catty," making frequent belittling remarks about Edith, her clothes and physical appearance. All this is understandable and natural under the circumstances. It is the tone at the end of the monologue that captures the reader's interest and makes it, along with the other stories in *Here Lies*, a reflection of the thirties. The girl appeals for her boyfriend's friendship because she cannot secure his love. She has a terrible fear of loneliness:

> After all, friends are the greatest things in the world, aren't they, Fred? Gee, it makes you feel good to know you have a friend. I feel great, don't you, dear? And you look great, too. I'm proud to have you for a friend. Do you realize, Fred, what a rare thing a friend is, when you think of all the terrible people there are in this world? Animals are much better than people. (127)

The story ends with the couple deciding to adopt a pet, a dog or cat or even a horse, but "just a little one" (128).

This ending is also reflective of the inherent problem most of Parker's characters have in finding love and companionship. The problem is that they are terribly egocentric (as is evident in the girl's persistent monologue), and it is this quality that prevents them from falling in love with anyone but themselves. The narrator of the above tale wants a pet, but only a little one, as if there is a qualifier for her limited capacity to love. Over and over again, Parker's characters desperately seek out love but are unable to give it themselves. Communication between couples, the primary requirement for any stable relationship, often breaks down or is lacking altogether.

In "New York to Detroit," a woman's desperate attempt to communicate with her lover not only is hindered by a bad telephone link-up but her lover's inability to understand her audibly, as well as figuratively. Her reason for calling is to obtain some assurance that he loves her. But her pleas for his affection are continually interrupted by his failure to understand what she is saying. When he finally does understand her message, he cuts her short by telling her how hard he is working and how he may have to delay coming home further because of another business deal. Then a group of "friends" suddenly barge into his apartment, making it even more difficult to talk. He tells her to write a letter, but she has already done so, to no avail. She becomes increasingly desperate:

"Listen!" she said. "Jack, don't go 'way! Help me, darling. Say
something to help me through tonight. Say you love me, for God's sake
say you still love me. Say it. Say it."

"Ah, I can't talk," he said. "This is fierce. I'll write you first thing in
the morning. 'By. Thanks for calling up."

"Jack!" she said. "Jack, don't go. Jack, wait a minute. I've got to talk
to you. I'll talk quietly. I won't cry. I'll talk so you can hear me. Please,
dear, please——" (298)

"All through with Detroit?" the operator asks her. At first, she says "no"; she
wants the line reconnected. But then she gives up, knowing that it is hope-
less. No letter or telephone call is going to be able to save this relationship or
make these people care for each other.

Women as victims of inconsiderate men is evident in many of Parker's
stories. Female counterparts to Benchley and Thurber's "poor boob," the
women are not physically abused or subjected to psychological control as
are the men in Thurber's stories, but instead suffer largely from their own
supersensitivity to comments and asides made by men who, although not
deliberately malicious, are blatantly insensitive and callous.

Such is the case of the man and woman in "The Last Tea." It opens with a
young girl waiting at a tea bar for her boyfriend who is forty minutes late.
When he arrives, he tells her he feels awful, and she makes the mistake of
thinking he is sick. Actually, he is suffering a serious hangover from a wild
party the previous night. She is concerned; she is solicitous; she hopes he
will soon feel better. Then he "slips" by telling her he met a fantastic girl at
the party, a Carol McCall. Immediately the girl's tone becomes antagonistic
as she hears more and more about this girl from her boyfriend. First he tells
her that she is a real "looker." "Oh, really?" she responds: "That's funny—I
never heard of anyone that thought that. I've heard people say she was sort
of nice-looking, if she wouldn't make up so much. But I never heard of anyone that thought she was pretty" (324–25).

The dimwitted boyfriend, however, fails to take the hint and continues to
describe the other "attributes" of Carol—her wit, her intelligence, her being
asked to go into the movies. The girl shoots back:

> There was a man up at the lake, two summers ago. . . . He was a director
> or something with one of the big moving-picture people—oh, he had
> all kinds of influence!—and he used to keep insisting and insisting that
> I ought to be in the movies. Said I ought to be doing sort of Garbo parts.
> (326)

Thus, they continue their conversation at cross-purposes, or as Edith Wharton once said, looking at each other through the wrong ends of the telescope. Parker's characters are all desperate for love, but their failure to communicate effectively dooms them to solitary lives.

It also prevents successful marriages. Simply because a couple has been able to weather the rocky shoals of courtship does not mean they are capable of handling the stormy sea of matrimonial affairs. For Parker, marriage simply compounds the problems that already exist. In "Here We Are," a couple on their honeymoon make the same mistakes we have seen couples make in previous stories; the husband compliments the looks of one of the bridesmaids, which in turn makes the wife angry. The ensuing "fight" takes numerous turns and twists with each accusing the other of insensitivity or trying to spark jealousy until their train finally nears its destination, New York. They resolve never to fight again. "Ah, baby. Baby lamb," says the husband, "We're not going to have any bad starts. Look at us—we're on our honeymoon. Pretty soon we'll be regular old married people. I mean. I mean, in a few minutes we'll be getting in to New York, and then we'll be going to the hotel, and then everything will be all right. I mean—well, look at us! Here we are married! Here we are!" To which the wife responds somewhat reluctantly, "Yes, here we are. . . . Aren't we?" (66).

For the wife, the uncertainty of the times makes her fear for her own future happiness. Thinking of the millions of people worldwide who get married each day fills her with a palpable sense of doom and despair. She thinks of them "all over everywhere, doing it all the time. At least, I mean—getting married, you know. And it's—well sort of such a big thing to do, it makes you feel queer. You think of them, all of them, all doing it just like it wasn't anything. And how does anybody know what's going to happen next?" (53–54). Her mistake is in thinking that people change for the better after they are married, but they often do—for the worse.

Such is the case of Mr. and Mrs. Weldon in "Too Bad." The story opens up with two ladies breathlessly wondering how their friends, the Weldons, could be getting a divorce; they seemed so devoted to each other—he the good provider, she the consummate housewife. "[T]hey got along so beautifully together—why, it just seems as if they must have been crazy to go and do a thing like this," says one lady to her friend (99). What these ladies don't know is that Mr. and Mrs. Weldon have never communicated with each other. Even during courtship they had little to say, as Mrs. Weldon recalls:

> . . . she hadn't worried about it then; indeed, she had felt the satisfaction
> of the correct, in their courtship, for she had always heard that true love

was inarticulate. Then, besides, there had been always kissing and things, to take up your mind. But it had turned out that true marriage was apparently equally dumb. And you can't depend on kisses and all the rest of it to while away the evenings, after seven years. (94)

When they visit friends or strangers, they are animated and lively. But with each other they reside behind curtains of silence, except for the occasional nod of acknowledgment. Their innermost thoughts remain forever locked within their minds—the husband hating his wife's long fingernails, she disliking the way he never sits down with her at the same time for dinner. They never fight, but neither do they love. They are soulless and emotionally dead products of the modern age.

Even the traditional values of the earlier paterfamilias have become sullied with time. Such a father is Mr. Durant. In the story, "Mr. Durant," the central character of the same name is portrayed as a benevolent, hardworking businessman who is apparently entrenched in married life, devoted to his two children and a wife who makes excellent fish chowder. But he has a roving eye. He likes to flirt with women he casually meets during his daily commute to the office, and at the office he has engaged in a long-standing affair with one of the secretaries, a natural thing to do, he feels, because he is, at fifty-nine, at the prime of his life. However, one night his children confront him with a dog they wish to adopt—a bitch. This gives him concern, and a sense of prudery overcomes his benevolent, fatherly wishes for his children's happiness. Such a dog, he feels, will soon be the object of the amorous attentions of all the male dogs in the neighborhood: " 'Disgusting,' he repeated. 'You have a female around, and you know what happens. All the males in the neighborhood will be running after her. First thing you know, she'd be having puppies—and the way they look after they've had them, and all! That would be nice for the children to see, wouldn't it,' " he berates his wife. She protests, but he keeps the upper hand, resolving the problem by throwing the dog out and lying to the children that it ran away (119–20). For Parker, the benevolence of the paterfamilias is merely an illusion, based on lies and deceit in a male-dominated world. The thirties did not destroy it; they merely showed it for what it really was all along.

The lack of communication, general destructiveness, and decline of values within modern marriage were views in accord with most of the Depression humorists besides Parker.

Don Marquis's celebrated duo, Mehitabel the cat and Archy the cockroach, often paint a dim portrait of marriage in their exploits in *archys life of mehitabel*. After a particularly bad experience with a tomcat named Percy who leaves her with a litter of kittens and false promises, Mehitabel sums up her view of all such relationships:

> the next four flusher that
> says marriage to me
> i may really lose my temper
> trial marriage or companionate
> marriage or old fashioned american
> plan three meals a day marriage
> with no Thursdays off
> they are all the same thing
> marriage is marriage
> and you can't laugh that curse off (217)

In Day's "The Owl and the Pussycat," from *After All*, a confirmed bachelor owl is hoodwinked into marriage by a crafty pussycat who hurries him off to a Turkey on a hill "who was the nearest thing to a clergyman that could be found, or even better—more like a bishop." They end up eating

> [an] indigestible wedding breakfast, as prescribed by tradi-
> tion—"mince, and slices of quince," nothing could be more dyspeptic
> than that—and the Cat inaugurated the petty thrifts of married life right
> at the start by allowing only one spoon for the two of them. Or it may
> have been merely her unhygienic sentimentality. And then, each think-
> ing his own weary thoughts, they went back to the shore, and danced
> with the abandon of lost souls.

"So," concludes Day, "the curtain goes down on them" (20–21).

Part of this confusion concerning marriage and the relations between the sexes for the Depression humorist stemmed from radical changes in the way men perceived women during the decade. As men were toppled from their traditional pillars of economic dominance and authoritarian rule, the "new" women were often viewed as either sexually aggressive or, at least, blandly uncaring.

For E. B. White, the advertising media was partly responsible for this confusion. A short essay, "Ravished Lips," from *The New Yorker* questions the strange moral ambiguity that surrounds the advertising of cosmetics targeted for women. For White, it becomes a reflection of man's general confusion as to what the "ideal" woman should be. Maybe in the old days the "ideal" was for her to be a wife and a mother, but today the key to her appeal is to appear "ravishing yet virginal," as one advertisement would have it:

And there is the daring new odeur, Gabilla's Sinful Soul, exotic and naughty. One would say that ladies are now enabled to ask, in the language of the odeur, for love licit or illicit, for enduring fidelity or for the wanton tweak. Let us hope that the ladies, with their fragrances, are not embarrassed by a too great confidence in the New York male's sense of smell, debauched as it is by blowing dust, burned motor fuels, and desiccating office heat. (Dale, 153–54)

For some humorists, however, the portrait could be grim and unsettling.

The great American humorist and political commentator, Will Rogers, would note in a 1933 article that the traditional view of women as the "gentle sex" could no longer apply in the modern age. He comes to the defense of a friend and publisher of the Chicago newspaper, Robert McCormick, who has been criticized for claiming that an astonishing number of women seem to be spearheading the war momentum in Germany.

Now I don't want to bring any more "she" condemnation down on him, but out here in California a couple of months ago, when they put on that lynching, women were the rooting section, and the original encouragement of the thing came from the "she" sex. So I guess, Mr. McCormick was about right at that. Many a man has got a licking because his wife has said: Go on, get him, John, you ain't a-going to let him say that, are you? (Sterling and Sterling, 230)

It seems only logical, concludes Rogers, to expect women behind any war effort. "They enter a thing with more spirit and enthusiasm. You let a woman get up at a recruiting meeting and denounce the whole thing, and defy the boys to join up, and I will lay you a bet that the first fifty hands that tore her asunder, would belong to the fair sex" (231).

"Tough" girls frequently surface in the humor of Damon Runyon and especially in one sketch, "That Ever-Loving Wife of Hymie's" from *Blue Plate Special*. The "guy" in this story, Hymie Banjo Eyes, is married to a blond "doll" named "Lasses." Neither can be considered reputable or exemplary examples of an ideal marriage. Hymie, an untidy racetrack gambler whose eyes "bulge out as big and round as banjos," has a penchant for promoting over-the-hill horses and marrying dames such as "Lasses," short for "Sweet as Molasses," an "adago dancer" out of some nightclub. As far as our narrator is concerned, she is about as sweet as green grapefruit and is about as cuddly as a porcupine, but Hymie puts up with her whims and pouty petulance like any browbeaten husband out of Benchley or Thurber. That is until Florida, at Hialeah, where he, being short on cash, agrees to use her as collateral against a bet of $500 put up by Brick McCloskey, a bookie, and, unbeknownst to Hymie, the sometime lover of "Lasses." The bet centers on Hymie's horse, Mahogany, winning at the track, a seemingly improbable occurrence.

The day of the race, our narrator encounters "Lasses" up in the grandstand, apparently unperturbed by her husband's making her part of a bet. As the race commences, Hymie's horse first leads then falls back a bit until it is running neck and neck with another horse. At this point "Lasses" begins to shriek for the jockey to speed up, and our narrator finds it necessary to distance himself from her, wondering how Hymie could have ever considered her fragile and delicate.

> Well I wish to say that "Lasses" voice may be all right if she is selling tomatoes from door to door, but I will not care to have her using it around me every day for any purpose whatever, because she yells so loud I have to move off a piece to keep my eardrums from being busted wide open. (367)

When Mahogany is declared the winner, "Lasses" lets out a screech and falls over in a faint. Everyone, including our narrator, assumes that she has swooned under the emotional tension of having come so close to being lost in a bet. But what they don't know, and only our narrator finds out at the end, is that the jockey she was rooting for was not the jockey on Mahogany but, instead, the one on the other horse, Side Burns. So much for the "ever-loving" wife of Hymie Banjo Eyes!

In Christopher Morley's account of the Depression family and the American man, *Human Being*, the chief character, Richard Roe, not only is dominated by his wife while he is alive, but, after his death, is soon forgotten as she pushes out of their apartment all remembrances of him: "Except for a photograph, firmly encaged in silver on Mrs. Roe's dressing table, and a few forgotten cigar ashes now covered by cigarette stubs in the shank of an untippable scarlet smoking-stand, there were no evidences in the apartment of Richard Roe" (16). Furthermore, his breakfast bowl is now being used by the family dog.

In fact, as a father and husband from the thirties, Roe rarely exercised any authority in the family unit. It seems only natural that our knowledge of him after his death would too be limited. How many men, Hubbard wonders, pass through life like a breath on the wind? How many of one's concerns of the present become the preoccupations of future generations? Man's ability to be remembered stems primarily from his ability to achieve dominance over his environment while he is alive. But the modern age and the changes and erosions created within the family unit during the Great Depression have precluded the continuance of the traditional paterfamilias, substituting in its place the nondescript man in the business suit, Richard Roe. No longer an idol in his family's eyes, the modern man inevitably slips into a benevolent obscurity. They even forget his birthday, as is the case in Roe's family.

Evident throughout Morley's novel is women's insatiable thirst for power, power and control over a traditionally male-dominated environment. The home is the first to fall under complete female control. The woman becomes supreme lord and dictator of what was once referred to as "the man's castle," adjudicating authority and bestowing praise rarely. Roe's wife, Lucille, has grown with time into what Morley calls one of those "aggrieved females" who must prove their husband wrong at every opportunity, believing that anything that gives him pleasure must be deducted from her own enjoyment.

The need to nag also affects the children of the house, for they soon learn from where power comes. In Richard Roe's case, the daughter, Gladys, who essentially gets along with her dad, soon realizes that to lubricate the wheels of domestic tranquillity and to insure her independence within it, she must always side with the dominant parent, her mother:

> To take a strong line against Richard was sure of maternal approval. What psychological effect this may have had on the girl herself would be too long an inquiry to pursue. It will work itself out in her own life, as these lessons must. At the time of her father's death, when she had to turn to and look for a job, she began to suspect that there was something both humorous and tragic in the misunderstanding. The notion that man is the workhorse, destined by divine allotment to toil for woman's luxury, received some drastic revision in her mind when she undertook earning for herself. (210)

Thus, independence does have its drawbacks. As in Gladys's case, it involves economic responsibility, for one cannot rule without power. And in the thirties, power spelled money.

Furthermore, the traditional retreats for men, the former bastions of male dominance—clubs and the world of business—are falling under feminine influence.

> Like the small efficient Japanese in the crumbling continent of China, women had invaded the old easy-going empire of man, burst open its flimsy pagodas and antique fortresses. Upper Broadway was a street in

a conquered city. In almost every window were the emblems of the vic-
tors. Flowers, perfumes, ribboned steamer baskets of rich unwhole-
some nougats, aphrodisiac movies, trashy novels—all designed for
women. Their most personal and psychological requisites flaunted
everywhere in shameless display. Even the cigar store, the barber, the
shoe-shine stand, old havens of masculine retreat, lay open to their tri-
umph. Men were as helpless as the crabs packed in trays of ice and sea-
weed in the chop-house window, doomed and yet still bubbling a last
heroic disdain. (67)

But not every morsel on the man's dish of life has been tasted by women, for
there still remains many a tasty tidbit, tantalizingly appealing but unfail-
ingly beyond her grasp. According to Morley, it is at such times the modern
woman still finds herself powerless and frustrated, resigned to retreating to
the washroom downstairs, "woman's only safe retreat in the stone world of
business. What unguessed stories of tears and tantrums those bleak sanctu-
aries could tell" (41).

For men, the sanctuary is more within the world of dreams or romantic
asides. In Morley's world, men are more likely to engage in the spontaneous whim, the unpredictable gesture of chance, rather than stick to the
path of prudence and levelheaded thinking, as do the wives. In many ways,
it is the world of the child, but children in the modern age are much older
than their years, and it is *they* who scold or are more embarrassed by a parent's behavior than the other way around. Thus, Roe's daughter recalls
what for her was a painful incident involving her father and a singing blind
man:

> "If a blind man can sing I don't see why we shouldn't," he said. He
> started singing, right there on the pavement. Of course I was dreadfully
> embarrassed, because he had no idea of music. His favorite tune was
> *Dorothy, Old English Dance*, that crazy thing they always give children
> to practice on the piano. I was learning it then, and he used to ask me to
> play it I don't know how many times. When he started to sing it on the
> street I was so ashamed of him I ran home. (75)

Interestingly enough, he sings a song of innocence and of a childhood long
since vanished and embarrassing in the modern age.

Like Morley, other writers of the Depression era often portrayed childhood with harsher colors. Gone were the "illusions" of innocence and pu-
rity. Gone too were any notions of tranquillity and even happiness. With the
collapse of the traditional values of the paterfamilias, a modern child
emerged—tough, flexible, and resilient—capable, at times, of assuming a

parental role. Like Richard Roe's daughter, the modern child is frequently embarrassed by a parent who "acts like a child" and is unable to maintain his or her sense of decorum and authority in the adult world. For the Depression adult, the modern child often becomes a "brat" or, at least, a mystery.

Ogden Nash's poetry frequently explores the complexities of adult-child relationships from two perspectives—that of the adult and that of the child. In "To a Small Boy Standing on My Shoes While I Am Wearing Them," we are addressed by an adult who has given up trying to understand the modern child. Indeed, he wishes they would universally disappear and especially get off his shoes.

> I do not like the things that you say
> And I hate the games that you want to play
> No matter how frightfully hard you try,
> We've little in common, you and I. (Smith and Eberstadt, 18)

He concludes that while the child's antics may delight some people, "keep your attentions to me in check, / Or, sonny boy, I will wring your neck" (18).

Depending on which way one interprets its enigmatic message, "My Daddy" can be said to offer a rather disquieting view of parent-child relationships:

> I have a funny daddy
> Who goes in and out with me,
> And everything that baby does
> My daddy's sure to see,
> And everything that baby says,
> My daddy's sure to tell.
> You *must* have read my daddy's verse.
> I hope he fries in hell. (41)

But the obscurity of its tone further enhances Nash's humorous dichotomy found in many of his poems dealing with children or marriage. Unable to completely embrace the "family" values of the past, he establishes an uneasy truce with what appears to be a Freudian ambiguity in the present.

In one poem, "Song to be Sung by the Father of Infant Female Children," he adopts the persona of an outraged father who, like some modern perversion of King Herod, plots infanticide as a way of protecting his own property, in this case, his daughter. His fear surrounds the process whereby little boys grow up to marry little girls:

> Yes, I loathe with a loathing shameless
> This child who to me is nameless.
> This bachelor child in his carriage
> Gives never a thought to marriage,
> But a person can hardly say knife
> Before he will hunt him a wife. (30)

The only way to arrest the habitual process is through torture or infanticide: "A fig for embryo Lohengrins! / I'll open all his safety pins. . . . Then perhaps he'll struggle through fire and water / To marry somebody else's daughter" (31).

Better yet, Nash notes in another poem at his iconoclastic best, why bother to have children in the first place? Who, he asks in "Did Someone Say 'Babies,'!" started the rumor that "just by being fruitful / You are doing something beautiful, / Which if it is true / Means that the common housefly is several million times more beautiful than me or you" (15). People would certainly be better off financially if they did not have children. They would have a chance for "fame and financial independence" if they did not have to support a family of "unattractive descendants." Thus, the best solution for the betterment of mankind is to wage war on traditional values and long-term objectives in favor of immediate economic satisfaction: "To arms, Mr. President! call out the army, the navy, the marines, the / militia, the cadets and the middies. / Down with the kiddies!" (15).

For Alexander Woollcott, however, the modern child is not merely a nuisance; it is unnervingly adult. His own goddaughter, he observes in "Hanson Is" from *While Rome Burns*, displays a decorum and presents opinions more typical of Lady Macbeth than the "vacuous" Dora Copperfield. One seven-year-old girl he knows by the name of Sally displays, at times, an unsettling animosity for another girl whenever the latter is within earshot. She croons a war song in which her rival is shot, brained, and skinned; the skin is then turned into a sleeveless dress to match Sally's tan shoes! "Well," concludes Woollcott, "there you have Sally, in a nutshell." He is thinking of writing a suitable bedside story for her, but wonders if her taste might be more for a history of two rival queens from barbarian times who, "in their squabble, killed off most of each other's children and grandchildren" (70).

Thus throughout the thirties, the nation's preconceived notions of what the family is or was during the age of the paterfamilias came under attack from the literary humorists no longer content to maintain the status quo in light of the social turbulence of the decade. Values had changed, and with them had our perception of ourselves as adults and children. Alongside the reversals of fortune had come a concomitant shift in the roles traditionally played by men and women. Some of the changes were viewed as beneficial; others were seen as detrimental, but all were unpredictable, and, like so many of the other changes that were to occur during the thirties, set the foundation for ideologies and beliefs from which there could be no turning back. As Benchley, Thurber, Parker, and others would frequently show us in their works, the best way to weather through these turbulent times was with a sense of humor, which, according to one of the most critical observers of the age, H. L. Mencken, was the indispensable attribute of any successful marriage, for the "woman who is amused by her husband, even if her amusement involves condescension, is not going to end by hating him. Nor is the man going to hate his wife who finds a trace of clownishness in her" (DuBasky, 133).

CHAPTER 3

Racial and Ethnic Humor

Racial and ethnic humor was not unique to the decade of the Great Depression. Its psychological and historical roots dated back to the very beginnings of the American republic. The eighteenth and nineteenth centuries had already produced countless varieties of wit and folktales aimed at specific cultural groups, from the British and Yankee New Englander to the African American and the Irish immigrant. Few, if any, ethnic or religious groups were totally immune from the occasional barbs of humor that were usually belittling and often vicious in content.

Similar varieties of humor were not uncommon throughout the world, but its evolution on the American scene was far more persistent and entrenched, owing, in part, to the new nation's ethnic ambiguity and lack of homogeneous cultural identity. During the Depression, its popularity soared with examples frequently appearing in the media as well as in literature. The nation, blessed with the increasing mobility offered by the automobile and a broadening cultural awareness stimulated by modern technology such as the radio, cinema, and, by the end of the decade, television, was rapidly becoming even more aware of its ethnic diversity and the mixed feelings this awareness engendered.

The fact that racial and ethnic humor can often be attributable to deep-seated, primordial emotions, such as clannishness, fear of those outside one's group, and other feelings of prejudice and intolerance, has resulted in its general condemnation within modern society, or at least within polite circles. This, however, does not mean that it has disappeared altogether, for its principal appeal lies among people who feel threatened by their surroundings and other ethnic groups. Negative traits, such as excessive sexuality, uncleanliness, gluttony, or criminality, are often projected by such groups upon anyone they feel threatens their physical, economic, or psychological security. Today such pockets of fear still exist; during the Great Depression, however, they were universal.

With the increasing unemployment and economic uncertainty of the times, ethnic stereotypes rapidly became for many a way to explain the incomprehensible. Unemployment in the major cities of the Northeast could be attributed to the "greedy machinations" of Jewish bankers or the "sly activities" of immigrants or black labor that had recently arrived in town. Humor deprecating specific ethnic or racial groups fostered increasingly strong prejudicial views that would later come to a crisis in America during the fifties and sixties, but during the thirties it might have served a salutary effect in helping defuse serious resentments and hostilities that would have otherwise exploded into race riots. Humor, even if it was mean spirited, helped many a victim feel like a victimizer and the one truly in power.

Furthermore, ethnic humor eventually helped the unassimilated become the assimilated in American society, especially during the thirties. For all of its drawbacks, this is the one principal trait of racial and ethnic humor of the Great Depression that made it a seminal influence in the growing liberal trends toward the civil rights movements of later decades. Such varieties of ethnic humor relied heavily on self-deprecatory humor and realism, as well as "revolving" stereotypes that become, with time, more heroic than pejorative in their attributes.

A good example of the above was the gradual change that had already occurred surrounding the "Yankee" image of previous centuries. Although at first a negative stereotype of American backwardness, it grew to become a symbol of American shrewdness and perspicacity. Southern stereotypes of the African slaves as shiftless, lazy, and sneaky evolved with time within the African-American community to become characters of instinctive cleverness and determination, survivors in a world the white race was slowly destroying. Similar trends are also evident in the ethnic humor directed at other groups such as the Irish, the Italians, and the Jews—all of which were to be equally represented in the humor of the Great Depression.

Changes within the context of racial and ethnic humor during the Great Depression were in part fostered by the gradual changes in how society in general and the ethnic or racial group itself were perceived. This was largely due to the ever-increasing influence of the movies and the newsreels that often preceded a main feature. Considerable ambiguity and ethnic confusion often appeared. A good example surfaces in one of the most popular films at the end of the decade, *Gone with the Wind* (1939). Blacks are uniformly presented as subservient and often incompetent and untrustworthy. Mrs. Wilkes's servant, played by Butterfly McQueen, assures Scarlett O' Hara that she is knowledgeable in midwifery only to panic and run amok when Mrs. Wilkes's moment of trial is at hand. But in another scene, Scarlett is saved from a "fate worse than death" by a courageous former slave. In countless other films of the thirties, the African American shuffles and bows to a dominant master race, eyes bulging and teeth grinning, but, at times, too, becomes a leader and the one in command.

The newsreels further jolted the sensibilities of complacent audiences with vivid depictions of racial intolerance and bigotry or outbursts of black anger. More lynchings of blacks were to occur in the South during the Depression than at any other time since the Civil War. The Harlem riots of 1935 left behind twelve dead (135 men, women, and children of all races in hospitals with serious injuries), eighty-nine men under arrest, and damage estimated at almost half a million dollars. The image of the fearful and self-effacing black depicted by the scriptwriters of Hollywood no longer logically followed the images flashed from the newsreels.

Similar conflicting portraits of other ethnic groups appeared often in the media of the thirties. Sportscasters gushed over the form of the Italian pugilist, Primo Carnera. The exploits and antics of New York's lovable mayor, Fiorello La Guardia, captivated millions. But lurking in the background was the darker side of Italian-American life—organized crime—and the shadowy figures of such types as deposed gangster Al Capone, now retired to Florida to spend out his last days, and new arrivals such as Lucky Luciano and Guiseppe (Joe the Boss) Masseria, leaders of Manhattan's underworld. Negative stereotypes of Italian-American violence were further compounded by the sensational attempt on President-elect Roosevelt's life in 1933 by a crazed anarchist, Guiseppe Zangara, who suffered from chronic indigestion and hated politicians.

German Americans had to contend with the conflicting images presented by a hero such as Colonel Lindbergh and the man charged with kidnapping his son, Bruno Hauptmann, during the disturbing trial of 1935. The humorous attempt of Arthur (Dutch Schultz) Flegenheimer to evade federal income taxes in a court case in upstate New York by pointing out to the jury that it was as much their fight as his, proved persuasive and made them sympathetic for a man who was also a partner in Murder, Inc.

Thomas E. Dewey, special prosecutor appointed by New York State's Governor Lehman to break the hold organized rackets had on New York City, had his hands full prosecuting the likes of Dutch Schultz and Lucky Luciano, and he quickly established a reputation as an amazingly thorough and diligent investigator. Old stereotypes of the Irish as humorous, sly, and naive would resurface in the press releases detailing the amazing adventure of Douglas "Wrong Way" Corrigan, who in 1938 soloed across the Atlantic in a rundown airplane carrying 320 gallons of gasoline and sixteen gallons of oil. He made the flight nonstop in less than twenty-seven hours and was greeted by Ambassador Joseph P. Kennedy. Returning home, he was treated to a hero's welcome in New York City and dubbed "Wrong Way" Corrigan by the press because the first words out of his mouth when he landed at Baldonnel airfield in Dublin were, "Isn't this Los Angeles?" When he was told it was Dublin, he responded, "Well, what do you know! I must have flown the wrong way!" It seems that Corrigan had asked federal authorities for permission to fly the Atlantic in 1937 but was refused on the grounds that such a flight in the plane he presented would be suicidal.

When the Bank of the United States failed on the eve of the Great Depression, it was a media sensation. Its collapse involved four affiliate corporations, in excess of $200 million, and more than a million stock units. Thousands of depositors, including many small merchants on New York's East Side who refused to believe that such a thing could ever happen, found their life savings gone. At the heart of the collapse were three individuals, Bernard K. Marcus, president; Sol Singer, vice president; and Isidor Kresel, an attorney, who together were charged with masterminding a pyramid scheme that went well beyond the bounds of prudence and sound banking laws. Although Kresel was exonerated, both Marcus and Singer were convicted and sentenced to terms in Sing Sing Prison. The event not only foreshadowed future bank failures, it also reinforced conventional stereotypes of the Jew as a swindler.

Many of these and countless other images of racial and ethnic groups presented in the media would resurface again in the literary humor of the age. But many authors often adapted the stereotypes to convey a particular message, as did those who used them to reinforce existing prejudices. Some even relied on current events for their source of inspiration, as was the case of Damon Runyon in his sketch "Broadway Financier" from *Money from Home*.

Loosely based on the above scandal surrounding the collapse of the Bank of the United States, its central figure is a "doll" named Silk who "scores a big one" and collects a sizable financial estate from her boyfriend, Israel Ib, a Jewish banker from the Lower East Side of Manhattan. As is evident in the narrator's description of him, Israel Ib is reflective of many of the stereotypical views that Americans in the thirties had of Jews. Ib is involved with money; he has a large nose and is as "homely as a mud fence"; and, as the story progresses, he is a swindler who will rely on the bank's funds to keep his girlfriend in jewelry and fur coats, including a few apartment houses and some real estate.

In other ways, as our narrator will also point out, he is a man like most men. He runs a thriving bank and has a reputation for being a "quiet, industrious guy, who has nothing on his mind but running his jug and making plenty of scratch" (259), until, that is, the day he first meets Silk. Henceforth he joins the rest of mankind by making a fool of himself and getting into a lot of trouble over a woman. Our narrator observes that it is sad when a person as smart and as shrewd as Ib lets himself get hopelessly involved with such a streetwise girl as Silk. But he also recollects that there are many others who are undoubtedly much smarter and similarly involved in precarious situations involving women, "so it is all even" (259).

Most of the depositors in Ib's bank are also Jews who, like Ib, reflect both negative and positive traits of the typical Jewish stereotype. When Silk pays a visit to Ib's bank later in the story, she encounters the depositors gathered outside the failed bank and a strong smell of herring in the air which simultaneously surprises and disgusts her. These people, our narrator comments, are unable to "understand about such matters as busted jugs. They are apt to hang around a busted jug for days at a time with their bank books in their hands, and sometimes it takes as much as a week to convince such people that their potatoes are gone for good, and make them disperse to their homes and start saving more" (262). One fellow, "a short, greasy-looking guy with bristly whiskers and an old black derby hat jammed down over his ears," happens to spot Silk in the crowd, and a riot ensues in which she is almost beaten to death by the frenzied mob of depositors who also blame her for the bank's failure. Despite her ordeal, however, Silk sympathizes with the crowd because she herself was once the victim of unscrupulous bankers that fraudulently squandered her mother's savings.

The story ends on a happy note with Silk telling a kindly Jewish judge, Judge Goldstein, that she wants to voluntarily turn over to the depositors all the holdings Ib gave her. She does and everyone is satisfied. Even Israel Ib reforms, returning to his conscientious ways and his old job as the bank's president!

Runyon's dual view of the Jewish stereotype is not atypical of ethnic humor during the Great Depression. Nor is its negative image indicative of a general bias against Jews as a race. Instead it serves as a reflection of society's combined fear and admiration for a race that was, in the thirties, still relatively unknown and unappreciated. In fact, Runyon's humor is not that much different from the ethnic views presented in Jewish folk humor that frequently combined negative and positive elements within the same stereotype.

A similar situation is again presented in the Jewish tale "Sam Kravitz, That Thief," by Michael Gold. "Why did I choose to come to America?" a father responds to his questioning, native-born children; "I will tell you why: it was because of envy of my dirty thief of a cousin, that Sam Kravitz, may his nose be eaten by the pox" (Ausubel, 42). As our story progresses, a morality play unfolds in which the virtues of our narrator are contrasted against the deceptive and underhanded behavior of his cousin, Sam Kravitz. The virtues of our narrator are not necessarily ethnic specific. In fact, his naiveté, optimism, and hardworking attributes might apply to almost any new immigrant in America then or now. But he is also Jewish, and in being Jewish helps dispel the traditional negative stereotypes of the Jewish community.

Our narrator transforms the negative image of Jewish persistence into the virtue of an unbending optimism and faith in the future. Even though some of his earliest illusions are somewhat shaken by the unpleasant realities he encounters in the New World (a "rich" friend turns out to be quite poor and disagreeable, and his surroundings in New York City are not as pleasant as he had hoped they would be), he remains convinced that the future is inevitably going to be better if not for himself, at least for his children. Despite his own bitter disappointments, he proudly tells his son and daughter that someday they will be a doctor and a teacher, respectively.

Contrasting sharply with him is his cousin, Kravitz, a swindler and a thief. Pictures of him sent to the family in the Old World presented another portrait, a man who wore "a fine gentleman's suit, a white collar like a doctor, store shoes, and a beautiful round fur-hat called a derby" (42). But our narrator discovers that his cousin is actually a sour, disagreeable manufacturer of suspenders who is disliked by other merchants and is barely able to keep his own shop financially solvent. Our narrator is given a position of the most menial sort in his cousin's establishment, but is soon made a "partner" when his optimism and easygoing manners make him a favorite with potential buyers and business increases. However, while on a trip with his wife at Niagara Falls, to see "that big water with the rainbow and Indians," Kravitz steals the entire business and its profits away from him, leaving him penniless. Our narrator confronts his cousin who merely laughs at him: "He showed me paper from a lawyer proving that the shop was his. All my work had been for nothing. It had only made Sam rich," he confides in his children (47).

In another story, "Bluff," by B. Kovner, the *Schacher-Machers* and *Finaglers* (manipulators and petty swindlers) are exposed for what they are but not entirely condemned in light of the times in which they live. The main character of the story, Beril, is a man who complains of his poverty if he feels he is about to be tapped for a loan, but just as quickly boasts of his wealth when the opposite is true. When confronted by an old friend on the street who inquires of his state, he laments, "One doesn't live, one doesn't eat, one is dressed in tatters." But when he finds out that his friend is doing well, he starts to boast:

> Since you're well provided, I'll tell you the whole truth: I too am well off! My heart told me long ago that a depression would come and that I would be out of work, so I saved a bit of cash in the good days. No, I didn't trade on Wall Street, neither did I deposit my few dollars in the Bank of the United States which went flop. Believe me, I didn't throw my money around. That's why I'm getting along now. (Ausubel, 152)

Once again his friend asks him for a loan, only again to hear the "real truth," which is that he is not really rich but very hard up. Incensed over Beril's deception, his friend berates him:

> Just out of curiosity I wanted to feel your pulse, to see whether it's possible to get a loan of a few dollars from you in time of need. But it hasn't come to that point yet, Beril! Since you've just told me the *truthful* truth, I too will tell *you* the truthful truth. I really don't need anybody's help. I had enough sense in my head to provide for a rainy day. Yes, Beril, thank God I'm provided for! And even if I had nothing I'd never come to ask you for a loan. I know you and I know your character too. I know that you don't like to do anybody a favor. Even if you were a millionaire I wouldn't come to ask you for a loan. I'd rather go to bed without supper than depend on you. (153)

But is Beril to be blamed for being such a liar? The Depression, he claims, has made him fearful of telling the truth:

> But where do you find fifties rolling around today? Nobody has anything. Take Chaim-Hersh, his tongue already is hanging out; Usher-Menasch stands in the breadline; Shachne-Lemmel goes around begging; Mechel-Moishe goes out like a candle. . . . And who is willing to

> lend money nowadays, who can and who dares? These days, if you
> lend somebody a few dollars, you can forget about them. (152–53)

In good times Beril would be just another *Schacher-Macher*, but in the thirties he is simply another frightened man of the street.

By the end of the thirties, however, events in Europe greatly altered the
perception of the Jew in much of the literary humor. With Hitler's persecution and obvious intent upon a "final solution," many humorists put aside
even their friendly barbs and adopted a more sympathetic and serious tone
needed for a world on the brink of darkness. Don Marquis's celebrated
cockroach, Archy, would rise to the occasion in "the ballyhoo":

> every time a european dictator
> gets at the end of his string
> and cant think of any other ballyhoo
> to attract the attention of the people
> he begins another attack on the jews
> centuries of persecution
> have so hardened and sharpened the jew
> that he survives his persecutors
> and outsteps them and outthinks them
> if these guys were smart
> they would give the jews a chance
> to disintegrate through luxury and ease
> instead of which they toughen
> the hebraic moral fibre
> through the ages and they will wind up
> by making the jews in the end
> what they were said to be
> that is the chosen people (281)

Thus, for Don Marquis, the stereotypical images of the Jew as shrewd and
persistent are the virtues of a race that over the ages has been able to survive
and endure despite countless persecutions.

Literary humor concerning African Americans, during the thirties, often
exhibited similar traits with the humor dealing with Jews. This was partly
due to a common ground of long-term persecution, whereby each ethnic
community had learned to rely on humor as a means of self-expression
within a society too powerful to overtly control.

One humorist, Zora Neale Hurston, based her writings on the folklore of
the rural South during the Great Depression. A graduate of Barnard College, she was also a student of the Haitian and British West Indian cultures

and a scriptwriter for Paramount Pictures. Among her works are *Jonah's Gourd*, *Their Eyes Were Watching God*, *Dust Tracks on a Road*, and *Mules and Men* (1935) in which she collaborated with Langston Hughes and from which our following story, "Talking Mule Story" is taken.

The story is derived from a black folktale she heard in her hometown of Eatonville, Florida, and is a classic example of how racial anger can be defused through humor. The story begins with a farmer telling his son to go and fetch the family mule, Ole Bill, for the day's work. Prior to putting on its bridle, it has been customary for the farmer or his son to address the mule with, "come round, Bill," upon which the mule compliantly acquiesces to the task at hand. But this time the mule acts differently; it rolls its eyes and talks back: "Every mornin' it's 'Come round, Bill! Come round, Bill!' Don't hardly git no night rest befo' it's 'Come round, Bill!' " When the farmer, mistrusting his son's explanation for not bringing the mule, goes to investigate, he, too, gets the same response from the animal. The mule, like a normally compliant black field hand, has done the impossible; it has talked back to its masters and has gone on strike! But this is not the end of the tale, for the farmer's dog also begins to talk to him, and when this happens, the farmer becomes so frightened he runs off. "Dat man is runnin' yet," our narrator concludes as the masters are driven off (Tidwell, 392–93).

The black as a tireless worker against impossible odds is portrayed in another Hurston tale, "Competition for a Girl." Three suitors for a pretty girl are told by her father that the one who wins her must perform "de quickest trick." One fellow takes a bucket to fetch some water from a spring ten miles off. When he is halfway back, he happens to notice that the bottom of the bucket evidently fell out while he was filling it: "[S]o he turned round and run back to the spring and clapped in dat bottom before de water had time to spill" (415). The second fellow asks for a "grubbin' hoe and a ax and a plow and a harrow," then proceeds to cultivate ten acres of woodland, plant a crop, and serve green peas for dinner. But it is the last suitor who wins the girl. He takes a high-powered rifle, goes off into the woods about seven miles, and shoots *at* a deer. Then he runs back to the girl's house, puts the gun down, and dashes back to the forest in enough time to hold the animal so the bullet will hit it!

This ability to transform negative situations and stereotypes into something positive is often encountered in the African-American folklore of the Great Depression. In an age where powerlessness was endemic, any image of strength or fortitude, no matter its origins, was something to be admired. Within the white man's culture, similar parallels were evident in the glorification of gangsters and bank robbers. For the rural black man of the South, there was the legend of Annie Christmas, as a WPA anthology of American folklore noted:

> Annie was a black gal who stood six feet eight inches without shoes, weighed over two hundred pounds and wore a neat mustache. She could carry a barrel of flower under each arm and another balanced on her head. Once she towed a keelboat from New Orleans to Natchez on a dead run. She wore a necklace of every ear, nose and eye she had gouged off of men in fights. Usually she dressed and worked as a man, but sometimes she primped up, shaved her mustache, filled her barge with fancy women from New Orleans and operated a floating brothel up and down the Mississippi. When she died her body was placed on a barge by her twelve coal black sons and all of them floated down the river and out to the sea, never to be seen again. (Weisberger, 236)

For the Southern black, Annie, the "Mississippi Madam" as she was also known, became another symbol of power and rebelliousness—as much so as Hurston's talking mule. Humor in both is able to channel otherwise negative stereotypes into something appealing and positive for the intended audience.

Nevertheless, stereotypical images of African Americans tend to dominate the pages of ethnic humor produced by white humorists during the Great Depression. Unlike black folklore humor of the rural South, white humor was intended for a different audience and as such catered to long-established prejudices, both derogatory and laudatory, regarding the black man. It appealed to an audience largely ignorant of the African American and his customs. Although the migration of blacks to the North during the thirties was not uncommon, many, either from choice or due to white prejudice, found themselves living in culturally isolated ghettos within the main Northern cities of Chicago and New York. As has been noted earlier in this chapter, the Harlem riots of 1935 shocked and frightened a white populace that knew next to nothing about conditions within the black community and its pent-up anger. Whites, whose only conceptualization of the black man was one derived from the movies and newspapers of the day, were frightened by images of violent destruction that belied their complacent beliefs that all blacks were subservient and easily manipulated by their "betters."

White American humorists were too caught up in this confusion, unable to clearly understand what this other race was like or needed. Some retreated within the well-worn clichés of previous generations, regarding the African American with fixed values which are often offensive. Others attempted to portray the black man in a more favorable light. Both groups were often confused and realized that what they wrote had to appeal largely to their own race.

The ambivalence is quite evident in James Thurber's "A Sequence of Servants" from *My Life and Hard Times*. The story details the qualities and activities of the most memorable servants within Thurber's childhood home; over the years they number upwards of 162! Among the blacks are two, Vashti and Mrs. Robertson. Of the two, Vashti is more the negative black stereotype. She rolls her eyes when she is frightened; she has a sexually promiscuous stepfather and an unmarried mother; she uses sex as a way of maintaining her boyfriend's interest in her; and there is even an allusion to her being something of a sneak thief:

> She was a comely and somber Negress who was always able to find things my mother lost. "I don't know what's become of my garnet brooch," my mother said one day. "Yassum," said Vashti. In half an hour she had found it. "Where in the world was it?" asked mother. "In de yahd," said Vashti. "De dog mussa drug it out." (84)

Far less stereotypical is Mrs. Robertson, a "fat and mumbly" old woman who had been a slave down South and often saw Union and Confederate troops marching by but never understood what they were fighting for. Totally apolitical, Mrs. Robertson exists more within the time frame of her own eccentricity, possessed by a feeling that something ominous is about to happen. Thurber recollects how she once drove his father to distraction by warning him that death was near while he recovered from a particularly unpleasant dental operation. Although she is proud of her race, she remains ambivalent about her position in the scheme of things, a casual observer on a day-to-day basis. "Mrs. Robertson had only one great hour that I can think of," Thurber recalls, "Jack Johnson's victory over Mistah Jefferies on the Fourth of July, 1910." She took a prominent part in the "colored parade through the South End that night, playing a Spanish fandango on a banjo" (90). Her minister claimed that the victory proved the superiority of the black race, but she later confesses to Thurber's mother that she still doesn't quite understand what he meant by saying so.

A similar ambivalence toward black domestics is again evident in S. J. Perelman's story "Kitchen Bouquet." Philomene Labruyere, an Amazonian housemaid with "the rippling muscles of a panther, the solidity of a water buffalo, and the lazy insolence of a shoe salesman," is the central character of this tale. A fitting parallel to the celebrated Annie Christmas of Southern lore, she accidentally picks up the family car when taking her suitcase out of the trunk. A suspicious and somewhat shifty individual, she barricades herself in her room at night where her employer is certain she engages in Caribbean voodoo rituals directed against him. Her sneakiness is only supplanted by her "consistency of cuisine":

> Meat loaf and cold fried chicken succeeded each other with the deadly precision of tracer bullets. At last, when blood and sinew could stand no more and I was about to dissolve the union, I discovered that this female Paul Bunyon had grown to womanhood under the bright skies of Martinique, and I knew a moment of elation. I let it be bruited through the servants' hall that I would look tolerantly on fried plantain, yams, and succulent rice dishes. That afternoon the kitchen was a hive of activity. The air was heavy with saffron, pimento, and allspice. I heard snatches of West Indian Calypsos, caught a glimpse of Philomene's head swathed in a gay bandanna. With the care befitting a special occasion, I dressed negligently but with unimpeachable taste in whites and cummerbund, mixed myself several excellent stengahs, and sauntered in to dinner for all the world like an up-country tea planter. A few moments later, Philomene entered with what might be called a smoking salver except for the circumstance that it was stone cold. On it lay the wing and undercarriage of an even colder chicken, flanked by two segments of meat loaf. (Namlerep, 5–6)

Our narrator discovers, however, that his maid's apparent failure is intentional because she has saved the best parts of the meal—*potage Parmentier avec croutons*, a crisp *gigot*, *salade fatiguee*, and *pot de creme au chocolat*—for herself! He dismisses her on the spot and sends her packing for St. Pierre.

As is quiet evident, Perelman's portrait of his black cook reflects an odd combination of admiration for her strength and anger for her deceptiveness. His view is not too distant from those imposed upon the African Americans by other white humorists of the thirties. In fact, it is so typical of the genre, it is difficult to attribute a definitive bias on Perelman's account until the end of the story, for it is here the author ends with an unfortunate cliché of his age: "And speaking of spades, could anybody put me on to one named Uncle Pompey, with a frizzy white poll and a deft hand for grits?" (8).

Negative images of African Americans are not restricted to Perelman, however. Demeaning references to blacks as "filthy Hottentots" surface in Clarence Day's immensely popular *Life with Father*, even though they are intended as a reflection of Father's bigoted point of view and not Day's. Ethnic or racial humor, especially when it enters into the realm of satire, is a double-edged sword at best, easily misunderstood and misinterpreted within the context of a politically correct age. Day's "Sic Semper Dissenters" from *After All* is a good example.

In it, Day employs the typical satirical persona of a white bigot who applauds the federal government's efforts to stifle free speech among blacks, "during the war-time censorship" of President Woodrow Wilson's postmaster-general. The infringements on habeas corpus during the national crisis are not unknown, but in Day's work they are principally directed at an aged "Hottentot" named "Hottentotten-tillypoo," who has the audacity to protest his plight, "grubbing up potatoes in an aimless sort of way, / Which really was the only way he had" (77). Arrested for sedition, for claiming "his neighbors didn't always do exactly as they ought," he is sentenced to twenty years in "all the local jails." The last we hear of him, he has forsworn off thinking, has "tied a piece of string around his tongue," and stands when any song is sung, which, according to our narrator, is inadequate: "When anybody differs with you, dammit, treat 'em rough, / Why, they ought to be bub-boiled alive and hung!" (78).

It is a sad legacy that similar negative images of the African American, images not necessarily reflective of the author's point of view but that of society in general, echo from the mouths of characters in other stories—Damon Runyon's street-smart narrator in *Money from Home* being one example. Blacks are frequently referred to as "jigs," "coons," "shines," and "smokes." In one tale, a racehorse that has been conditioned to allow only a black jockey on its back, lets a white man in greasepaint mount, but, afterward, some people claim "this is a knock to the way [the white jockey] smells" (194).

Fortunately, most of the images of African Americans depicted in the humor of the thirties tend more to the positive. In a decade where considerable reforms were being made in social issues, except for those involving racial or ethnic equality, some literary humorists helped set a new trend, often rejecting outright the preconceived notions of earlier generations. This was generally not the case in other forms of entertainment, such as the movies or the radio, where traditional stereotypes predominated almost exclusively. Appealing to a more literate and better educated audience, the Depression humorist found inspiration in the numerous WPA anthropological studies of the age that, for the first time in American history, attempted to bridge the gap not only between the various geographic regions of the United States, but its ethnic pockets as well, which, as late as World War II, still remained uncharted, terra incognita, for most Americans.

Day's "Portrait of a Lady," in *After All*, strikes out in this direction. It chronicles the exploits of a white friend who, with the spirit and drive of an

intrepid explorer, embarks on a journey to some islands off the coast of
South Carolina in search of local folklore from the poor black fishermen
and farmhand inhabitants. Her first mistake, she later admits, occurs when
she puts herself in the trust of a "white family on one of the more civilized
islands." While they are interested in her plans, they also feel she is in immi-
nent danger and follow her wherever she goes, insulating her from that
which she seeks. "I got the impression," Day continues, "of her tramping off
into the wilds, after breakfast, to look around for what she was after, in her
business-like way; and of worried hostesses panting along, following her"
(244).

Eventually freeing herself from their control, she lands on one of the islands by herself but has no place to stay. Still keeping within the traditional
bounds of discretion, she attempts to find shelter with a white family, only
to be rebuffed by the master of the household who refuses to take in a
strange lady when his wife is away. Her local guide, a black native named
James Bone, insists he can find shelter for her at a friend's house. But when
they arrive there, the family and relations of his friend, Peevie, have arrived
for a funeral and are occupying every room:

> But James Bone was insistent. He went indoors and stirred them up and
> made lots of talk and excitement, and never stopped until the funeral
> guests rose and went away, in the rain; and with them all the relations
> except old Aunt Justine and her nieces. These and the regular family
> somehow packed themselves into three rooms, and gave up the two
> best to Elsie, who promptly retired. I don't know where Mr. Jack slept.
> Maybe under the cart. (248)

Nor does their hospitality and kindness end here, for they assist in Elsie's
research, telling her tales of native folklore, and even pulling in a passerby
to supplement her collection. Their friendliness, however, is not automatic with all strangers, especially whites, as James Bone later informs
her: "We don't have no traffic with the white folks, only buying and sell-
ing. They keep to themselves, and we keep to ourselves, 'cept for that"
(249).

On another island, where Mr. Jack has relatives, Elsie encounters some
native women opening oysters, and who, with Elsie and Mr. Jack, sit down
to an impromptu picnic of seafood and bran cookies, talking until midnight.
Mr. Jack then escorts Elsie back to the mainland, leaving her at the dock
with the parting, "I stayed wid you to de en" (250). Day concludes with the
hope that his tale has afforded us a glimpse into his friend's life, but it simul-

taneously introduces its white audience to a world it rarely saw and genuinely feared.

If white racism is treated somewhat benignly in Day's story, it falls under a scathing attack in Dorothy Parker's, "Arrangement in Black and White" from *Here Lies*. The main character is a "liberal" society lady who enjoys ceremoniously applauding her "absence" of racism by frequently alluding to her husband as the bigot in the family: "Well, you know, he comes from Virginia, and you know how they are," she confides to a party friend (4). Her true nature, however, is frequently exposed during the course of her one-sided conversations, first with the hostess and then with the guest of honor, Walter Williams, a famous singer and a light-skinned black man.

She wants to meet the singer, but a mixture of social reserve and explicit bigotry prevents her from doing so. She confesses to the hostess that she has absolutely "no feelings whatsoever" regarding black people who are after all "just like children—just as easy going, and always singing and laughing and everything." And she *does* argue, she emphasizes, with her intolerant husband who says he "wouldn't sit down at the table with one for a million dollars." She is of a mind like her hostess, "giving this perfectly marvelous party for him, and having him meet all these white people, and all. Isn't he terribly grateful?" To which the bored hostess curtly responds: "I hope not" (5–6).

She continues to gush on with the hostess, perpetually exposing her cliché-ridden mentality, until the moment arrives and she meets the artist himself. It is now when she makes her biggest gaff, speaking with "distinctness, moving her lips meticulously, as if in parlance with the deaf." Across the room she chances to spot another black celebrity, a famous actress, and being off guard for the moment blurts out in the presence of Mr. Williams that she "looks almost like—," but catches herself. "I was just going to say Katherine Burke looked almost like a nigger," she later admits to her hostess. Of course, even if she had slipped he probably would not have said anything: "You know, so many colored people, you give them an inch, and they walk all over you. But he doesn't try any of that. Well, he's got more sense, I suppose" (9–10).

Besides Parker's tale, the tolerance of African Americans within a dominant white society of manipulators is evident in the humor of other Depression writers, such as Will Rogers and James Thurber. It was evidently not intended to serve as a clarion call to arms—to rebellion—as was often the case with much of the socialistic rhetoric of the day. It is doubtful that the many who rioted in Harlem in the midthirties had been inspired by the writings of Parker and others. Reality alone served as the chief motivation. But humorists like Parker were sounding an alarm for the potential of even more deadly future riots, which many in the decade were still too deafened by their prejudices to hear.

Will Rogers once claimed that he did not like to write humor that hurt anyone. This, unfortunately, is the main reason why modern criticism has apparently dismissed him as an inconsequential social critic. But one story, "Fisticuffs in Portland," is more than a gentle look at the African-American experience.

An otherwise direct account of a retired black boxer and now movie extra, Sam Baker, one has to carefully search between the lines for its serious racial theme, mingling with the general folksiness of Rogers's style. Rogers lets Baker narrate an account of a fight up in Portland, Oregon, some years past. It seems Sam, then semiretired, was minding his own business in Hollywood as a doorman at a local nightclub when a fight promoter approached him about taking a few rounds up in Portland because "another Colored boy was to go out in the fourth round, and didn't. He stayed till the sixth and could a stayed for a week, but his seconds throwed in a towel, when all that had happened to him was that he was jes goin' against de rules. He jes wouldn't lay down" (Sterling and Sterling, 182).

Unlike his predecessor, Sam quickly learns upon arriving in Portland that he is going to have to play by the promoter's rules or face serious consequences:

> I is called on by a couple of gun men, who inform me that there is one thousand dollars, and it's mine to keep, hold or destroy, BUT, here the guns come into the scene—that I was to go out in the first round. First round, understand! Not to get my dates mixed and dive in the second, but the first! Another Colored boy crossed us, and we been hunting for him for two weeks. But we ain't going to hunt for you, you are right here where your body will be found. If you carried all this out accordin' to de aforesaid, you gets another thousand, and if you don't, you is carried out. (182)

Like his opponent, Sam now realizes that to survive in this world he is going to have to do a lot of good acting, just like the stars in Hollywood. Still, a sense of pride inclines him to put on a good show and "do . . . some Barrymore, when the time comes." During the actual fight, he and his opponent slip up so many times, with Sam sometimes falling before his opponent has delivered the punch, that the audience soon spots a ruse and begins to boo and laugh at their antics. "Den I sunk down easy," Sam continues, "glanced over at the gun men, and stayed down. I wasn't going to make any mistake about the round, and here I is, back in Hollywood, safe and sound, and still jes as good a actor as Mr. John Barrymore." Sam knows well the quintessential requisite for the survival of the black man in Depression America—good acting: "You see, he [Barrymore] acts when he don't have to. I acted when I had to act—or else" (183).

The struggle for blacks to survive within the white-dominated society around them comes up again in a work by Thurber, "I Went to Sullivant" from *The Middle-Aged Man on the Flying Trapeze*. Sullivant, Thurber's grammar school, is described as a particularly difficult school to get through, not because of its academics but because it has the largest concentration of bullies and street-wise toughs to be found anywhere in Thurber's hometown. Most of its students have been held back for years, including one white chap in the fifth grade who is twenty-two and sports a mustache! Thurber claims he never could figure out why the parents of this kid let him stay in school so long. "All I know is why he kept on in school and didn't go to work: he liked playing on the baseball team, and he had a pretty easy time in class, because the teachers had given up asking him any questions at all years before" (104). Even tougher, however, Thurber remembers, was a black student named Floyd:

> Nobody knew—not even the Board of Education, which once tried to find out—whether Floyd was Floyd's first name or his last name. He apparently only had one. He didn't have any parents, and nobody, including himself, seemed to know where he lived. When teachers insisted that he must have another name to go with Floyd, he would grow sullen and ominous and they would cease questioning him, because he was a dangerous scholar in a schoolroom brawl, as Mr. Harrigan, the janitor, found out one morning when he was called in by a screaming teacher (all our teachers were women) to get Floyd under control after she had tried to whip him and he had begun to take the room apart, beginning with the desks. Floyd broke into small pieces the switch she had used on him (some said he ate it; I don't know, because I was home sick at the time with mumps or something). (105)

Harrigan, however, is no help. Floyd whips him too and sits on his chest until he promises to be good and say, "Dat's what Ah get."

Ironically, it is this burly outcast of the halls of academia who in the end becomes a friend and protector of the delicate and easily picked on Thurber. Having grown up and survived on the mean streets of the city, Floyd can easily usher his new friend down the dangerous corridors of the school. His protective spirit seems to spring from an admiration of Thurber's intellectual achievement. "I was one of the ten or fifteen male pupils in Sullivant School," Thurber continues, "who always, or almost always, knew their lessons and . . . how many continents there were and whether or not the sun was inhabited" (105). Thus, in the end it is he and not Thurber who assumes the subservient role as the bodyguard and, as such, has been manipulated by the even stronger conventions of society that place mental achievement above physical ability. Like Rogers's fighter, he becomes Hercules tamed, a shorn Samson, a potentially explosive pawn for future decades.

One may have well asked during the thirties if the plight of the African American was destined for him by God. Had not the black man always been subservient to the demands of the white race? Was not Africa known as the "Dark Continent," mysterious and beyond the reach of modern civilization? Was not the entire creation of Western philosophical thought and scientific achievement firmly settled on the shoulders of the white race? The average white American during the thirties thought so. Some even looked afar, to the growing trends in Germany for support for their beliefs. Although it might be a bit exaggerated to label any of the major humorists of the Great Depression as closet fascists, many of the examples seen so far would seriously disturb the sensibilities of many readers, of any race, in a more liberal age.

Don Marquis, however, was different. Something of an outcast himself due to his heavy drinking, he was the lone white humorist of the thirties to clearly address the brutality of racism through the biting sarcasm of his artistically prolific cockroach, Archy, and even questions the "sanctity" of the American way of life by so doing. It all comes out in "the big bad wolf" from *archy does his part*.

Archy's inspiration is derived from recently watching a Disney cartoon about the three little pigs:

> how cruel i said to myself
> was the big bad wolf
> how superior to wolves are men
> the wolf would have eaten those pigs raw
> and even alive
> whereas a man would have kindly
> cut their throats
> and lovingly made them into
> country sausage spare ribs and pigs knuckles

The superiority of the species, claims Archy, must be an irrevocable mandate of Heaven:

> when a pig is eaten by a wolf
> he realizes that something is wrong with the world
> but when he is eaten by a man
> he must thank god fervently
> that he is being useful to a superior being

But that which applies to the beasts of the earth is applicable to the races of man as well:

> it must be the same way
> with a colored man who is being lynched
> he must be grateful that he is being lynched
> in a land of freedom and liberty
> and not in any of the old world countries
> of darkness and oppression
> where men are still the victims
> of kings iniquity and constipation

It can be extended to those who suffered from the speculators and investment bankers who brought about the great financial collapse and massive unemployment:

> we ought to be grateful in this country
> that our wall street robber barons
> and crooked international bankers
> are such highly respected citizens
> and do so much for the churches
> and for charity
> and support such noble institutions and foundations
> for the welfare of mankind
> and are such spiritually minded philanthropists
> it would be horrid to be robbed
> by the wrong kind of people

But are we to seriously adopt the conventional view of society that "what is" must be? How long will the poor, the black, or the oppressed in any shape or form remain silent believers in the status quo? Like many in the movie audience, Archy, who has been so depressed he often contemplates suicide by "impersonating a raisin and getting devoured as part of a piece of pie," claims he will continue to toe the line of convention, fixed in his belief of "our national blessing" and of the age as "a great period in which to be alive." But he seems a bit coy with his "boss," claiming that "god is on the side of the best digestion" (285–86).

Unlike much of the ethnic and racial humor dealing with Jews and African Americans that either questioned or assaulted many of the conventional stereotypes, ethnic humor focusing on Europeans tended to follow long-standing prejudices and adopt worn-out clichés. Literary humorists, many of European origin, took delight in passionate Italians, thrifty Scots, drunken Irish, arrogant Germans, and dim-witted Swedes who frequently set the tone and helped the reader anticipate the ending without difficulty. Like the proverbial "Polish joke," the reader could be assured of a conventional conclusion. Surprise was not intended, or wanted, in these stories. Nevertheless, they are not without merit, for in many ways they, too, like much of the humor already viewed, are the production of a nation balanced between the naiveté of 1920s isolationism and the global commitments of an impending world war.

The Irish had been a fixture in the American cultural scene as far back as the Revolution, but not until the massive emigrations of the 1840s, due to the Great Potato Famine in Ireland, did they dominate large sections of the population. Nineteenth-century humor directed at the Irish was amazingly vicious in content. Often portrayed as offish brutes, thoroughly uneducable, they were detested in a largely Protestant America for their Catholic beliefs. However by the 1930s, these images were significantly modified to accommodate an ethnic group that had been predominantly assimilated into mainstream American life.

The principal image that remained was that of the Irish alcoholic or, at the very least, heavy drinker. A typical example is presented in Clarence Day's *Life with Father*. Morgan, the family coachman, is called upon one hot summer's day to harness the family horse to the dogcart and fetch some ice in the village. The narrator and his brother are expected to accompany him as well, a requirement of Mother's that Morgan fails to appreciate and finds irritating: "When we boys were along he couldn't take off his stiff black high hat or unbutton his thick, padded coat. Worse still, from his point of view, he couldn't stop at a bar for a drink. That was why Mother had sent us along with him, of course, and he knew it" (70). Morgan somehow, probably because he is also a "crafty" Irishman, slips free of his masters during some negotiations for ice and reappears "coming out of a side door down the street" with his hat tilted back and an air of satisfaction on his face.

When a story called for a cheap penny-pincher or someone neurotically thrifty, a Scotsman was naturally brought on line. It was an image that was largely fixed in society, and frequently surfaced in the ethnic folklore archives of the WPA. One story features a thrifty father who tells his sons that, on the infrequent times they wear their new shoes, they should take especially long steps. He capitulates only when his wife voices her concern that such a measure will result in the children splitting their pants. In another tale, a Scotsman settling his account at a general store is about to receive the customary bag of candy for the children, a common practice in those days, when he declines the shopkeeper's offer and requests instead the same value in a bag of nails. Another has a Scotsman going out into his backyard on Christmas Eve, firing a pistol, then rushing into the house to inform his children that Santa Claus has just committed suicide! Here is one short sketch, "So Tight," in its entirety:

> A Scotchman in order to teach his small son thrifty habits gave him a penny each day and saw to it that he deposited them in a white piggy bank. As soon as the boy had five pennies thus saved, the father removed the coins and gave the lad a nickel in exchange and had him place it in a larger blue china bank. And when the five nickels had been accumulated again the father took the smaller coins and gave him a quarter for them which the boy was taught to place in a large red receptacle. But the LARGE RED RECEPTACLE was a quarter-in-the slot gas meter! (Tidwell, 565–66)

With Andrew Carnegie's largess notwithstanding, the Scotsman remained the perennial favorite for tightwad jokes, or as Ogden Nash would observe in "Genealogical Reflection"—"No McTavish / Was ever lavish" (Smith and Eberstadt, 3). Another type of stereotype was forced upon the Swedes of the Midwest.

The term "dumb Swede" had been around for some time, at least since the nineteenth century, and probably stemmed from the language difficulties many of the early immigrants faced upon arrival in the New World. If assimilation did not occur rapidly, the general populace labeled the immigrant as "dumb." Because many of the Swedish immigrants tended to congregate in the upper Midwest where they found steady employment in the lumber industry and could easily maintain their language and customs at the same time, they were often stereotyped as being slow-witted. One tale, "Don't Monkey with the Buzz Saw," from a 1937 folklore anthology, presents us with a graphic example:

In the sawmills changes came quickly to meet the growing trade in fin-
ished lumber. The rotary saw replaced the crude "muley" saw and cut
twenty times as much lumber in a day's shift. Promptly millmen
learned how ruthless that whirling blade could be, and in time the familiar warning passed into common speech: "Don't monkey with the
buzz saw."

With the rotary saw splitting its spray of sawdust and the multiple
blades snarling through great logs, a mill crew was never far from danger. Every mill town had its men with mutilated hands. Over and over
they told the story of big Olaf's explaining to the foreman how he had
just lost a finger. The foreman thought the saws were guarded, but Olaf
demonstrated how it had happened: "Vell, Ae tak da boord dis vay wit
dis hand an dis vay wit da oder. Ae move de boord op to da machine lak
dat, and da first ting Ae know—YUMPIN YIMINY, DAR GOES ANODER
VON!" (Tidwell, 572)

Another immigrant group that was largely unknown and as such treated
with suspicion were the Finns. WPA studies of ethnic groups in the thirties
uncovered many an amusing anecdote detailing the cultural conflicts that
frequently arose when the Old World met the New. One involved the Finns
of Esko, Minnesota, and their neighboring farmers:

The Finns are a clannish people who cling to their Old World manners
and customs, and to a stranger may sometimes seem unfriendly. At one
time a suspicious farmer accused them of practicing magic and of wor-
shipping pagan deities. Entire families, he claimed, wrapped themselves in white sheets and retreated to a small square building set apart
from the dwellings and worshipped their gods, calling upon them to
bring rain and good harvests to Finns, and wrath upon their neighbors.
On investigation, however, it was discovered that although they did
wrap themselves in sheets and visit these "shrines" almost daily, it was
not in the zeal of religion but for the purpose of taking baths. The Finns
here are almost fanatical advocates of cleanliness, and each has his
own "sauna" or steam bathhouse. (Weisberger, 284)

It is unknown if the local farmers changed their attitudes toward the Finns
once they discovered the truth behind the strange happenings, but the epi-
sode does serve as a good example of the darker side of ethnic humor and
how it often evolves out of ignorance or suspicion of different customs.

The image of Germans, like that of the Irish, had been greatly modified
since the massive emigrations of the mid-nineteenth century. By the thirties,
they were largely assimilated and a dominant ethnic group in American cul-

ture, but besides the general views of them as being conscientious and hard-working, they were also stereotyped as arrogant and brutally fearless—an image fostered by the negative publicity they suffered during the First World War.

Many are the conflicting attributes of Thurber's German hired hand, Barney Haller, presented in "The Black Magic of Barney Haller" from *The Middle-Aged Man on the Flying Trapeze*. According to Thurber, Barney is one of the best hired hands he has ever had, "strong and amiable, sweaty and dependable, slowly and heavily competent" (159). But Thurber also fears that he traffics with the devil. On hot summer days when powerful and un-predictable thunderstorms fire up around his farm, Thurber hastily retreats to the safety of his home or barn, but not Barney, who continues to work out in the woods or fields as if nothing is going on around him. Unlike Barney, Thurber fears the power of the heavens and the wrath of God: "I always have a feeling that I am going to be struck by lightning and either riven like an old apple tree or left with a foot that aches in rainy weather and a habit of faint-ing." Barney, on the other hand, comes into the house during a terrible thun-derstorm merely to inform his boss that a huge bolt of lightning has cascaded down one of their lightning rods. "I should have dismissed it," Thurber continues, "but it had its effect on me. Here was a solid man, smell-ing of hay and leather, who talked like somebody out of Charles Fort's books, or like a traveler back from Oz. And all the time the lightning was zigging and zagging around him" (160).

With time, Thurber becomes convinced that not only is Barney immune to lightning, he creates it as well:

> About six o'clock next evening, I was alone in the house and sleeping upstairs. Barney rapped on the door of the front porch. I knew it was Barney because he called to me. I woke up slowly. It was dark for six o'clock. I heard rumblings and saw flickerings. Barney was standing at the front door with his storm at heel! I had the conviction that it wasn't storming anywhere except around my house. There couldn't, without the intervention of the devil or one of his agents, be so many lightning storms in one neighborhood. (162)

So when Barney eventually moves away, Thurber feels he might be able to rest a bit easier and put to sleep his fears of being struck by a bolt from one of Barney's storms. Unfortunately, the new hired hand is not as fearless as Bar-ney. Like Thurber, he is afraid of his environment and refuses to go up into the attic to clear out the wasps, whereas "Barney could have scooped them up in his hands and thrown them out the window without getting stung"

(164). The story ends on an ambivalent note with Thurber remaining convinced that Barney trafficked with the devil, but likewise unhappy that such a capable handyman is gone.

Along with the Germans, Italian Americans found themselves permanently associated with certain stereotypes, the most dominant being the gangster. This stereotype was in part fortified by current events and newspaper articles on such underworld characters as Lucky Luciano or Frank Costello; part of its successful permanence stemmed from an intrinsically romantic appeal to the lawless side in all individuals, then or now.

It seems only natural that such a stereotype would eventually surface in one of the stories peopled by Runyon's guys and dolls. Frankie Ferocious is one such stereotype, and he appears in "Sense of Humor" from *Money from Home*. Of course, his real name is not Ferocious. It's "something in Italian like Feroccio," but either way it's a suitable title for a man who engages in numerous vendettas. Our narrator is unhappy that Joe the Joker once gave Frankie the "hot foot," because Frankie will undoubtedly take it personally and maintain a lifelong grudge against anyone who lives within the borders of Manhattan. Heavy-set, swarthy complexioned, with hair "blacker than a yard up a chimney," and working as a "large operator in merchandise of one kind and another, especially alcohol," Frankie is a typical Italian-American stereotype of the 1930s (245).

Joe the Joker is the other stereotype. Jovial and easygoing, a practical joker of immense proportions, Joe represents the image of the Italian American as a buffoon, a clown, with a zest for the impractical or imprudent. "Sense of Humor" is a story about the conflict between these two men over the same woman, Rosa, who also happens to be Joe's wife. Rosa leaves Joe to go live with Frankie, a situation Joe is not too averse to because Rosa likes to spend lots of money on herself and her upkeep. "Do not feel sorry for me," he tells the narrator. "If you wish to feel sorry for anybody, feel sorry for Frankie Ferocious, and, if you can spare a little more sorrow, give it to Rosa" (247).

Joe soon finds out about a plot, however, whereby he is to be delivered to Frankie in a sack, because he refuses to give Rosa a divorce under any conditions. He decides to turn the tables on his adversary, employing a scenario not too different from the one found in the famous Verdi opera *Rigoletto*. He informs one of Frankie's gang, who is partial to him, that he will be delivered in a bag to Frankie, but alive, not dead, and when Frankie opens the sack he will be surprised by a gun opening fire on him. But sensing a double cross, which does occur, he changes his plan. A bag is delivered to Frankie who promptly pumps several shots through it because he has been tipped off about Joe's plan to turn the tables. No sooner has he done so than some police break onto the scene and arrest him for murder. And who is in the bag? None other than Joe's now ex-wife—Rosa! Revenge is sweet for Joe, and as an old Italian saying goes, it is a dish that people of taste prefer served cold.

Sometimes even obscure ethnic groups would appear on the pages of Depression literary humor. Day and Perelman present us with fleeting looks at Armenians and Latvians, respectively, even though most readers probably had never seen one in their lifetimes or even knew where they came from. An ominous portrait of an Armenian rug salesman appears in the chapter "Mother and the Armenian" from Day's *Life with Father*. His contradictory appearance is a foreshadowing of things to come, for his blue-black hair, dark skin, gleaming eyes, bad breath, and hooked nose immediately set him apart from the local gentry at the summer resort where the Day family is vacationing. But he does have perfect teeth, the kind of teeth Mother says most people would envy.

Mother's dealing with the Armenian possesses a similar dichotomy. She is a born shopper and is always in search of a "good buy," but the Armenian's repertoire of sales tactics alternatively appeals to her heart and offends her more delicate sensibilities. He claims to be a poor college student, working his way through school, and Mother is naive enough to believe his story, although she does wonder how in his broken English he can either understand or be understood by his professors. It is his aggressive bargaining over the price of a rug—groaning and shrieking over her offers, hissing through his teeth, and finally sinking into such a ghastly look that Mother fears he will fall into a fit—that forces her to close the deal and purchase the rug.

Understandably, her husband is infuriated when he finds out about the rug, claiming that he could purchase such rugs at "fifty cents a barrel on Front Street." Determined to throw both the rug and its salesman out onto the street, he marches off to the Armenian's establishment only to find the place locked up and a sign in broken English on the door: "BAK-NEKS-WEK." Years later, Day recalls, a news item was circulating about the terrible Turkish massacres of the Armenians, against which a local clergyman had been particularly outspoken. Father, despite having grown more tolerant on some subjects with age, still harbors deep-seated resentments against the Armenians. "That's just like a parson," he says to his son, "to sympathize with those fellows, without even asking first what they have done to the Turks" (139).

Equally ominous is the murderous Latvian maid employed by Perelman in "Kitchen Bouquet." Named Ilyeana, she so surprises Perelman with her eagerness to live in the country that he is convinced that she must be a fugitive from justice. He is right, for he soon discovers a newspaper clipping about a murder in Canada and how the authorities are searching for the victim's sister, the prime suspect, whom they believe escaped to Latvia. But, as Perelman continues, far from being there, "the victim's sister was standing at that exact moment peering over my shoulder in good old Tinicum township, Pennsylvania. I cleared my throat and edged a little closer to the fire tongs." "Ah, this happen every time I get good job," she responds in a matter-of-fact tone. "Always pickin' on me. Well, I guess I go up there and take a look at him. I know that head of hair anywhere." At the railroad station she gets a ticket to Savannah, which, as far as the author is concerned, seems a rather "circuitous route to the Dominion" (Namlerep, 8).

Events of the late thirties also introduced many Americans to ethnic groups that few understood or had even seen unless they lived in one of the major urban centers. One extensive but largely invisible class of citizens and aliens were the Orientals. Advances by the Imperial Troops of Japan against mainland China dominated much of the newsreels by the end of the decade, but even then the average white American knew little about the culture of either nation. New York and San Francisco had their Chinatowns, and many Japanese Americans were scattered throughout the West Coast where they had become successful, hardworking, and reliable shopkeepers and farmers. But partly due to the Oriental person's intrinsic reserve and self-effacing manners, he remained a mystery to the majority of other Americans. This reserve would later prove a liability, resulting in the internment of many Japanese in prison camps after the outbreak of World War II—a humiliating violation of civil rights that even today has not been properly addressed.

By and large, the Depression writer faced serious difficulties when incorporating the Oriental into a humorous sketch. As a race, their habits and lifestyle, except for their cooking, were so unknown to the average American, including the humorists, that it was difficult using them in a humorous vein. For Benchley, their lifestyle was too dull and nondescript for satire, although he is able to draw upon the Chinese reputation for wise sayings and the astute philosophy of Confucius for one essay, "Maxims from the Chinese," from *My Ten Years in a Quandary*.

It is largely composed of glib one-liners that read like the ramblings from some bizarre fortune cookie philosopher. "The wise man thinks once before he speaks twice" and "It is often difficult to tell whether a maxim means something, or something means maxim" are two examples. A short sketch of a Fan Lee from the same work, however, is more substantial, and presents us with some of the attitudes Americans largely held for the Orientals at that time. To begin, Fan is a remarkably dull individual who walks endlessly in the countryside, "with his hands on his elbows," thinking what comes after the letter, "W," and failing to interest us as a character, as Benchley notes. Suddenly he encounters himself coming in the opposite direction and philosophizes, "We are getting nowhere." Other asides, supposedly from Confucius ("the sensible man goes but a short distance with himself before taking his own temperature" and "eggs do not roll sideways") are equally pointless and eventually result in his double running away. As Benchley concludes: "Too much wisdom gets on the wise man's nerves" (216).

Although Benchley capitalizes on a carefree image of the Oriental as a philosophizing bore, Don Marquis presents a darker picture with xenophobic undertones in "hold everything," from *archy does his part*. Like much of Marquis's work, it is filled with Archy's usually pessimistic observations about life and mankind in general, but it is the ending that stands out, presenting us with an attitude that would dominate in the forties and preoccupy Americans even today: "when i was in hollywood / i ran across the ingenious theory / that the japs might make trouble / just because so many / americans had been coming in / to their state of california" (300).

Astonishingly prophetic, however, are Alexander Woollcott's observations in "How to Go to Japan" from his 1934 work *While Rome Burns*. In it he touches upon many of the little-known aspects of the Japanese lifestyle—unknown, that is, for the average American of the thirties. Having traveled extensively in the country, been a guest in numerous houses, and lectured at various schools there, Woollcott's presentation is remarkably evenhanded and quite perceptive for its time. He mentions the Japanese penchant for cleanliness, recalling how often he had to struggle to remove his own shoes before entering temples, homes, restaurants, and even the backstage of the theater. Nowhere in Japan, he claims, is one allowed to "trail the dust of the city onto the spotless mattings of the interior" (298).

Besides being immaculate about their environment, Woollcott continues, the Japanese are a friendly people who are fascinated by and imitative of American culture. The language barrier is not as acute in Japan, he notes, as it is in France. "If the French in a thousand years have learned less English than the Japanese in a hundred, it is not, of course, because they are slow-witted, but because they would really rather not know English" (299). The average Japanese child, however, is well versed in the favorite novels of

American children. At one school he forgets the name of Jo March's school in *Little Women* until he is rescued by a little girl "supplying 'Plumfield' in a stage whisper" (300). Japanese actors imitate the mannerisms of American thespians, often, as one Japanese stage manager observes, to their detriment, "expressing a mild dislike by such facial disarray as they formerly reserved for murderous hatred and indicating a slight surprise by calisthenic contortions reminiscent of epilepsy" (301).

Woollcott is in accord with the stage manager. The Japanese, he feels, are on the verge of losing the tranquillity of their own traditional culture in their haste to become Western. While visiting a pastoral retreat one beautiful spring day, enjoying the quiet interrupted only by the hum of children's voices or the echo of a distant temple bell calling Buddha's attention to a sinner's prayers, he becomes saddened when the peace is disturbed by the rasping sound of a radio reporting the closing prices on the silk exchange. Woollcott's friends, he further notes, see no future exchanges between the two countries except the military kind. Such talk, he feels, can only help foster increasing prejudice and misunderstanding on our part, but if war does come, he hopes that we, the ultimate victor in such a contest, will remember that we won the war "because we were larger, richer, and more numerous, and therefore not feel too proud about it. For I have seen just enough of Japan and the Japanese to suspect that such a victory might be only another of history's insensitive triumphs of quantity over quality" (305).

Almost as misunderstood as the Oriental were two other racial groups that had for a long time been a part of the American landscape—the Indians and the Mexicans. Although our failure to appreciate the Oriental stemmed, as Woollcott implies, from ignorance based on psychological isolation and geographic separation, false images of Indians and Mexicans were too deeply rooted to be easily excised. For more than a hundred years, white America had been raised on the traditional view that because both groups had opposed what most accepted as the manifest destiny of westward expansion, they were inherently bad and not to be trusted. Such views had been and still often are reinforced in the movies and textbooks. Most of the literary humor involving these groups came from folklore, possibly because the major humorists were either entirely ignorant of them or viewed them as too established in the public's consciousness to bear further comment.

Indians, in humorous folklore, are often presented in conflicting images. At times sly or lazy, as one tale reveals, they can also be remarkably stoic when compared to a white man:

On a cold dreary day an Indian and a white man were making a journey together. The Indian had on no clothing except a blanket, while the
white man was bundled up in all the clothes he possessed. The white
man continued to complain about the cold and to wonder why the Indian was not freezing. He said to the Indian, "I don't understand it.
With all my clothes I am about to freeze, and you, with only a thin blanket, do not seem to be cold at all."

"Is your face cold?" asked the Indian.

"No, my face is not cold, but I'm just about to freeze everywhere else."

"Me all face," said the Indian. (Tidwell, 573)

In a 1939 tale titled "The Lazy Indian and His Pet Trout," an Indian becomes
tired of having to constantly change the water in a barrel where he keeps a
pet trout, Tommy, and instead teaches it to exist, like the Indian, in an alien
environment.

He commenced by taking Tommy out of the barrel for a few minutes at
a time, pretty often, and then he took him out oftener and kept him out
longer, and by and by Tommy got so he could stay out a good while if
he was in the wet grass. Then the Indian found he could leave him in the
wet grass all night, and pretty soon that trout could live in the shade
whether the grass was wet or not. By that time he had got pretty tame,
too, and he used to follow the Indian around a good deal, and when the
Indian would go out to dig worms for him, Tommy would go along and
pick up the worms for himself. The Indian thought everything of that
fish, and when Tommy got so he didn't need water at all, but could go
anywhere—down the dusty road and stay all day out in the hot
sun—you never saw the Indian without his trout. (Tidwell, 402–3)

But adaptability has its limits, for one day when Tommy is following his
master into town, he falls through a chink on a bridge and disappears. When
the Indian goes back to find him, he discovers his beloved fish belly-up in
the stream below—drowned!

Outside the folklore of the thirties, few of the major humorists even
touched upon the American Indian as a fitting subject. Too remote and distant, a concern for earlier centuries, the Indian, as E. B. White notes in *One
Man's Meat*, had become with time something greater than himself—something "half way between DiMaggio and Christ" (24). For an earlier America, the Indian had been "agreeably bloodthirsty" and "definitely suspect,"
but in the modern age, thanks to "progressive education and some apprecia-
tive artists and writers in the Southwest," that image had become a Romantic cliché. "His pottery, his dance, his legends, his profile," White continues,

"are cultural and good. To my own son the American Indian is a living presence, more vivid than Popeye. To my boy, next month isn't December—it is the Month of the Long Night Moon" (24).

Mexicans, too, were largely ignored, but when they did surface, it was mainly within the folklore. Like the Indian, they represented, as a race, a "simplified" living style, which for Depression-weary Americans was preferable to the hectic and, for many who were unemployed, unapproachable material lifestyle of the North. Indeed, for many of the unemployed, the Mexican easily came to symbolize the plight of the dispossessed and downtrodden in an America where the class distinctions between the have and have-not's were increasingly apparent. One story recorded by the Federal Writers Project of the WPA for the state of California clearly shows the class divisions. It's titled "Give Him Time."

In it, a Mexican comes North of the border and falls into drinking with an American he meets outside a bar. The Mexican is used to his native mescal, but knows nothing of whiskey, which he starts drinking with the man and which soon gets him very drunk. The two fellows rent a room for the night, and, in the morning, the Mexican, still suffering the effects of a hangover, accidentally puts on his partner's shirt, which also happens to have a watch in one of its pockets. The Mexican hasn't wandered far from the hotel when the American summons the police. The "perpetrator" is soon captured and hauled before a crusty old judge who turns a deaf ear to the Mexican's plea for clemency due to his unfamiliarity with American alcohol. "Well you people ought to get familiar with American ways before you come up here," is the judge's response, whereupon the Mexican acquiesces, "Si, senor, send me to San Quentin." The startled judge asks him why he wants to go there. Has he ever been there before? Are his friends and family already "guests" of the state? The Mexican replies in the negative to these and other questions. The reason he wants to go to a notorious prison such as San Quentin is because he's heard on the street it's the best place "to learn all thees American ways." An unamused judge sentences him to a year in prison or ten months "on good behavior." "Caramba!" responds the Mexican in disgust as he's led off in handcuffs, "What you theenk I learn in ten months?" (Tidwell, 569–70).

Regional stereotypes also surface in the humor of the Great Depression, and although not in the truest sense classifiable as either ethnic or racial humor, do, nevertheless, share many of the characteristics of the two. Regional differences were far more distinct during the thirties than they are today. A population that remained largely within geographic boundaries from generation to generation, despite the advent of the automobile, was becoming increasingly fascinated with areas that had remained until recently as alien and unexplored as the dark side of the moon. One such area was the American South. Rich in native folklore humor, it became a prime source of material for WPA-sponsored anthologies of quaint and relatively unknown traditions and customs of the American people.

Southern folklore was certainly not unique to the thirties, having been a part of American literary culture since the Revolution. Much of it was based on an oral rather than a written tradition, publishing houses being somewhat scarce in the South until the twentieth century. As such, much of the folklore humor that was well known in the country had to do with only one part of it—New England. The Yankee was a persona everyone was familiar with. But who was the Southerner? What were his characteristics and eccentricities? In what ways was he similar or different from his fellow Americans? These were some of the questions people were asking in the thirties.

Kentuckians liked to capitalize on their reputation for fine bourbon, a characteristic observed in a 1932 "recipe" called "A Kentucky Breakfast." When in Kentucky, a Northerner is bound to be asked if he ever has had a Kentucky breakfast. The answer is likely to be in the negative, claims the narrator, whereby his Southern host will clarify: "A Kentucky breakfast is a big beefsteak, a quart of bourbon, and a houn' dawg." Now the Northerner can understand two thirds of this recipe, but not the last part. When he inquires as to the third ingredient, "What is the dog for?" he gets a "straight" answer—Southern style: "He eats the beefsteak!" (Tidwell, 568).

Other humorous stories from the South exhibit a similar "tall tale" form of exaggeration. One in particular, titled "Lead Go," presents a gun duel with a most unusual outcome:

> It happened down in the brush country. Two genuine Texas frontiersmen got into a difficulty and decided to shoot it out. They were both for a strictly ethical duel. Each had a long rifle. They met in a little opening, stood back to back, and then each took ten long steps straight out from the other. Simultaneously each turned around and with his right eye drew a bead on his opponent's left eye. Such precision was never seen even in the army. It wasn't considered sportsmanlike to shoot out the other man's right eye, and thus spoil his aim. So, as has been said, each shooter aimed at the other's left eye.
>
> Well, they fired at the same instant, and much to their surprise, and to the surprise of several men who were watching, neither bullet took effect. They shot a second time. The result was the same. To make a long story short, they stood there, reloading and aiming and firing until they had shot ten rounds.

"By grabs, there's something spooky about this," one of them finally said.

"There shore is," the other replied. "Speerits in the air or something."

"I'm just about ready to shake hands," announced the first speaker.

"Shake. Here's mine," agreed the other.

The two men advanced, each of them taking ten long steps, so that they met face to face exactly where they had parted back to back. After they had shaken hands and each had bit a chew off one plug of tobacco to pledge their good will, one of them happened to look on the ground.

"Shades of Jericho!" he exclaimed, "What is that?"

"Lead, by grabs, and still hot."

In fact, the ground was spatted with a pile of melted lead. So accurate had been the aim of the frontiersmen, each sighting his long rifle at the left eye of his opponent, and both firing simultaneously, that the two hot lead balls had met midway, stopped each other, and melted down to the ground. (Tidwell, 504–5)

Such surprises, however, were not uncommon in this state, as a short note on an event in Sherman, Texas, recorded by a WPA writer, reveals. It seems a log structure that served as the courthouse was once torn down in the town to settle a bet as to whether an old gray duck had made her nest under the building. History never recorded if she did. The next day the sheriff came by with a notice that had to be posted on the courthouse front door. Unfazed by the scene that presented itself and conscientious about his duties, "he dug the door from the debris, propped it up, and affixed the notice" (Weisberger, 334).

Examples of humor focusing on regional differences and racial and ethnic distinctions would proliferate throughout the Great Depression years. However, by the mid to late thirties, a new focus, devoted solely to the immigrant experience, would appear. Immigration to America had dwindled significantly during the postwar years largely due to severe limitations and quotas imposed during the 1920s. But with the increasing unrest in Europe during the thirties and the expansion of fascism abroad, a new wave of immigrants began to appear on America's shores. This new wave was not as poor or dispossessed as were those who had arrived a half century earlier, but it, nevertheless, suffered under the same hardships and cultural disorientation. American humorists often sympathized with the difficulties these new Americans faced, either having been immigrants themselves or the son or daughter of one. They well knew the confusion and humor that is frequently encountered in the acclimatization process.

Clarence Day was among this group, as is evident in his story "From Noah to Now" which appears in *After All*. In it, the American government has fallen under despotism, and, as a result, many who once despised immigrants have decided to "sail away and go to work in a new land themselves" (157). Their desires to flee, however, are tempered by feelings of loss, saying good-bye to old friends, relatives, and familiar neighborhoods. Emotions are temporarily uplifted by the prospect of a new beginning in a land called Atlantis, but their treatment upon arrival is not what they expected. Surly guards herd them from one holding bin to another, refer to them as "Hoogs" (which, as Day notes, is like Americans saying "Chinks" for Chinamen), and examine their eyes and pocketbooks before they are at last set "free."

Freedom has a price. The new Atlantin soon discovers that the dirtiest and worst smelling sections in the neighborhood are where he is expected to live. There he encounters many a prominent, well-educated individual from the "old country" who has been reduced to begging or holding a cheap, unskilled job simply because he has not yet mastered the new language. Even more perplexing are the cultural differences, many of which the American considers silly but which are necessary for him to know if he wishes to survive. He adopts so many new customs that he soon forgets what or who he is. His old friends drop away, but his children, who have been raised within the new culture, continue to spot his mistakes and look down upon him as a greenhorn.

> The natives of Atlantis would help you along, once in a while, by giving you lectures and telling you not to read your home paper. But you, who had felt so adventurous and bold, when you started, would have to get used to their regarding you as a comic inferior. Not even your children would know what you had had to contend with. Not one of the natives would try to put himself in your place. (61–62)

And where does Noah fit into all of this? Well, he was an immigrant too in search of a better land, but faced none of these problems—where he was going was uninhabited!

Some of the arguments presented by Day surface in other Depression humorists as well. E. B. White's "Anything Like That" (1932) from *The New Yorker* briefly mentions the xenophobic questioning of immigrants by Immigration Department personnel, questioning White feels is insultingly undemocratic although it doesn't seem to bother an immigrant friend on whose behalf he is a character witness.

> A young lady, born in Russia, confided to us that she was about to become an American citizen, and would we be her witness, for she needed someone to testify to her good character and good intentions. Greatly touched, we dressed in a semi-formal manner and accompanied her to a sort of barn over on the North River. Here we were tossed about from one United States naturalization clerk to another United States naturalization clerk, and eventually wound up before a bench, an American flag, and a grim, chilly examiner. After a few routine questions, the man suddenly speeded up his voice and inquired: "Do you believe in Communism, anarchism, polygamy—or anything like that?" And before we could pry into the phrase "anything like that" —which we felt it our duty to do—our young friend had blithely answered no, and it was all over. (Dale, 53)

White's friend is now an American citizen, he concludes, thoroughly Americanized like everyone else and "sworn never to believe in Anything Like That."

Leo Rosten's 1937 work, *The Education of H*Y*M*A*N K*A*P*L*A*N*, focuses more on humorous semantic misunderstandings between speakers of American English and those trying to learn it. The principal characters are Hyman, a recent arrival in the United States, and his teacher Mr. Parkhill, an instructor of a beginner's English class at the Night Preparatory School for Adults.

Kaplan's difficulty with the English language is reflective of his general inability to smoothly assimilate into the mainstream of American life. An apparently conscientious student, he nevertheless remains a thorn in his instructor's backside, not from a lack of perseverance or attention but more from a perpetual difficulty with vocabulary and meaning. Parkhill's frustration with his pupil is a reflection of the irritability that many Americans might feel when encountering someone living in the United States but unable to speak English. In one scene, Parkhill asks if anyone can tell him the meaning of the word "vast":

> Mr. Kaplan rose, radiant with joy. " 'Vast! ' It's commink fromm *diraction*. Ve have four diractions: de naut, de sot, de heast, and de vast."
>
> Mr. Parkhill shook his head. "Er—that is 'west,' Mr. Kaplan." He wrote 'VAST' and 'WEST' on the blackboard. To the class he added, tolerantly, that Mr. Kaplan was apparently thinking of "west," whereas it was "vast" which was under discussion.
>
> This seemed to bring a great light into Mr. Kaplan's inner world. "So is 'vast' vat you eskink?"
>
> Mr. Parkhill admitted that it was "vast" for which he was asking.

"Aha!" cried Mr. Kaplan. "You minn '*vast*,' not"—with scorn—
" 'vast.' "

"Yes," said Mr. Parkhill, faintly.

"Hau Kay!" said Mr. Kaplan, essaying the vernacular. "Ven I'm
buyink a suit clothes, I'm gattink de cawt, de pents, an' de vast!" (24)

Kaplan's lack of command of the English language by no means signifies a
loss of self-respect or sacrifice of high ideals.

Like most immigrants, he is confident in his own potential, a confidence
reflected in his signature on a classroom assignment. Distinct from the assignments the other students submit, Kaplan's has his name in bold letters
of "red-blue-green glory." Parkhill, like most Americans, has a hard time
appreciating this distinction, seeing it more as foolish bravado, the "youthful ambition" of a man who wants to become a "physician and sergeant"
(24).

This immigrant's belief in utopias engenders within it a concomitant
radicalism that native Americans might have seen as subversive during the
twenties. Kaplan's awkward and misspelled composition for labor reform
in which he asks, "Why should we slafing in dark place by laktric lights and
all kinds hot for $30 or maybe $36 with overtime, for Boss who is fat and
driving in fency automobile?" mirrors closely the growing labor movement
and social consciousness it created in the thirties. In this respect, he could be
said to be more American than his instructor who fails to understand its significance and instead complains that it fails to "meet the assignment" and is
not a simple exposition.

Kaplan, like his fellow classmates, eagerly anticipates his assimilation into
the American lifestyle. But assimilation is not always without peril, as Clarence Day previously noted. Cultural transition is often accompanied with un-
derlining feelings of loss and disorientation. This dilemma is beautifully
presented in another story, "Mushrooms in Bronx Park" by Michael Gold.

Gold's story is a portrait of his mother, who, as he claims, lived most of
her life on the Lower East Side, on the same street and in the same tenement,
possessed of a "peasant's aversion to travel." "In her Hungarian village no
one ever traveled far, except to America" (Ausubel, 350). Her husband has
assimilated better with his adopted country. He enjoys swimming every
Sunday during the summer at Coney Island. He enjoys the "razzle-dazzle,
the mechanical blare, the gaudy savage joys" of the amusement park; his
wife would rather walk in the fields and woods, as she did as a child in her
native country.

One Sunday they decide to go to the Bronx park, but the elevated train
ride is unpleasant and makes her feel sick:

> Her face flushed purple with heat and bewilderment. No wonder; the train was worse than a cattle car. It was crowded with people to the point of nausea. Excited screaming mothers, fathers sagging under enormous lunch baskets, children yelling, puking, and running under everyone's legs, an old graybeard fighting with the conductor, a gang of tough Irish kids in baseball suits who persisted in swinging from the straps—sweating bodies and exasperated nerves—grinding lurching train, sudden stops when a hundred bodies battered into each other, bedlam of legs and arms, sneezing, spitting, cursing, sighing—a super-tenement on wheels. (351)

She becomes happier as the train gets closer to its destination. Tenements disappear, replaced by small houses in weedy lots, and there are trees.

When they arrive at the park, she initially has to overcome a fear that she will be arrested if she takes off her shoes and walks barefoot on a grassy knoll. But there are no signs warning her to the contrary, nor are there any policemen nearby to apprehend her, so she does and immediately becomes alive and youthful to the astonishment of all her family.

When she enters some nearby woods to pick some mushrooms with her children while her husband remains behind, sleeping, she is completely transformed, and, for the first time in the author's memory, ushers her children into a secret garden of knowledge and folklore they never knew existed. She tells them about the different types of mushrooms she used to pick in the woods back in Hungary, and how mushrooms take on the aroma and color of the woods around them. When her son innocently asks: "Do they come on a string?" she snorts in disgust, "Those are the grocery store mushrooms. . . . Ach, America, the thief, where children only see dry, dead mushrooms in grocery stores!" (353). She and the children pick mushroom after mushroom, marveling at the texture and color of each. Just when they are about to return to where their father is sleeping, she flings her arms around them and kisses them impulsively. For the first time since her arrival in America, our author concludes, she is genuinely happy.

For another writer, however, an immigrant's overassimilation into the American way of life may result in his becoming a busybody, a "know-it-all" American. In Leo Katz's short story, "The Technical Expert," a recent immigrant finds himself being "educated" by one of his former countrymen, now an American, who feels he is best suited to be his teacher. The attempts of others to stop what amounts to be a boring, one-sided conversation are to no avail: "He was so filled with his mission, with his desire to smooth the newcomer's path in America, that nothing could stop him" (Ausubel, 517).

During the course of the story, the "greenhorn" is introduced to the modern miracles of the New World—the electric lightbulb, the gas stove, and central heating. But when the newcomer is told about the telephone, he stares back in disbelief. This motivates his "teacher" to go out, despite a heavy snowstorm, find a public telephone, and call him up. The technical expert also alerts his wife to be certain the disbeliever knows how to pick up and speak into the receiver. The entire apartment house is alive with curiosity as everyone gathers around to see the newcomer become "Americanized," according to the expert's wife. Increasingly annoyed by all the attention he is receiving and the prevailing attitude that he must be a fool without the wit, the immigrant deliberately refuses to acknowledge that he can hear a voice from the receiver after it's thrust into his face. The story concludes on the moral that a "pseudo-scholar is like a donkey that carries a load of books" (521).

Thus, the portrait of the immigrant, like most examples of racial and ethnic humor during the Great Depression, grew to reflect the increasing diversity of the American population. By encompassing both negative and positive features and amalgamating them into a unified portrait of each group, it effectively served, often unintentionally, as a window not only into our past but our future as well. Americans were beginning to learn in the thirties that what had previously been negatively perceived as one's backwardness and cultural diversity were actually the virtues of a new race on the verge of discovering itself.

CHAPTER 4

The Icons of the Past—
The Professionals

Nothing eroded more rapidly during the years of the Great Depression than the average American's belief in those who had come to represent the prosperity and stability of the decade that had preceded it. Among these icons of the past were the nation's politicians, policemen, professors, doctors, lawyers, businessmen, and bankers—individuals who up to that time had reflected and maintained an order of economic expansion unprecedented in the nation's history. Upon their shoulders had rested the faith of millions who had relied on their predictions of the seemingly invincible economic boom of the twenties and an age that predestined that virtually all schemes, financial and otherwise, could not help but be successful. If the average man and woman failed to understand the complexities of Wall Street investing, it mattered not. All they had to do was to follow the support and advice of those assuredly more knowledgeable in these matters to secure a toehold on the golden ladder to wealth.

In an age where everything seemed within reach, where a pervasive "can-do" attitude prevailed within the minds of most Americans, where the newspaper headlines frequently touted the amazing exploits of individuals such as Lindbergh or Babe Ruth, the skeptic who announced his reservations about man's limitations was bound to be labeled as something dangerous, possibly subversive, possibly a communist, or, at least, someone who had absolutely no faith in the American way of life. The fact that the nation's prosperity had in a large part been born out of its having been sheltered from the horrors of the world war failed to impress many. If the nations of Europe that had suffered most from the economic and social devastation created by the war—England, France, Russia, and Germany—failed to find a postwar prosperity, it was due to their lack of perseverance and hard work. War debts were expected to be repaid on time—an issue of contention that would later lead to loggerheads between an recalcitrant Congress and the French people.

That the problems of Europe could not, must not, become the problems of an American people was a deep-felt sentiment that would later resurface during the late thirties in the isolationist rhetoric of many fearful of another world war. It was a sentiment that had always had a deep hold on the American consciousness. Immigration quotas imposed during the twenties were more the products of a Congress fearful of new ideas than a concern for overburdening the nation's infrastructure—although such laws were often proposed with such intentions in mind.

At the heart of it was the principal fear of a profoundly conservative American business and political establishment—communism. Between 1920 and 1927, communism had surfaced during the notorious trial of Sacco and Vanzetti, two Italians who had immigrated to the United States in 1908 and who were charged with a robbery and double murder in South Braintree, Massachusetts, on April 15, 1920. Despite their claims of innocence, they were subsequently condemned to be executed by a judge and a jury angered and shaken by numerous protests and rallies, many of them sponsored by the Communist Party and supported by the socialists, which had broken out here and abroad in defense of the two defendants. Governor A. T. Fuller, on behest of the defense, appointed a panel of distinguished authority figures—A. Lawrence Lowell of Harvard University; President Samuel W. Stratton of the Massachusetts Institute of Technology, and Robert Grant, a former judge—to investigate the case independently, but despite a sworn confession from a Celestino Madeiros in 1925 that he and not the defendants was responsible for the crimes, the two men were not granted an appeal and died on August 23, 1927, in the electric chair, still maintaining their innocence.

Radical intervention into the American way of life became an increasingly important issue for the American businessman, but many failed to appreciate the foundations of labor unrest. Between 1933 and 1937, almost three hundred companies would spend over $9 million for munitions used in breaking up strikes. General Motors, alone, would spend over $1 million during that time period. San Francisco would witness one of the longest and bloodiest strikes in American labor history when the International Longshoreman's Association attempted to organize the West Coast waterfront in 1934. In certain circles, years later, rumors would surface that the initials J.S. on the Roosevelt dime indicated the secret control Stalin had over the American president, as well as the passage of bills related to labor and business.

Further damaging to the image of the American businessman were widely publicized newspaper accounts of corruption, political payoffs, bribery, and graft within the business community. A Federal Trade Commission probe revealed that many utility magnates had milked operating companies to amass profits for holding-company empires and had corrupted state legislatures in doing so. Such activities prompted the popular humorist Will Rogers to quip that a "holding company" is a "thing where you hand an accomplice the goods while the policeman searches you" (Horan, 34).

Other stories circulated, such as that the National City Bank had provided its speculating officers interest free loans and Samuel Insull ruined thousands of small investors through abuses in his fraudulent utility empire. Such escapades dominated the front pages and American minds of the thirties. Unfortunately, few knew of those within the business community who revealed the finer angels of their characters in their secret diaries and letters. One such man was Marriner Eccles, who headed a Utah economic empire on the verge of collapse. Confused and frightened as much as any common man on the street, he confessed to his friends in private letters that everyone expected him to "find a way out of the pit," not knowing that he himself was just as frightened and exhausted by the pretensions of knowledge he was "forced to wear in a daytime masquerade" (Horan, 8). It is doubtful, however, that if such sentiments had gone public they would have had much impact. Those within the business community were among the icons of the past, and, as such, had to now face a new age that was increasingly suspicious and distrustful of those who for so long dominated their respect through power.

Still, Eccles's concern would have been ameliorated in part by the observation that he and others of the business fraternity were not destined to shoulder alone the entire burden of responsibility for the economic crisis. The American public's suspicion and anger found other icons to topple from their pedestals. Among these were the nation's politicians, policemen, and professors.

Corrupt politicians and violent policemen would become the celebrated characters in the WPA-sponsored paintings of artists, such as Philip Evergood, Jack Levine, and William Gropper. Evergood would highlight in one canvas the excessive brutality of the police in breaking up a serious strike on Memorial Day, 1937, in which ten were killed and scores hurt. Jack Levine's painting, *Three Corrupt Men*, featured a politician, policeman, and banker in a state of moral atrophy. Gropper's *The Opposition* presented to the world a Congress filled with tired old men bent on fulfilling personal agendas.

Professors might have been spared a bit more than the above, but they too were viewed as principal characters in deciding economic or political policy, and, as such, had to incur some of the blame if things did not work out as expected. One magazine article from the thirties claimed that on a "routine administration matter," Cabinet members could be consulted, but if matters of policy and "higher statesmanship" were involved, then one had to consult the professoriate. Of course, if they erred in judgment, they could always retreat back to the university, secure within the arms of tenure (Horan, 50). H. L. Mencken's philosophy about professors in Washington matched those of the general public; for him, they were the "sorriest lot of mountebanks ever gathered together at one time . . . professional uplifters and do-gooders . . . poor dubs," or, in short, "blatant and intolerable idiots" (DuBasky, 50). Nor were the above determiners of economic and social polity alone in being held up to ridicule. As the Depression persisted, such others as doctors, lawyers, authors, the clergy, and newspapermen, would be linked with those in more exalted positions and satirized by the American humorist as major contributors to the escalating crisis.

At the top of their list, however, the politician reigned supreme. He and he alone was reserved for the majority of complaints registered in their pages. Part of the complaint stemmed from a developing philosophy in the thirties that evolved out of the Roosevelt administration—namely, that it was the principal duty of government to protect the average citizen from the unscrupulous and criminal behavior of those in power. The average man could not be an authority in all matters and instead had to rely on those in government to protect him from the fraudulent. Unfortunately, this was not always the case—a lesson learned early during the Depression years.

For Thurber, the politicians, along with everyone else in authority, had been painfully negligent in anticipating the stock market collapse in 1929—a view implied in his story "The Day the Dam Broke" from *My Life and Hard Times*. It reflects a sentiment Will Rogers expressed four years earlier when he said that it came as quite a shock to the politicians to discover that the Lord "not only closed the stock market on Sundays, but . . . could practically close it any day of the week" (Sterling and Sterling, 158). The reason they had failed to anticipate the crisis was due to their inability to think independently and contrary to general opinion. In Thurber's tale, the entire citizenry of a town are stampeded into a frenzy when someone is inadvertently seen running down main street, and the word "dam" is mentioned. Fearing that a nearby dam may have broken, everyone from the most eminent and educated to the most ignorant and foolish rushes to high ground, although they are already on high ground and no dam has indeed broken:

> The fact that we were all as safe as kittens under a cookstove did not, however, assuage in the least the fine despair and the grotesque desperation which seized residents of the East Side when the cry spread like a grass fire that the dam had given way. Some of the most dignified, staid, cynical, and clear-thinking men in the town abandoned their wives, stenographers, homes, and offices and ran east. There are few alarms in the world more terrifying than "The dam has broken!" There are few persons capable of stopping to reason when that clarion cry strikes upon their ears, even persons who live in towns no nearer than five hundred miles to a dam. (40–41)

For Thurber, those in power are in no way different or possess greater judgment than those who are not, and if this is an absolute truth, then how could anyone again trust authority? Thus were planted the seeds of doubt that would flourish and bear fruit in other Depression writers.

In Benchley's cynicism they suitably found ample room to grow. "Black Magic" in *From Bed to Worse* peers further into the darkness and asks if anyone is actually capable of pulling the nation out of the Depression. Maybe a return to primitivism is in order?

> In the hurly-burly of modern life I sometimes wonder if enough attention is paid to the old-fashioned rites of demonology. We have tried almost everything else to get ourselves out of the jam that we got ourselves into, but it never seems to occur to anyone that a little polite attention, accompanied by incantations and a sprinkling of wolfsbane in the general direction of several of the more influential demons might work wonders. (122)

Of course, Benchley's cynicism regarding the outcome of political reform stems largely from a prevailing view during the Depression that most politicians were by nature scoundrels bent upon lining their own pockets and those of their friends. Notwithstanding elections, the common man did not stand a chance against the lords of Capitol Hill. Republican or Democrat, liberal or conservative, their behavior was prompted by greed.

The principal spokesman for Don Marquis, Archy the cockroach, has some interesting observations on this subject. In "destiny" from *archy does his part* he contemplates the outcome of suicide which seems to be always on his mind. He regards it as a generally favorable way to end the suffering and turmoil that afflict us during our lives, except, that is, for one problem. Like Hamlet, he is not certain of the outcome:

> . . . what body will
> the soul of archy transmigrate
> into now i asked
> myself will i go
> higher in the scale of
> life and inhabit the
> body of a butterfly
> or a dog or a
> bird or will i sink
> lower and go into the
> carcase of a poison
> spider or a politician (429)

His negative view of politicians, lower than his estimation of poison spiders, springs from a trip he made to Washington, D.C., during the previous summer. He took up residence at the Smithsonian bug collection, being careful to look like a dead bug if anyone passed by, but found no need to disguise himself at the Capitol "because there are so / many insects around it gives you a / great idea of the / american people when you / see some of the / things they elect" (248–49).

The Depression humorist's distaste for the contemporary politician was fired in part by a confusing array of laws and regulations flowing from an alphabet soup of governmental agencies. For Archy, the only solution for ending the world's chaos is to abolish all grand schemes, as he notes in "conferences":

> you cannot get a millennium by
> laying a whole lot of five year plans
> end to end if governments would just let people
> alone things would straighten out of themselves
> in the course of time (282)

It is a sentiment similar to one expressed a few years earlier by Will Rogers in "The Congressional Record." "Compared to those fellows in Congress," he smiles, "I'm just an amateur. And the thing about my jokes is that they don't hurt anybody. You can take 'em, or leave 'em. You know what I mean. You can say they are not funny, or they are terrible, or they are good, or whatever it is, but they don't do any harm. But with Congress, every time they make a joke, it's a law! And every time they make a law, it's a joke!" (Sterling and Sterling, 256).

One ritual, perceived as a joke, that reappeared every ten years with the tedious regularity of an unloved season was the national census. But, given this year and season (1930), Rogers feels it might be appreciated: "[I]t's an old Spanish custom, and it does give work to the ones that count, and that's what we got to do this year, to do something that will give everybody something to do" (165). Unfortunately, it was about all the government would do that year!

Benchley is less sanguine about statistical taking. Governmental statisticians, he feels, have hopped the track in a frenzy to gather data and draw charts. What the country *really* needs is *less* data on productive labor and *more* on "unproductive labor," a point he argues with firm conviction in "A Few Figures for Unproductive Labor" in *From Bed to Worse*:

> All plans for a new economic order are drawn up in terms of the number of men it will take to tan hides in fifteen minutes, or construct dams in four days, or open oysters in a year. Hide-tanners, dam-builders, and oyster-openers are going to be sitting pretty in the Golden age. But no one has a plan for those of us who just copy figures from one book to another, or draw borders for photographic layouts, or poke at the letter "x" on typewriters all day. No new order is arranged for us. (220)

Data on unproductive labor, he concludes, are far more fascinating and worthy of governmental study. Such data would reveal (in the argot of the bureaucrat) that the "*phenomena* involved in the *functional operation* of a *social mechanism* are *constant*, and, at the same time, *variable*." "Indeed," he pontificates further, "this means that the postulate that *energy determinates* which are *variable to themselves*, thereby nullifying the whole goddamned thing" (224).

The irrationality of the bureaucrat and governmental concerns for establishing production quotas fuels the wrath of Ogden Nash in "One from One Leaves Two":

> Mumbledy pumbledy, my red cow,
> She's cooperating now.
> At first she didn't understand

> That milk production must be planned;
> She didn't understand at first
> She either had to plan or burst
> But now the government reports
> She's giving pints instead of quarts. (Smith and Eberstadt, 74)

As a gentleman farmer, E. B. White, too, becomes increasingly alarmed by the profusion of governmental restrictions on the books. One in particular dictates plant reproduction and is mentioned briefly in his essay "Prohibited" from *The New Yorker* in 1936. "The plant-patent business is taking right hold, apparently," he writes. "We know a man who received a birthday present of a nice little azalea. Tied around the azalea's stem, like a chastity belt, was a metal tag from Bobbink & Atkins, reading, 'Asexual reproduction of this plant is illegal under the Plant Patent Act.' " The man, obviously angered by the tag, tears it off, feeds it to his dog, and sends the plant to a friend in Connecticut with instructions to "bed it down warmly next to an old buck hydrangea" (Dale, 3).

Even more alarming for White is the fact that more and more of the regulations seem to be evolving from an intense desire on the part of the bureaucrats to impose their concept of morality and "right" thinking on others. The American virtues of individuality and independent thought are giving way to an Orwellian mind control of the masses. In "Anything Like That," noted in a previous chapter, he details the experiences of a young lady, recently emigrated from Russia, who cannot become a citizen in her adopted land until she agrees to eschew anything that does not meet with the government's official stamp of approval.

Similarly, Don Marquis voices a concern over the rising efforts of those in political circles in creating agendas based on moral issues and prompted by autocratic pretensions. For Marquis, America had suffered enough under the legislation of prohibition during the twenties. (Who but Don Marquis would have so argued!?) Archy sees that if he, like the politicians, is ever able to "put things over" on others, he must start as they do by "singing loudly about reform and censorship." It always stampedes the ignorant into compliance (291).

Even when prompted by the best of intentions, governmental regulations often presented a calliope of conflicting values. E. B. White's confusion in "Frontier," also from *The New Yorker,* echoes what many Americans must have wondered at the time. The efforts on the part of the Department of the Interior to maintain the Great Smokies as the "last frontier of the East" was inevitably at odds with the agency's parallel efforts to eliminate poverty and introduce technology to such regions in the Untied States:

> They want to preserve [the native] just as she is—her speech, her
> homespun garments, her bare feet, her primitive customs, even her re-
> bellious nature (she doesn't like the North). Well, who's right? If busi-
> ness is to revive, this old lady has got to buy our American products;
> she's got to spruce up her person and her home. She's got to have an
> electric orange-squeezer and a suitable tray for serving canapés. She's
> got to quit grinding her own meal and buy herself a bag of Gold Medal.
> She's got to trade the ox for a Pontiac, and she certainly must quit talk-
> ing like a hick and get herself a radio, so that she can hear the pure ac-
> cents of the American merchandiser. Yet if she does, the Great Smokies
> will be spoiled. (Dale, 217)

Truly, White concludes, a nation intent on increasing both its standard of
living while simultaneously preserving its frontier and quaint traditions "is
in the devil of a fine fix" (217).

Also at odds with the federal government's desire to raise the average
American's standard of living was its increasing need to raise revenue
through taxes. Early into the Depression, Will Rogers threw up his hands in
disgust, claiming that the only thing the government had failed to tax was
optimism. He is not opposed to taxes in general, but it seems, he claims, that
the majority of the revenue ends up fueling a bureaucracy, a bureaucracy
that is "not a bit better than the government that we got for one-third the
money twenty years ago." At the heart of his complaint is his anger over the
failure of those in government to protect the common man and alert him of
the impending disaster in 1929: "Was our government, or our prominent
men warning us? If we had had a 'prominent' man he would have, but we
just didn't have any" (Sterling and Sterling, 201).

Even more infuriating for Don Marquis is how the government wastes
what it picks from the pockets of its citizens. With people on bread lines,
was it really essential for the government to subsidize a "rediscovery" of the
South Pole?

> it seems admiral byrd has to discover
> the south pole all over again
> every little while
> that comes of not discovering it
> hard enough the first time
> so it would stay discovered
> we insects are superior to you men
> in many ways
> it would never have occurred to us
> that the south pole cared whether it was

> discovered or not
> the thing that amuses me
> is that the country is so busted
> that a lot of people have no jobs
> or food or clothes or shelter
> but there is money enough to keep on
> discovering the south pole
> over and over again (288)

Archy can see no profit arising out of such governmental expenditure, but he does mention an interesting proposal from an associate of his—a radical flea.

It seems that back in 1928, "when things were boomin," your average flea wouldn't have bitten into anything less than a "dachshund with a pedigree as long as himself." But nowadays, the flea protests to Archy, the pickings are not that choice. What the government should spend its money on is creating a better tasting dog for fleas. "If there was any justice in this country," he claims, "they would give us russian wolf hounds." "I find a lot of discontent among / insects in these days," Archy concludes (327).

Along with the politicians in Washington and his radical friend, Archy occasionally proposes schemes for extracting the nation out of the Depression that cannot be, he feels, worse than anything the federal government has proposed. In one poem he advocates the abolition of Bridge:

> the administration ought to get wise
> to one thing about the hard times
> and recovery from them
> the country was getting along all right
> until everybody in it
> took up contact bridge in a big way
> a few years ago
> everybody stopped work and did nothing
> but play bridge
> and the country hit the chutes
> they don't know they are loafing
> because there is just enough mental effort
> connected with bridge so they can kid themselves
> they are busy all the time
> and smart and clever as the dickens
> when the bridge fever subsides
> the country will automatically recover itself (287)

As busy as any politician on Capitol Hill, Archy and his friends are always quick to offer plans for the general recovery—even if the recovery is intended for the insect population! One scheme involving relocations, however, sounds suspiciously similar to something already hatched in Washington.

In an attempt to eliminate poverty, inhabitants of particularly poor neighborhoods were moved into modern, federally built, housing developments. All too often, unfortunately, the problems of inner city crime and unemployment followed the poor into their new neighborhoods and effectively prevented any long-term benefits from occurring. The criminally intent and socially irresponsible members of the old community continued to flourish within the new one, and, within a short period of time, the politicians who had initially hailed the new projects as the way of the future found the outcome not that certain. In short, more than a move was needed to change the quality of life.

A friend of Archy's in "statesmanship" offers one such "relocating" scheme. If cockroaches find it impossible and dangerous within the city—move to the country and become grasshoppers!

> i was astonished
> at the simplicity of the
> solution but as i
> thought it over it occurred
> to me that
> perhaps it sounded more
> statesmanlike than it
> really was
> how i asked him are
> cockroaches to become
> grasshoppers
> that is a mere
> detail he said which i
> leave to you for
> solution . . .

In the end, Archy feels the city best suits him, and his friend's solution to the "bug" problem offers nothing more than most of the "easy schemes for the improvement of the human race" (467–68).

For E. B. White, cockroaches have actually done more than any government plan in bringing people together. After all, he writes in an observation in *The New Yorker*, statesmen and historians "have long known that a common enemy is the most solidifying thing a nation can have, welding all the people into a happy, united mass." Such was the case in his own family, evidently, when a few weeks back some cockroaches were discovered in the pantry. Since then, the household has warred against them with a "high feeling of family unity and solidarity, sniping at them with a Flit gun, rubbing poisonous paste on bits of potatoes for them to eat," and otherwise acting "full of great singleness of purpose and accord" (Dale, 79–80). One may wonder how Archy would have responded to that!

But the best satire of a politician's "foolproof" scheme for recovery appears in Benchley's "Wear-Out-A-Shoe Week" from *My Ten Years in a Quandary*. Unfortunately, Benchley is no fool. There is a "movement on foot," he claims, whereby people will be encouraged to wear out their shoes faster, "thereby giving employment to 186,000 people in the shoe industry alone."

> Why are economists always so concerned with shoes? It amounts to fetishism. When they want to make a point it is always illustrated by the number of pairs of shoes that a given number of people will wear out over a given period. Just as in the old arithmetics it was always that A and B were sawing wood or swimming up-stream, in practical economic problems it is always that shoes are being worn out. Doesn't anyone ever care about socks? (56)

The plan just might work for most Americans, but, unfortunately, he is more the "sedentary type" who prefers to stay put. Why not let people like him, he asks, remain at home, but while listening to the radio or reading a book simultaneously "hold a pair of shoes against a grindstone?" This, he feels, is more to his liking except for one last reservation:

> Every theory of economic good is based on *my* wearing out shoes, on *my* looking in store windows, on *my* spending money. I have never encountered a plan for an economic Utopia which included anyone's reading a piece by Benchley in the paper or even asking Benchley out to dinner. In the Perfect State, Benchley pays. (59)

Still, he concludes, he will do his part like everyone else, even if he is "just a parasite—a paying parasite" (59).

Besides politicians, the police too fell increasingly under the scrutiny of the Depression humorist. The traditional view of the policeman as an upholder of justice and a protector of the defenseless rapidly eroded during the thirties. What replaced it was a cynicism that often portrayed the police as corrupt syncopants of the well-to-do establishment or, at least, bungling incompetents who always arrested the wrong man. Such views were commonly found in the movies and newsreels of the day. Movies as varied as *The Bank Dick* and *The Grapes of Wrath* depicted unflattering scenes where officers were held up to ridicule or condemnation. A scandalous book of 1930 generated the most interest on this subject—*I Am a Fugitive from a Georgia Chain Gang* by Robert Eliot Burns—which, in turn, was also turned into a sensational movie in 1931, starring Paul Muni.

Burns, an unemployed veteran of World War I, was convicted by the State of Georgia of petty theft in the twenties and sentenced to serve ten years on one of the state's notorious chain gangs. Enduring extremely harsh and inhumane punishment at the hands of the police and prison guards, involving such "corrective" devices as "sweat boxes" or small barrels where convicts who were considered "insolent" were confined on brutally hot days, Burns managed to escape to the North where he eventually became an editor of a national magazine in Chicago.

However, a spiteful ex-wife notified the authorities in Georgia of his whereabouts. The authorities demanded his return, promising that he would receive a speedy pardon. Burns returned voluntarily, only to find himself locked up in an even worse prison, serving the remainder of his complete sentence. Escaping again to the North, his case gained national notoriety with the appearance of the film in 1931; Clarence Darrow headed his defense, and state policies regarding the criminal justice system came under greater scrutiny as a result. In 1945, after years of bitter negotiations and legal wrangling, Burns returned to Georgia, and in the state house in Atlanta, Governor Ellis Arnall commuted his original sentence to the time he had served. Burns, at last, was a free man.

Other stories that depicted the police as foolish and neurotic in their zeal to uphold law and order abound during the Depression years. Accounts frequently appeared in the newspapers of their merciless attempts to break up WPA strikes and of even chasing down a truck in Salinas, California, that had a red warning flag attached to its load because they feared that subversive "reds" were aboard. Little Audrey, a folklore character about whom thousands of nonsensical tales circulated during the thirties, frequently had odd altercations with the police. The tales were immensely popular on the college campus.

In one, Little Audrey is confronted by a policeman who asks her why she is crying. She informs him that she has lost her father. "I wouldn't cry about that," he comforts her. "There's your papa right across the street leaning against that bank building." The overjoyed little girl then proceeds to dash out into the street only to be run over by a two-ton truck. "The cop just laughed and laughed" (all the stories end with somebody laughing). "He knew all the time that that was not Little Audrey's papa leaning against the bank building." In another, her jailbird brother breaks out of prison, and the sheriff puts bloodhounds on the trail. This makes Little Audrey laugh, " 'cause she knew all the time that her brother was anemic" (Tidwell, 537–38).

At times fiction mimicked life, as does Damon Runyon's tale "The Old Doll's House" from *Blue Plate Special*. Loosely based on the accounts of Ella Wendel, one of the richest women in New York City, whose holdings in real estate amounted to $36 million at the time of her death in 1932, Runyon's tale captures all the spinster's eccentricities (she would not allow any radio antennas to be attached to any of her buildings for fear of hurting birds in flight) and offers a rather glib view of "New York's Finest" as well.

In Runyon's tale, a con artist and small-time thief named Lance McGowan escapes from some pursuers bent upon shooting him with their "sawed-offs" by jumping over the backyard stone wall of a large old house owned by Abigale Ardsley, a rich old recluse who inherited her father's real estate empire and about whom strange stories circulate. Upon entering the house, he encounters the old lady, sitting alone and surrounded by the memorabilia of her past and, like Miss Haversham in *Great Expectations*, frozen in time with all her clocks stopped at twelve o'clock in mute testimony to her having been jilted by a lover when young. After a long chat with the "old doll," Lance eventually leaves and gets his revenge by killing his pursuers, only to be arrested the next morning by Johnny Brannigan, a plainclothes policeman, for having done so with witnesses present. There is great rejoicing, continues the narrator, among the police because they have been under attack in the press for being largely incompetent or unwilling and unable to stem the ever increasing crime statistics (449).

The case, however, never makes it past the grand jury because when Miss Abigale is questioned as to what time Lance was in her home, she responds twelve o'clock, the very time he was supposed to be plugging his enemies. Of course, the police fail to notice that all the clocks in her house have been perpetually at twelve o'clock for the last forty years!

For Thurber, however, the police are more than simply incompetent—they are destructive as well. In "The Night the Ghost Got In" from *My Life and Hard Times*, they arrive at the Thurber home, having been informed by the family that a burglar or ghost is on the loose. What appears to be the entire police force arrives in a Ford sedan, on motorcycles, and in a patrol wagon "with about eight in it and a few reporters" (59). When no one in the household is able to immediately respond to their cries of "open up . . . we're men from Headquarters," the front door with its thick beveled glass is broken down.

> I could hear a rending of wood and a splash of glass on the floor of the hall. Their lights played all over the living-room and crisscrossed nervously in the dining-room, stabbed into hallways, shot up the front stairs and finally up the back. They caught me standing in my towel at the top. A heavy policeman bounded up the steps. "Who are you?" he demanded. "I live here," I said. "Well, whattsa matta, ya hot?" he asked. It was, as a matter of fact, cold; I went to my room and pulled on some trousers. On my way out, a cop stuck a gun in my ribs. "Whatta you don' here?" he demanded. "I live here," I said. (59)

Unable to find the perpetrators who would after all most likely be invisible, they proceed to tear through the house looking for evidence, yanking open doors, pulling out drawers, throwing over furniture "with dull thumps," yanking clothes off their hooks in the closets, and throwing boxes and suitcases off shelves in a wild frenzy of fulfilling procedural duties:

> One of them found an old zither that Roy had won in a pool tournament. "Looky here, Joe," he said, strumming it with a big paw. The cop named Joe took it and turned it over. "What is it?" he asked me. "It's an old zither our guinea pig used to sleep on," I said. It was true that a pet guinea pig we once had would never sleep anywhere except on the zither, but I should never have said so. Joe and the other cop looked at me a long time. They put the zither back on the shelf. (62–63)

In the end, disappointed over not being able to get their hands on any evidence, they conclude that the family is suspicious. "This guy," says one of the policeman to the others and pointing at our author who was previously spotted dressed only in a towel at the top of the stairs, "was nekked. The lady," he concludes about the author's mother, "is historical" (63). And with this the police investigation more or less comes to a rather undignified end.

Benchley sympathizes with the plight of the Thurber family, and offers his own observations on the police in "Tell-Tale Clues" in *From Bed to Worse*. In modern America, Benchley claims, the average criminal "has no idea how careful he has to be in order to keep on being a criminal and not just an ex-" (260). For example, he continues, at Illville, Illinois, robbers blew up the vault of the Lazybones National Bank and Fiduciary Trust Company, made a deposit of two hundred shares of Goldman Sachs to the bank's one hundred, and on the way out pulled off the handle of the front door: "It had evidently been pulled off in pique by one of the robbers when he found that the door would not open as easily as he thought it ought to" (261). The police promptly respond by rushing first to the Farmers' and Drovers' Bank and then to the First Congregational Church before arriving at the Lazybones National, "where the explosion had taken place" (261). Captain Louis Mildew comes to the conclusion that if they can find the doorknob they will have the robber, and his prophetic prediction comes true when they arrest a man in Zanesville a week later carrying a doorknob that corresponds in every detail with the one missing. Despite the man's protesting that the knob belongs to him and that he was carrying it as a cure for rheumatism, he is arrested and "confesses" under police questioning.

In another case, a murder victim is found clenching an artificial leg in his teeth. A detective promptly makes an arrest in a local bar of a one-legged customer enjoying his drink, but not before customarily "turning back his lapel where he had forgotten to pin his badge" (263).

But the best example of detective work surfaces in Mistick, California, where a man by the name of Potts abducts an elephant that had formerly been a camp follower of a circus but preferred the town and stayed behind when the rest moved on. Since then, the town had whitewashed her and "spread the report about that she was sacred," charging "two bits to take a walk around her, once around one way and back around the other" (264–65). Potts, however, does not get too far with his "ill-gotten gain," for a shrewd constable spots him on a country road with white elephant powder on his sleeve. When questioned about it, Potts claims he has just left his girl:

> "Does your girl wear white elephant powder?" asked the constable, very comical. "That's white elephant powder and it's off that elephant."
> "What elephant?" said Potts in surprise, looking behind him. "Oh, *that* elephant?" (265)

The thief tries to escape by hiding behind the elephant, but the constable can see his legs from the other side and places him under arrest. "So you will see," Benchley concludes, "that it is the little things that count in successful police evasion, and the sooner our criminals realize this the fewer humiliating arrests there will be" (265).

For Will Rogers, troubles within the criminal justice system are more a reflection of our liberal times than police incompetence. In "Crime Made Easy," he complains that in the old Wild West days a bandit always faced some opposition, having to "back out shooting, and make it to his horse by the blaze of his guns." But in our modern times, a "robber, or killer, or whatever his day's work might be, why, he does it all casually, just in the regular routine of things. If there is a bank to rob, why, he just saunters in, and the only way he can possibly be noticed is that he will perhaps be dressed better than the banker." Another problem for Rogers is the availability of automatic weapons: "It's made no practice necessary to be an outlaw. Give any young egotist two shots of dope, and an automatic, and he will hold up the government mint" (Sterling and Sterling, 187).

Murder, too, has proliferated, claims Rogers, within this age of progress:

> All of our boasted inventions, like the auto and the automatic, and our increased dope output, terrible liquor, lost confidence in our Justice, graft from top to bottom, all of these have made it possible to commit anything you can think of, and in about 80 per cent of the cases, get away with it. He can get away quick in a car. He can't miss with the gun he's got. If he is caught he knows it will be accidental. Then, if he is caught, his connections with his gangs get him out. So it's not a dangerous business, after all, from the looks of it. (188)

About the only detriment to crime in our liberal age, he notes, is the difficulty in finding somebody who has something to steal! What is going on in Los Angeles is going on in the rest of the country, too, he concludes, making the last observation so he will not be accused, "like all these Californians," of bragging (188).

Thurber, also adopts a more conciliatory view towards the police in a later story titled "The Topaz Cufflinks Mystery" from *The Middle-Aged Man on the Flying Trapeze*. It involves an eccentric, middle-aged couple who attract the attention of a passing officer by trying to see if a human's eyes glow in the dark like an animal's. When the officer stops, the man is down on his hands and legs, crawling and barking like a dog by the side of the road while his wife slowly passes by with the lights on in the family car. At first embarrassed, they tell the officer they are looking for some cufflinks, but the officer remains suspicious until they finally confess what they are up to. The husband believes that a man's eyes won't reflect the light; the wife does, claiming that the reason her husband's eyes won't in this situation is because they are higher off the ground. It remains with the officer to pass the final judgment of Solomon by telling the lady that he drives along the road every night, passing hundreds of people and animals, and "people's eyes don't shine."

"The people are never close to the ground," said the lady.

"*I* was close to the ground," said her husband.

"Look at it this way," said the cop. "I've seen wildcats in *trees* at night and their eyes shine."

"There you are!" said the lady's husband. "That proves it." (22)

"Smart guy," he concludes, as the officer rides off into the evening, even though the woman would like to pursue it further: "I said it all depends on how *high a man's eyes*." *(23)*.

Even more than the police, bankers frequently incurred the wrath of the Depression humorist. Unrelenting in their pursuit of mortgage payments, bankers were often depicted in the media as not only the instigators of the Depression but the principal factor in its continuance. Countless thousands who had lost their savings considered safe within the bank's vaults now faced the added burden of paying back loans that had been thrust upon them during the carefree twenties. For many Americans, the bankers had not equally born the brunt of the economic downslide. Farmers in the dust bowl regions of Oklahoma and Texas grimly noted that the incessant windstorms hadn't blown *everything* away—they still had their mortgages!

For Nash, the banker as the epitome of evil during the thirties is abundantly clear in "Ma, What's a Banker?"

> The North wind doth blow,
> And we shall have snow,
> And what will the banker do then, poor thing?
> Will he go to the barn
> To keep himself warm,
> And hide his head under his wing?
> Is he on the spot, poor thing, poor thing?
> Probably not, poor thing.
>
> For when he is good,
> He is not very good,
> And when he is bad he is horrider,
> And the chances are fair
> He is taking the air
> Beside a cabana in Florida.
> But the wailing investor, mean thing, mean thing,
> Disturbs his siesta, poor thing. (Smith and Eberstadt, 52)

If he is to plunge into the pool, continues Nash, it is only with his "kith and his kin" with whom he often gets out when the "widows and orphans get in." Maybe, concludes Nash, the bankers will leave America altogether someday and retire to a temple in Greece, letting "Athens and Sparta / Play host to the martyr." If the joyful day ever comes, the rest of us will be able to "cling to our fleece, Hot Cha!" (53).

In another work, "Bankers Are Just Like Anybody Else, Except Richer," Nash is at his surly best. Bankers, he claims, "dwell in marble halls" because they "encourage deposits and discourage withdralls." They uniformly observe their golden rule of never lending money to anybody who needs it: "If people are worried about their rent it is your duty to deny them / the loan of one nickel, yes, even one copper engraving of the martyred / son of the late Nancy Hanks; / Yes, if they request fifty dollars to pay for a baby you must look at them / like Tarzan looking at an uppity ape in the jungle" (114). Of course, if someone who has capital requests more, the bankers "brim with the milk of human kindness," and only ask if the "borrowers want the money sent or / do they want to take it withm." But, he concludes, one must not be too harsh in judging bankers. They do, it seems, perform one valuable public service by "eliminating the jackasses / who go around saying that health and happiness are everything and money isn't essential" because as soon as these people get ill or have to borrow money, they're denied and mercifully starve to death. *Then* they know that "good old money" is "nothing short of providential" (114–15).

Not all portraits of bankers in the writings of the Depression humorists were as virulent as Nash's, however. Runyon's tales feature bankers who are no better or worse than the average man. Israel Ib misappropriates funds but is still able to reform and regain the trust of his depositors, as has been previously noted in "Broadway Financier." In another story, "It Comes Up Mud" from *Money from Home*, a banker by the name of Paul D. Veere is a smooth-talking philanderer who is one step ahead of the law. The details of his banking practices are never mentioned, but he appears at the end of the tale desperately trying to catch a train so as to get back to his bank and straighten things out before the federal authorities put him in jail. When his car breaks down in the rain on a country road, he borrows a racehorse from our central character in the story, a down-and-out fellow named Little Alfie. Veere gets back to the bank in time to avoid prison and, surprisingly, makes good on a promise to give Alfie $50,000 for the use of the horse. Of course, one may well wonder where that money came from, but, at least, he is a man of his word!

For another writer, Irving Cobb, bankers were more than just men of their word; they were voices of reason in a wilderness of financial panic that followed the stock market collapse. In his story, "One Way to Stop a Panic" published in 1933, Cobb details how one town was able to avoid general panic thanks to the quick-witted maneuverings of a few bankers.

The bankers of the town, Comanche City, are men who are motivated more by finer principles than personal profit. Unlike Nash's, they have not retreated to the security and comfort of a cabana in Florida, preferring instead to do their "share to combat the effects of the prevalent industrial depression that covered the land as with a vast wet blanket. Within their own section they had wrestled with the aftermath of a drought which all through the trans-Mississippi Southwest turned fertile farms into parched deserts and solvent planters into bewildered paupers" (Churchill, 312). Their main concern for the moment, however, is with a skittish and panicky public that has lost its faith in the banking system and has been closing all its accounts in numerous runs on banks across the country. This is exactly what the bankers of Comanche City do not want to see happen in their town.

The only obstacle they encounter is an elderly gentleman "so extensively whiskered-over that he rather suggested some sort of game sanctuary" (313). In short, he is an old fool who is so overly concerned about losing his savings that he periodically withdraws all his money from his account and deposits it in a safe deposit box until he feels another "crisis" has been averted. If he is to do this now during the national predilection for "bank runs," he might, the bankers agree, precipitate a citywide panic, forcing all the banks in town to close.

When he appears at the teller's window at his own bank with the intention of repeating this foolish stunt, he is told by a bank official that the safe deposit boxes are no longer available. Furious, he pulls his money out of the bank and proceeds to call upon one bank after another in a vain attempt to have it secreted in a safer spot. But all the bankers are on the alert, and prevent him from depositing his money in their institutions. Frustrated and nervous, with a large contingent of townspeople following at his heels, and fearful that he might be robbed at any minute, he seeks out the shelter of a local post office with a "large sign set there by a paternal government to advertise the desirability of postal savings for safe and guaranteed investment" (324). Much to his surprise, they no sooner have given him a receipt for his deposit than they immediately redeposit it in the bank he had originally withdrawn it from! As the postal clerk tells the protesting man, the post office will gladly accept a deposit, but when it does "we ain't such fools as to keep 'em there in the safe once we get 'em; we bring 'em right down here to this regularly designated government repository and deposit 'em permanently where the stuff can earn a little something" (326). Furthermore, the man also learns that because the redeposit will constitute a new account, it will earn less interest than his old account, and he would have been a lot better off leaving it there in the first place! Thus the ever-vigilant bankers of Comanche City are able to avoid a panic, and an old fool learns a lesson.

The average American's attitude toward business and businessmen varied during the Depression years. No one could deny that the working class had borne the major brunt of the economic collapse, but entire businesses also folded, displacing people of every capacity. Everyone from the president of a corporation down to the average assembly line worker could easily find himself on an unemployment line. Although there were many who favored the initial role of government in revitalizing the economy during the first few years of the Depression, there were many who, by the end of the decade, had revised their former opinions and returned to the more conservative philosophy of leaving businessmen to run business. This dichotomy of view, in turn, generated a mixed bag of humor concerning businessmen. In the press they were either hailed as champions of American homespun values or criticized as a deceitful pack of con-artists who dupe the consumer with slick advertising.

Samuel Goldwyn's malapropisms and humorous asides, frequently heard in the hallways of the MGM studio, became the gist of a popular book, *The Great Goldwyn*, by Alva Johnson, published in 1937. In its pages, one could enter into a private world of privilege and power that had been largely untouched by the Depression years and encounter a man who seemed more a grandfather type than the powerful tycoon he actually was. His observations on such a commonplace thing as a sundial ("My, my, what won't they do next?") and his wife's beautifully cared-for hands ("Yes, I'm going to have a bust made of them.") were innocent enough to delight the multitudes and seemed more befitting the man on the street than the producer of Hollywood blockbusters (Tidwell, 562).

A more negative view of businessmen, however, appeared in an anecdote about the automobile industry. Evidently the governor of Michigan was invited to one of the factories, and in his presence, they assembled a complete car in exactly two minutes. The event was given lots of press coverage. About a month later, however, a man telephoned the factory and asked if what he had read in the papers was true. Had they assembled a car in two minutes in honor of the governor? " 'Absolutely true,' came the reply. 'Damn your hides,' shot back the irate citizen, 'I'VE GOT THAT CAR' " (Tidwell 448).

His complaint was not unique, for it reflected a fundamental shift in the way many Americans viewed domestic products and how they were produced during the thirties. People began to question the conflicting values that seemed to be inherently behind all moves toward progress in American industry. Gone were the days of handcraftsmanship—now replaced by "more efficient" automated production methods and slick advertising, which touted new products as the best engineered and constructed in the world.

Benchley, for one, is amazed at the amount of effort and money American businesses spend on advertising—even more, it seems, than they spend on the assembly line! In "Fatigue without Work" in *From Bed to Worse*, he marvels at the "copy-writing, art-work, conferences, re-copy-writing, re-art-work, more conferences, inter-office communications, conferences between the advertising agency and the advertiser, re-copy-writing, re-art-work, random suicides," and what not that go into producing some jingle on the side of a bus (178). Just thinking about it makes him tired and somewhat depressed: "Does it make life seem hardly worth struggling through? When you see what actually came out of all this, do you wish you had never been born?" (180).

Advertising also bothers E. B. White, but for a different reason—its seeming lack of ethics. In "Truth in Advertising," from *The New Yorker*, he voices his amusement with the "Truth in Advertising" movement's celebration of its silver jubilee:

> Most types of enterprise never give truth a second thought, but advertising people are not like that: they keep truth in front of them all the time, brooding dreamily about it while writing the long, long drama of mouth hygiene. They worry so furiously about truth, one suspects they read each other's copy. All this is confusing to the consumer, who has a double responsibility toward advertising, being obliged to read it and keep up with it and buy products on the strength of it, and at the same time sympathize with the advertiser's devotion to truth. (Dale, 151)

We should be proud of advertising, continues White, because it is without a doubt America's undisputed contribution to western civilization. It parades the very values we all hold close to our hearts—integrity and honesty. American business is on the verge of a new millennium:

> Advertisers are the interpreters of our dreams—Joseph interpreted for Pharaoh. Like the movies, they infect the routine futility of our days with purposeful adventure. Their weapons are our weaknesses: fear, ambition, illness, pride, selfishness, desire, ignorance. And these weapons must be kept bright as a sword. We rise to eat a breakfast cereal which will give us strength for the tasks of the day; we vanquish the excesses of the night with an alkaline fizz; we cleanse our gums, stifle our bad odors, adorn our diseased bodies, and go forth to conquer—cheered on with a thousand slogans, devices, lucubrations. (152–53)

Why, he concludes, should the industry be so concerned with truth when it is through fiction the average American approaches and masters each day!

Besides the consumer, it has mislead even the world of business by creating a false image of success through competition. The modern attitude that competition demands a Darwinian approach to life or, as White puts it, a "dog eat dog" mentality, is largely self-defeating: "The fact that about eight-five per cent of the dogs have recently been eaten by the other dogs perhaps explains what long ago we noticed about business: that it had a strong smell of baloney. If dog continues to eat dog, there will be only one dog left, and he will be sick to his stomach" (147).

The failure of the business community to instill confidence in the American public becomes, for some of the Depression humorists, a serious obstacle to recovery. For if they are as deceitful and as cutthroat as people have been led to believe, how can the American consumer place any trust in their predictions of an economic recovery or improvement in the stock market? Just as the future consumer would suspiciously eye each new product, so too would the investor view new stock options. Such is the position Don Marquis's celebrated cockroach adopts in "a warning" from *archy does his part*:

> i am glad to see business
> picking up again but when i hear
> that the stock market is on the rise
> there is a bit of a chill
> creeps over my flush of optimism
> for i can remember way back
> millions of years back
> to the days when the stock market
> was up in the stratosphere
> in a wild balloon
> and it came down without a parachute
> if it does that all over again
> we will reach a situation
> where the hard times of the last few years
> will look so good by comparison
> that they will resemble
> an ice cream party on the pastors lawn (283)

Archy's concern is not unique. It reflects the cautious optimism that accompanied most of the economic reforms that formed the nucleus of the Roosevelt administration, as well as the predictions from the business community that they alone, without the intervention of the federal government, could effectively stimulate a recovery. Americans now, more than ever before, were beginning to carefully scrutinize their once blind trust in the leaders of the economic community who had already let them down and could do so again.

Clarence Day, for one, ponders over the rapidly changing image of the American businessman—an image firmly rooted in a capitalistic system that had created the nation's wealth but had simultaneously failed in 1929. How was one to reconcile the opposites? Were businessmen to be praised or pilloried—a point discussed in "As They Go Riding By" from *After All.*

In it, Day draws a whimsical parallel between the knights of old England and the modern-day tycoon. The knights, he claims were overly romanticized by such writers as Tennyson and Malory. For them, there were very few "wicked, villainous knights, who committed crimes such as not trusting other knights or saying mean things, but that even they were subject to shame when found out and rebuked, and that all the rest were a fine, earnest Y.M.C.A. crowd, with the noblest ideas" (163).

The truth, for Day, is not as kind in its assessment. Paging through encyclopedias has altered his perspective of the past and shaken his illusions of youth. The knights in reality, he concludes, were actually a disreputable lot of thieves and bullies who terrorized the local citizenry when not off fighting in some crusade against the infidel. Closely allied to the church and in positions of wealth and privilege, they were above the laws that they themselves had created. They were a closed society, exclusive in its membership and possessed of a "loathing for the people [that] seemed almost akin in its intensity to color prejudice" (165). But modern man fondly subscribes more to the illusion than to the reality, visiting reliquaries and strolling down halls filled with armorial splendor.

Such may be the fate of America's tycoons, Day ponders: "Some day when our modern types of capitalists are extinct, in their turn, will future poets sing to their fine deeds and make young readers dream? Our capitalists are not popular in these days, but the knights weren't in theirs, and whenever abuse grows extreme a reaction will follow" (169). Man's inherent predatory instincts and need for romantic heroes will favor the resurrection. The facts will not be consulted by future poets. Their inspiration will not be derived from the pages of newspapers:

> He will get his conception of capitalists out of his heart. Mighty men who built towers to work in, and fought with one another, and engaged in great capitalist wars, and stood high above labor. King Carnegie and his round directors' table of barons of steel. Armour, Hill and Stillman, Jay Gould—musical names, fit for poems. (170)

The men of the future will wish they had lived in such times and try to recapture the past in pageants where they can dress up as capitalists, "some with high hats and umbrellas (borrowed from the museums)" and engage in games of golf and polo "carrying the queer ancient implements." Little boys will gaze in wonder on the events and hurry back home to "play they are great financiers" even if some histories refer to their heroes as "not all noble, but a mixed human lot, like the knights" (171).

In his attempt to heal the divisions and dispel the conflicts that had arisen between the business community and the American public during the thirties, Christopher Morley would humanize and clarify the businessman in *Human Being*. The main character, the recently deceased Richard Roe, is a nondescript but, nevertheless, decent, hard-working, and, in some ways, exemplary fellow whose biographer, Hubbard, learns to admire. Like all traveling salesmen, Roe possesses, according to Hubbard, an almost Whitmanesque "nobility of purpose." In the Pullman train car, he sings his song of the open road, "rhyming the unlikely with the impossible":

> He consoles fatigue and disgust with some telephone number in his little memo-book. Sparkle comes back into his nerves. He has a word of comedy for the porter. He goes to the stale smoking-washroom to deal wits against other companions of chance. So he matches against the impossible odds of life, and is Lord of his event. (38)

Whether he is the frightened beginner or the seasoned professional, the traveling salesman is the master of "comedy and cajolery; persistence, tact, evasion; knowing when to sidestep and when to strike" (38). In short, he is a man to be admired and not shunned as one of the principal forces behind the Great Depression.

Then, too, Hubbard continues to philosophize, no man is more qualified to feel the shame, fear, and disillusionment of those years more than those associated with business. While taking his daily walks with the family dog, Roe becomes increasingly alarmed with the large number of almost completed and then abandoned apartment buildings he passes along Central Park West. Such scenes, Hubbard notes, might give "ironic and malicious amusement" to the poets and radicals of the thirties, but for a man of business like Roe, they contradict a "fundamental piety." Half-completed construction sights, with their "rusting iron girders of the unfinished door-canopies projected over the pavement like gibbets," foreshadow the collapse of Western civilization and all its dreams for the future: "A dangerous ghost lived in those dark rooms, the wraith of some economic law that men had transgressed. What was that grim veto: Not to Bite Off More than

You Can Chew?" (71). Even more distressing for Roe are the times he is forced to shut down his own factory or lay off some of the workers. His wife Minnie secludes him from the many letters he gets from disgruntled workers, "letters of threat or of anguished appeal," for she feels there is nothing her husband can do (339).

The disheartening aspects of the Great Depression can also fire the imagination of businessmen like Roe. Such men are familiar with downswings in fortune, and when faced with seemingly impossible odds, display a resilience not uncommon to the species. Such men, Hubbard writes, "are tough mountaineers":

> With ice-pick and hob-nails, roped together in catenations of credit, they bridge many a crevasse. The southernmost deposit of the great glacial epoch is that mysterious little stone in the middle of Battery Park. It is encouraging, it says COAST AND GEODETIC SURVEY, BASIC BENCH MARK. Perhaps to many a poor devil, touching bottom on a park bench, it seems only tragic irony. But there is meaning in that lowest curve of the tall city. Standing there, you can feel energy growing and roaring behind you. The God's-eye view would be that even an Ice Age could not shatter these industrious bipeds. They used it for tobogganing. (84)

Business might not play the role it did twenty years ago, but it is, nevertheless, hard to kill. The spirit of success is too strong within the heart of the businessman.

Perhaps, however, their dreams are based more on fantasy than reality. Their conception of success is unable or unwilling to admit to inevitable defeat. For Hubbard, the businessman can then become too much of a dreamer, unaware of real life and its pitfalls, or, at worst, a drudge of Madison Avenue, eking out a "small timid career of bargain and bicker" (269). Such men become unhappy men—unhappy with their careers and their lives—hiding behind a facade of the "Good Old Times . . . humanity needs its Good Times so much that when they don't exist it invents them" (232). Such men pursue the "phantom of Better Business like the jolly horsemen of England chasing the fox across the shires and through other people's cabbages. They cry *Yoicks*! and *Gone Away* (or whatever the catchwords are) and the whole hunt, led by some lively publicist in a red coat, goes careening over fences" (232–33). In the end, Hubbard concludes, many fall by the side or end up standing on the windowsills of the very buildings they have built.

For a number of the Depression humorists, an individual far more worthy of the businessman's precarious position atop the windowsill was the average medical doctor. Maybe their complaints stemmed from the unrelieved aches and pains of middle age to which a few such as Benchley had grown accustomed. For whatever reason, no other profession outside the groups previously discussed fell under as much criticism and, sometimes, outright scorn. The fact that the medical profession existed within what the average man might have considered to be almost a secret society did not help matters any. Like the politicians or police, they were a closed fraternity which, in this case, dealt with the science of healing and which was for the most part incomprehensible for many and therefore open to condemnation or ridicule.

For Ogden Nash, the average man was a victim of *all* professionals simply from the fact that unlike the average man, they had not suffered as much during the thirties. The arrogance of the educated is the target for Nash's pointed and barbed wit in "I Yield to My Learned Brother." For him, "Professional men, they have no cares; / Whatever happens, they get theirs." No matter how important or rich a man may be, it is the professional who controls destiny:

> The noblest lord is ushered in
> By a practicing physician,
> And the humblest lout is ushered out
> By a certified mortician.
> And in between, they find their foyers
> Alive with summonses from lawyers. (Smith and Eberstadt, 70)

His only real complaint now is that his parents had not been more forceful in encouraging him earlier to enter one of the professions, for, if they had, he would now be driving a "Rolls or an Isotto," instead of wearing out his shoe leather as a poet. He learns too late in life that certain segments of society will always be immune to economic downswings, for doctors "were doing fine / in '29, / And they're doing fine today" (70).

One can detect a note of jealousy in Nash's observations, but none in Thurber's "Draft Board Nights" from *My Life and Hard Times*. For Thurber, the medical doctor is simply another fool, another misguided member of the human race, excepting one major difference from the average man. Doctors are often the ones in authority, so their judgments impact not only on themselves but those around them as well. Like the politicians, they too seem to be inevitably the decision makers in the common man's life. In Thurber's tale, the decisions involve who is or is not to be drafted into the army during World War I. Thurber, however, is faced with another predicament; the draft board keeps calling him in for a physical although he has previously been granted a 4–F on account of his poor eyesight. Frustrated with having to return time and time again for the physical only to be told that his poor eyesight disqualifies him for active service, Thurber decides to break the monotony by borrowing a stethoscope and joining the other doctors in the examining process. Much to his surprise, none of them recognizes him as an impostor. In fact, one of the physicians, Dr. Ridgeway, with whom he frequently works alongside in the "chest-and-lung section," later recalls him to be a "good pulmonary man" and possibly a relative! (143).

For S. J. Perelman, the more specialized the doctor the bigger the fool. The activities of a plastic surgeon, for one, become a suitable script for a grade B thriller in "Midwinter Facial Trends." Perusing the doctor's brochure on cosmetic surgery, Perelman encounters terrifying scenes worthy of a Boris Karloff. One in particular titled "The Formation of the Dimple" catches his eye. The good doctor, after scrubbing down the cheek with antiseptic and inserting a hypodermic needle in a likely spot for a dimple, proceeds with an operative method "strikingly similar to fishing for perch through a hole in the ice." "The Doctor," Perelman continues, "lowers a line with a bobber and a bit of red flannel, builds a fire on the patient's forehead, and sits down to warm his hands till a dimple is hooked. The patient lies there softly whimpering, 'I didn't have enough trouble, I had to have dimples like Robert Taylor yet!' " (Namlerep, 117).

Dentists likewise come under attack in "Nothing but the Tooth." In it, Perelman claims that nothing would satisfy him more for a birthday present than a free subscription to *Oral Hygiene*: "Through its pages runs a recital of the most horrendous and fantastic deviations from the dental norm. It is a confessional in which dentists take down their back hair and stammer out the secrets of their craft" (68). Of particular fascination is the question-and-answer column. It has opened Perelman's eyes and altered his conception of the profession:

> I had always thought of dentists as of the phlegmatic type—square-jawed sadists in white aprons who found release in trying out new kinds of burs on my shaky little incisors. One look at *Oral Hygiene* fixed that. Of all the inhibited fumble-bunnies who creep the earth, Mr. Average Dentist is the worst. A filing clerk is a veritable saber-toothed tiger by comparison. Faced with a decision, your dentist's bones turn to water and he becomes all hands and feet. He muddles through his ordinary routine with a certain amount of bravado, plugging a molar here with chewing gum, sinking a shaft in a sound tooth there. In his spare time he putters around his laboratory making tiny cement cup-cakes,

substituting amber electric bulbs for ordinary bulbs in his waiting-room to depress patients, and jotting down nasty little innuendoes about people's gums in his notebook. But let an honest-to-goodness sufferer stagger in with his face out of drawing, and Mr. Average Dentist's nerves go to hell. He runs sobbing to the "Ask *Oral Hygiene*" department and buries his head in the lap of V. C. Smedley, its director. (69)

Dentists, Perelman continues, plead for advice on how to stop teeth grinding at night or how to eliminate thumb sucking in toddlers to exotic dilemmas such as a teenager whose right cuspid tooth turned black after being struck by lightning! Enough of this, Perelman concludes. From now on he alone will control the destiny of his bicuspids, and dentists will never get him into their chairs again: "I'll dispose of my teeth as I see fit, and after they're gone, I'll get along. I started off living on gruel, and, by God, I can always go back to it again" (72).

The last batch of specialists to come under attack by Perelman is the podiatrists as seen in "Boy Meets Girl Meets Foot." What attracts his attention here is a recently published book by an eminent foot doctor, a Dr. Nelson. Its uniqueness lies not in its being published because it is evidently not an uncommon trend for physicians to publish a book nowadays. Indeed, he notes, it becomes their particular concern on the road to fame and fortune: "It would seem from the publishers' spring lists that the entire Hippocratic fraternity had forsworn the art of healing in favor of letters" (155). But this book is decidedly different, for the "reader becomes so acutely aware of his feet that he spends his day listening with a rather cunning expression to his toes meshing into gear" (156).

The doctor especially shines in his ability to portray his patients as dim-witted creeps, which, Perelman suspects, is a "deep-seated conviction among doctors about their patients" (156). One patient, a flustered housewife with burning feet, is characterized as a simpleton, and her husband, the doctor "gratuitously insinuates," is nothing more than a "red-faced, bull-necked extrovert who taunts his wife with her malady" (157).

Another woman patient is reduced to humble adoration when the doctor cunningly diagnoses the calluses on her feet before she has even taken her shoes off. What's amiss is that her second toes are distinctly longer than her great toes. When the lady confesses that she has always considered it to be an indication of a perfect foot as noted in ancient Greek sculpture, the doctor responds curtly: "What was ideal for the women of ancient Greece is definitely not ideal for the modern woman who wears high-heeled shoes." Of course, Perelman concludes, "Old smarty-pants Nelson knows what

Grecian women wore on their feet; he was there. Everybody remembers *him* around the agora, arm in arm with Pericles. Oh, you wine-dark, loud-thundering, many-throated Nelson, you!" (158).

Benchley would agree. Doctors are always quick to give advice on matters of health, he feels, but fail miserably when confronted with the common ailments of life. Even more aggravating is the dilemma created by contradictory medical reports, widely disseminated in the press and supported by opposing camps of physicians and medical scholars, all of which leaves the average sufferer bewildered and floundering for a cure. As a body, the profession is fueled by fear—fear, on the doctor's part, that patients will get well and no longer need help, and fear, on the patient's part, of impending disaster if a prudent lifestyle is not immediately followed.

Now it seems, according to Benchley, some doctors are saying that fear is *good* for the constitution as he notes in "Eat More Worry" from *My Ten Years in a Quandary*. " 'When we worry,' says the doc, 'every gland in the body pours energizing juices into the brain. It is the body's way of preparing the mind to meet an emergency. The biological purpose of worry is to enable you to get up steam' " (148). So much for Roosevelt's dire prediction in 1934 that the nation had nothing to fear but fear itself. It's mother's milk for the infirm. In fact, Benchley includes a list of "worrying exercises," guaranteed to get the average man back on his feet in no time:

> *Position No. 1.*—On arising stand facing an open window. (Not too wide open, as, if you get to worrying too well, you may fly out.) Place the hands lightly on the hips and think: "On the fifteenth that big insurance premium comes due. On the fifteenth the income tax is due. On the fifteenth I shall be just eight hundred dollars short of meeting them." Repeat this ten times and then exhale.
>
> *Position No. 2.*—Lie flat on your back, with your legs in the air, and run over in your mind the age at which you find yourself, the amount of money you have saved, the probable number of years left, and what chances you will have of getting a ten-year guest-card at the Home for Aged Men. As soon as the energizing juices have reached your feet lower them and adopt a sitting posture on the floor. Sit that way all day, with your chin in your hand.
>
> *Position No. 3.*—Stand in front of a mirror and look at your stomach.
>
> *Position No. 4.*—Wake yourself up in the middle of the night, lie flat on your back in bed and look at the ceiling. Then figure out just how you would get out of the house in case of fire, what you would do first if that pain in your side should turn out to be acute appendicitis, or how you would face an actual werewolf.
>
> *Position No. 5.*—Just stop to think about *anything*. (149–50)

If you follow these simple exercises and the doctor's advice, Benchley claims, in no time you will become a new man—one you will not like!

An alarming bit of medical news, for Benchley, surfaces in "Health and Work." He is disturbed by a report that with "proper attention to health" an average person can remain active in business up to the age of eighty. Indeed, he ponders, "I know that there are supposed to be veterans who simply have to patter down to the office or the foundry every day, just out of sheer love of the thing, but they must also have some other reason for their devotion to work. There must be someone at home who gets on their nerves" (191–92). Work, Benchley concludes, is merely another form of nervousness. Far more reasonable for him would be to make enough money to retire before thirty and then devote the rest of one's life to health. After all, "what is the sense of being in good health if you have to work?" (193).

In "My Trouble," Benchley points out that despite all the learned advice he has received from numerous doctors, none has been able to cure his medical problem—when he lies down his throat closes up and he stops breathing! Concluding that it must not be a normal condition ("do all boys of 46 stop breathing when they go to bed?"), he decides to get another medical opinion. "It is a form of jumpiness," the doctor tells him further, adding that he must not be breathing when he lies down. "I know that," Benchley responds. "I was the one who told you." Finally the doctor labels it as a phobia, and the cure is simple but effective: "All you need to do," he says, "is to breathe when you lie down."

> "You mean inhale and exhale?" I asked.
> "That's one way of putting it," he said, smiling tolerantly.
> "I guess you're right at that," I said. "Just inhale and exhale."
> "When you are lying down," he added
> "Ah—there's the catch," I replied, catching.
> "You are just making things more difficult for yourself," he said. "Go home, and come back to me tomorrow." (126)

Benchley doesn't bother to return, and we leave him still wondering about his malady at middle age.

Benchley finally comes to the conclusion in "Do Dreams Go by Opposites" that possibly the answer to our medical problems lies in our dreams. Behavior is not created out of logic but instead the illogic of the subconscious. A good example of this is evident in one study where a man had a dream that he was in a public dining room, was not running for a train, and, according to Benchley, illogically had all his clothes on. Upon awakening he is so unnerved, he takes off his clothes, goes to a public dining room, and runs for a train, but misses it. In another example, a woman dreams of being in a greenhouse moving up the side of a mountain, tapestry-weaving in the presence of a deaf elk that has climbed in through a hole in a screen: "Now the amazing thing about all this was that exactly the opposite thing happened to the woman the very next day. She was *not* in a funicular greenhouse; she did not see a deaf elk, and she knew nothing about tapestry-weaving" (51–52). Such is the progress of medical science!

But it would be left up to the father in Clarence Day's *Life with Father* to register the definitive sentiment regarding doctors and the medicine they practice. When a physician is speedily summoned by Mrs. Day to her husband's bedside, fearing that he might have pneumonia, he summarily dismisses the visitor and shows him the door: "I know all about doctors. They think they know a damned lot. But they don't. Give your pills and things to Mrs. Day—she believes in them. That's all I have to say." Ironically, the doctor is able to get the upper hand in the end, convincing the old gentleman that he is *indeed* quite ill, which in turn makes him think he is in need of spiritual guidance. From the hallway, the conferring doctor and Mrs. Day overhear her husband calling on God for assistance: "Have mercy. . . . I say have mercy, damn it!" (65).

Interestingly enough, Father does not call upon the assistance of a clergyman, probably holding them in less regard than he does physicians. If such were his sentiments, they were equally shared by a number of the Depression humorists who displayed a broad range of attitudes toward the clergy in their writings.

Will Rogers adopts an "evenhanded" approach in one observation entitled "About the Churches." In it, he responds to a letter he has received from a clergyman up in Minnesota who says he is going to be speaking about Rogers in his next sermon. "There is an awful lot of different ways to speak on me," Rogers writes back to the pastor, "and all of 'em pretty near true, at that." But there are a few points about himself he does want to make clear. Concerning religion, he is merely a believer in God. Raised predominantly as a Methodist, he has traveled so much and mixed with so many people in all parts of the world that he is no longer sure what religion he is except for the fact that he is not a nonbeliever. "But I can honestly tell you," he informs the minister, "I don't think that any religion is *the* religion" (Sterling and Sterling, 233).

> If I am broad-minded in any way—and I hope I am in many—I do know that I am broad-minded in a religious way. Which way you serve your God will never get one word of argument, or condemnation, out of me. There has been times when I wished there had been as much real

religion among some of our creeds as there has been vanity, but that's
not in any way a criticism. (233)

He comes to an end, wishing the minister well and hoping he will be understanding of the ones in his congregation who have not "paid up" on time:
"They got just as much religion, as the paid up ones. So you will just have to
trust 'em, and give 'em a little preaching 'on time' " (234).

E. B. White's encounter with a minister, however, is more sinister than
sanguine. In "Camp Meeting" from *One Man's Meat*, he attends a fund-
raiser for a Dr. Francis E. Townsend of California. He first notices the rever-
end under a "God Is Love" sign, busy soliciting funds from the local farmers
and small-town merchants who have paid their admission for the honor of
seeing the great man. The people in attendance are from the surrounding
farm area of upper Maine—"honest, hopeful folks, their faces grooved with
the extra lines that come from leading godly lives" (93). The woodland retreat where the meeting is being held possesses, for White, a general "disreputable air," being like most buildings in the wilderness, largely
unoccupied for the majority of the year except for woodpeckers, sneak
thieves, and lovers in season. Such matters do not bother Dr. Townsend
who, as we soon find out, is a man with a mission; he has come to do good,
and he will do well indeed.

He is a man with a political agenda, riddled with enough hackneyed clichés and sentimental overtones as to moisten many a dry eye and receive the
approving nod from the average man on the street. He speaks to his audience of the terrible plight of the elderly and of a nation, possessed of unlim-
ited resources but unable to care for its own. Its failure lies, he feels, within
the political philosophy of the Roosevelt administration and its New Deal
agencies. "Do you want to be taxed for these useless and futile activities?"
he exhorts his audience. His audience shakes their heads in unison: "No, of
course not!" (95).

His plan is so simple and logical it immediately converts his listeners:
"Levy a two per cent tax on the gross business of the country and divide the
revenue among persons over sixty years of age, with the one stipulation that
they spend the money ($200 a month) within a certain number of days. 'And
mind you,' said the Doctor, with a good-natured grin, 'we don't care a rap
what you spend it for!' " (95). Murmurs of approval arise out of the audience as the doctor continues: "We want you to have new homes, new furniture, new shoes and clothes. We want you to travel and go places. You old
folks have earned the right to loaf, and you're going to do it luxuriously in
the near future. The effect on business, when all this money is put into circu-

lation, will be tremendous. Just let us have two billion dollars to distribute this month, and see what happens!" (96). The sound of such a huge sum further excites his hearers, White notes, but there are still questions to be answered, and now the doctor begins to look thoughtful and confused.

"How much will it cost to administer?" one old woman asks; "Can a person get the pension if they hold property?" queries another listener. These and other questions leave the good doctor floundering for answers. Ironically, no one bothers to ask him the effect his plan will have on inflation because it will undoubtedly be the response of business to pass any tax on to the consumer. But no one does, and the meeting comes to an end with a flurry of handshaking and backslapping. The chairman of the event arises to announce that today's take is over eighty dollars, and "life," White notes, "began to settle into its stride again" (100).

> The Doctor, waylaid by a group of amateur photographers, posed in front of an American flag, and then departed in a Dodge sedan for the airport—a cloud-draped Messiah, his dream packed into a briefcase for the next performance. On the porch of a cottage . . . three old ladies rocked and rocked and rocked. And from a score of rusty stovepipes in the woods rose the first thick coils of smoke from the kitchen fires, where America's housewives, never quite giving up, were laboriously preparing one more meal in the long procession. The vision of milk and honey, it comes and goes. But the odor of cooking goes on forever. (100)

And so too do con-artists like the doctor from California!

Con-artists of a different sort were the attorneys, who, as a class, are generally not mentioned in the writings of the Depression humorists with the exceptions, as usual, of Nash and Benchley. Nash briefly sums up his view in a short poem, "Family Court":

> One would be in less danger
> From the wiles of the stranger
> If one's own kin and kith
> Were more fun to be with. (Smith and Eberstadt, 3)

Benchley, on the other hand, likes to fantasize how well he would hold up under the extensive cross-examination from befuddled and confused prosecutors in "Take the Witness" from *My Ten Years in a Quandary*.

In such a courtroom Benchley would shine before the judge and jury, "calm in a nice way, that is—never cocky. However frantic my inquisitor may wax (and you should see his face at times—it's purple!), I just sit there, burning him up with each answer, winning the admiration of the courtroom, and, at times, even a smile from the judge himself" (5). Appreciating the fact that most sensational trials are molded into media events by attorneys, Benchley takes care to rebut questions with enough wit and sarcasm to make himself shine in the public's eye—and possibly get another book published. When the prosecution asks him how he knew an event took place at exactly eleven-fifteen, he responds: "Because I looked at my watch."

Q—And just why did you look at your watch at this particular time?

A—To see what time it was.

Q—Are you accustomed to looking at your watch often?

A—That is one of the uses to which I often put my watch.

Q—I see. Now, it couldn't, by any chance, have been ten-fifteen instead of eleven-fifteen when you looked at your watch this time, could it?

A—Yes, sir. It could.

Q—Oh, it *could* have been ten-fifteen?

A—Yes, sir—if it had been in Chicago. (8)

Such repartee would keep the media's attention riveted to the trial and Benchley's performance for weeks. The only thing he fears is that if he ever *really* has to testify in some case he won't be asked the "right" questions: "That *would* be a pretty kettle of fish" (9).

Benchley's "day in court," like many of the numerous attacks on doctors and lawyers in the writings of Depression humorists, was not entirely generated by what was considered to be abuses within those professions. Part of the impetus arose out of a groundswell of anti-intellectualism that paradoxically prevailed throughout the thirties—a decade that concomitantly considered itself to be at the forefront of modern technology and a better world as was seen at the 1939 World's Fair in New York City. Audiences at the various exhibits were enthralled with delightful miniaturizations of cities a mere thirty years into the future, where people tirelessly traveled along smooth uncongested highways or rode above on sleek monorails between towering skyscrapers of glass and steel. Such cities and the infrastructures that supported them would be the result of a seamless joining of government with the academic community. The cliché of the harmless, absent-minded college professor smelling of tobacco smoke and frequently misplacing his notes was rapidly fading before projections of "brain trusts" siphoned from the nation's leading institutions of higher learning and now securely enthroned within the highest levels of the decision-making process—federal, state, and local. Such a future gave many Americans, including the humorists, pause to consider the outcomes. A nation of people who had grown to mistrust the promises of the past could well harbor doubts for those of the future.

E. B. White certainly has his doubts about "certainties," a point he makes abundantly clear in an observation of the same title from *The New Yorker*. The new age, for him, is proliferating in "experts" who possess at their fingertips an encyclopedic understanding of the world's problems, as well as the necessary solutions for its ills. After one dinner party, where he finds himself nestled between two such "intellectual giants," he is borne to such an extent on the waves of their conversation that when he returns home and his wife asks him if he thinks the family dog has worms, he answers with a resounding "'Yes,' in a moment of vainglory pretending that here was a thing on which we spoke knowingly—though such was far from the case, as we both secretly knew" (Dale, 211).

As the decade progressed and academia became more and more a part of the decision-making process in government, the average man began to find his lifestyle increasingly predetermined for him by those who evidently knew better. Reduced to the status of a guinea pig, the modern man, some of the humorists feared, would lose his ability for independent thought, becoming instead a subject running through a maze of conflicting scientific theories.

Such is Benchley's fear in his essay "Those Dicta" from *My Ten Years in a Quandary*. In it, he expresses his frustration with a new crop of "busybody" scientists who are determined to make man predictable and therefore controllable. "Scientists," he claims, "would get a lot farther with me if they didn't generalize so dogmatically. For every general dictum that they issue, at least three exceptions can be found right in my own house" (282). He is furious with one scientist who claims that mankind "feels" better in the spring because the "sensitivity of the brain is greater." Now, claims Benchley, this may apply to some people, but what right does the professor have to ascribe such feelings to all mankind? Benchley, for one, is "peppiest in October. And I flatter myself that I am a member of that group which is known, euphemistically, as mankind" (283).

Even more infuriating is another professor of psychology who claims that all mankind finds the sight of someone slipping on a banana peel funny. Benchley doesn't. Nor do some of his friends. So what right does the doctor have in labeling it the "universal joke"? These, along with other theories, such as all dreams are based on sex and self-preservation is the first law of mankind, are, for Benchley, flawed, and the reason for their being so is quite simple: "The trouble with the specialists in what mankind does or does not do is that they don't get around enough with mankind" (284).

Instead, they prefer to putter around in their laboratories, spending government money and considerable time on useless projects—a complaint Benchley registers in another essay, "Robot Rats." It seems, Benchley claims, that someone has invented a motorized rat consisting of small motors, electromagnets, and switches. Such a rat, he feels, might be a considerable improvement over the average house rat: "It shouldn't send timid folks leaping into chairs at any rate" (249).

> But I still can't figure out the need for having done it at all. The robot rat is so constructed that, when set on a track and adjusted to take the wrong turn at a switch, it learns a lesson from having bumped up the dead-end and the next time takes the right turn of its own accord.
>
> This is very cute of it, but wouldn't it have been simpler to have adjusted it to take the right turn in the *first* place? Why subject it to the humiliation of bumping up the dead-end at all? (250)

As far as Benchley is concerned, he can think of several other mechanical appliances he would prefer for Christmas than a "deliberately maladjusted" robot rat!

Thurber agrees with Benchley's inability to appreciate the achievements of the academic world. His own experiences with college professors were less than promising, as detailed in "University Days" from *My Life and Hard Times*. The realm of science remained a mystery throughout his college years, and the study of botany became a nightmare in particular because, unlike the other students, he never could see anything through a microscope. This, of course, infuriated his professor who was certain that Thurber could see what he was told to see but, instead, preferred not to:

> "It takes away from the beauty of flowers anyway," I used to tell him. "We are not concerned with beauty in this course," he would say. "We are concerned solely with what I may call the *mechanics* of flars." "Well," I'd say, "I can't see anything." "Try it just once again," he'd say, and I would put my eye to the microscope and see nothing at all, except now and again a nebulous milky substance—a phenomenon of maladjustment. You were supposed to see a vivid, restless clockwork of sharply defined plant cells. "I see what looks like a lot of milk," I would tell him. This, he claimed, was the result of my not having adjusted the microscope properly, so he would readjust it for me, or rather, for himself. And I would look again and see milk. (111)

Thurber has equally unpleasant encounters in other subjects, such as economics and physical education, but it is compulsory military drill that sets aside his college for distinction. Even though the world war is in progress, the cadets train with old Springfield rifles and study the tactics of the Civil War era: "It was good training for the kind of warfare that was waged at Shiloh but it had no connection with what was going on in Europe," Thurber concludes, adding that it might have been financed by German funds. At any rate, it marked "the decline of higher education in the Middle West" (123).

Negative stereotypes of professors surface again in the writings of Ogden Nash and S. J. Perelman. A professor as insensitive as Thurber's botany instructor becomes the subject of one of Nash's short poems titled "The Purist." A conscientious scientist, Professor Twist, embarks on an expedition into the jungle with his loving bride only to find her missing from the camp one evening: "She had, the guide informed him later, / Been eaten by an alligator. / Professor Twist could not but smile. / 'You mean' he said, 'a crocodile'" (Smith and Eberstadt, 145). However, for S. J. Perelman, professors are not entirely devoid of feelings; they lust for their students! In "The Love Decoy" a sexually overactive coed lures one of her professors into her dormitory room with the intention of humiliating him for having ridiculed her during a class, only to find out that he is quite a lecher and not alone in his feelings for her because he is soon joined by an academic dean to form a ménage à trois! The professor is also noted for his unique way of "breaking the ice." When he invites pretty coeds up to his office to help him with his research, he tells them he needs assistance compiling a book of dirty limericks. As one pretty coed puts it: "In the twinkling of an eye we were in the gutter" (Namlerep, 124).

Fortunately, not all the humorists are as uniformly caustic as Perelman in their appraisal of the profession. Thurber champions teachers as upholders of high ideals in *The Male Animal*, where a hen-pecked English professor reaches a noble and heroic stature by reading Vanzetti's last letter of denial to an English class despite threats from the Board of Regents. Even Damon Runyon's world of deadbeats and ne'er-do-wells finds room for a sympathetic portrait of an absent-minded professor.

The professor, Dr. Woodhead from Princeton, New Jersey, surfaces in the story "Pick the Winner" from *Money from Home*. We find him in Florida for his health but frequenting Hialeah, fascinated by the track mob and what he considers to be the "greatest show" around. Within a short time, he is befriended by a track-side bookie and small time hustler named Hot Horse Herbie who makes a living by getting people to bet on certain horses and

taking a part of the winnings if they come in on top. Our narrator is somewhat amused when he sees the two together at the track each day, for it is not
often you see a bookie alongside a professor "puffing at his old stinkaroo
and looking somewhat bewildered" (310). But he gets to like the old fellow
more when he notices a wad of "coarse notes" in his possession and has
more respect for the profession even though the professor is so "ignorant
about racing that it is hard to believe he is a college guy" (311).

Hot Horse Herbie is desperately trying to get the overly cautious professor to place a bet on a horse called Breezing Along, and finally enlists the
services of his girlfriend, Cutie Singleton, who is to use her "clairvoyant"
powers and predict a "big wind" in the professor's future. While she does
so, she also happens to find out that the professor is single and lives by himself, except for his housekeeper, in a beautiful, white-shingled home with
green shutters and "vines all around and about" in Princeton.

Hot Horse Herbie is able to get the professor to bet $100 on the horse, but
on the day of the race the professor is nowhere to be found, much to Herbie's
delight because he loses the professor's money on the bet anyway. Surprisingly, Herbie can't find his girlfriend, Miss Singleton, either and doesn't
know where she has disappeared to until he receives a letter from the professor two weeks later with an explanation for their absence. It seems they got
married and are now living in Princeton, but the professor is the one who is
primarily apologetic for having won big at the race at Hialeah and for not
having shared some of the proceeds with Herbie, especially because he had
been nice enough to introduce the future Mrs. Woodhead to him. It seems
that on the day of the race the professor decided to place another bet on another horse, Mistral, which eventually came in ten to one. Our narrator and
Hot Horse Herbie can't figure out why the professor would have bet on this
horse until they decide to expand their vocabulary and look up its name in
the dictionary; it means a "violent, cold and dry northerly wind," which, according to the professor, seemed more in keeping with the predictions of
Miss Singleton who decidedly had an eye for the future!

The conflicting opinions of the Depression humorists toward the teaching profession are probably best summarized in the writings of H. L.
Mencken who had a well-established reputation as a curmudgeon by the
thirties. At times he lashes out at the "pedagogue," his favorite word, as little
more than a "nurse employed to instruct adolescents in the intellectual and
pseudo-intellectual equivalents of decent table manners." His chief source
of irritation, however, is reserved for the proliferation of teacher training
schools in America during the Depression. Such schools, he feels, are doing
more harm than good toward the development of an American educational

system. The professors of such schools, he claims, are arrogant and conceited eggheads, filled with grandiose plans on how to run the nation as well as its schools but whose "profound contributions" to the teaching art are "next to nothing" (DuBasky, 107).

Caught up in the midst of these new arbiters of American education is the average schoolteacher for whom Mencken has a genuine sympathy:

> The real villains are the quacks who now run the American school system . . . and they ruin her as a teacher. Every year she is beset by a series of new arcana and forced to struggle with them on penalty of losing her job. In Summer, instead of getting her holiday, she is driven into idiotic Summer schools and there required to master all of the nonsense hatched at Columbia during the preceding Winter. (110)

Thus, he concludes, "teaching becomes a madness and the children learn next to nothing" (110).

The proliferation of "experts" and "authorities" becomes for Mencken a major source for his complaint against America and a culture that prides itself on its ability to make the difficult easy and the complex simple. Correspondence schools and certificate programs, which had grown rapidly during the twenties, now hatched an amazing assortment of euphemistically titled positions. No other nation on the earth produces, he feels, such a variety of "engineers." Thus, the lowly *rat catcher* of previous generations is miraculously transformed into an *exterminating engineer* who can wear "buttons like the Elks, Shriners and Rotarians" and demand learned degrees from the universities and "the right to examine and license persons aspiring to their art and mystery" (242).

While pointing an accusatory finger at all the above icons of past and present, the Depression humorist frequently found himself in the uncomfortable position of reviewing his *own* performance and those of his fellow writers in shaping and directing the American consciousness. The Depression writer was not a spontaneous creation of the thirties; these satiric pundits had been poking fun at American culture throughout the twenties as well. It would have been grossly unfair if not undemocratic for them to discount their own responsibility for the current crisis. Had they not already established themselves as the arbiters of American taste and values? Were they too not among the authorities they so zealously vilified in their writings? Were not the contributors and editors of the nation's leading journals among the icons?

For Benchley, the printed word had not done much to dispel the gloom of the already troubled present. In his essay "Bad News" from *My Ten Years in a Quandary*, he condemns the obvious penchant in the media to focus on silly and inconsequential news items in a vain attempt to make readers "feel better." One item catches his eye, although he wishes it had not; it's an article about "fur-bearing trout" deep in the lakes of Yellowstone. "At first," he claims, "I thought that I wouldn't read about it. 'This is a free country,' I said to myself, smiling sadly. 'You don't have to read anything you don't want to read. Skip it, and go on to the next page. Keeping abreast of current events is one thing—masochism is another' " (43). But a perverse New England streak in him, "that atavistic yearning for a bad time," instinctively draws his eyes to the item and how the fur might be a feature in future fashionable wear. Such news should not be so easily bantered about, claims Benchley, for its effect on the reading public is incalculable. It could well drive brother against brother and dissolve the nation "rapidly into chaos" (45).

Another news item that has left him in a state of nervous exhaustion is whether there is such a thing as a "tribal pow-wow of prairie chickens" up in Canada. As he notes in "Waiting for Bad News," also from *Quandary*, he first read about it last summer but lost the article. Now winter is upon him and nothing since has been mentioned in the press, leaving him in a terribly anxious state, wondering if it is true that there are birds, somewhere, taking "steps forward and *then* backward—*in tempo*!" (258). If it is, he fears it may be catching, and he too will find himself "in the middle of my bedroom floor doing the steps myself" (258).

For Nash, such items, which were intended to boost the morale of the reading public, lumped newspapermen and comic writers with the irritating naysayers of his generation. In "Look for the Silver Lining," he criticizes such people for ignoring the realities around them, preferring instead to be "cheery souls who drop around after every catastrophe and think / they are taking the curse off / By telling you about somebody who is even worse off. . . . Life to them is just one long happy game, / At the conclusion of which the One Great Scorer writes not whether / you won it or lost it, but how you played it, against your name. / Kismet, they say, it's Fate. What is to be, will be. Buck up! Take heart! / Kismet indeed! Nobody can make me grateful for Paris Green in the / soup just by assuring me that it comes that way Allah carte" (Smith and Eberstadt, 36).

The condescending attitude of newspaper reporters also draws Benchley's ire. In "Isn't It Remarkable" from *Quandary,* he is miffed by a caption under a photo of a *"Remarkably Accurate and Artistic Painting of a Goose from Pharaoh Akhenaten's Palace, Drawn 3,300 Years Ago"*:

> What I want know is—why the "remarkable"? Why is it any more re-
> markable that someone drew a goose accurately 3300 years ago than

someone should do it today? Why should we be surprised that the people who built the Pyramids could also draw a goose so that it looked like a goose? (46)

Such attitudes seems to be endemic, claims Benchley, in modern American culture:

> We are constantly being surprised that people did things well before we were born. We are constantly remarking on the fact that things are done well by people other than ourselves. "The Japanese are a remarkable little people," we say, as if we were doing them a favor. "He is an Arab, but you ought to hear him play the zither." Why "but"? (47)

Of course, Benchley concludes, the reason we must do this is to reaffirm our own superiority. If we didn't, we would be just like the ancient Egyptians!

Along with the journalists, writers of novels and short stories come under increasing attack from the Depression humorists. Whether it's the potboilers from the pen of James Cain or the obscurantic verse of Gertrude Stein, the humorists always find something to question. Thurber ridicules the gutsy prose of James Cain's popular novel, *The Postman Always Rings Twice* in "Hell Only Breaks Loose Once," from *The Middle-Aged Man on the Flying Trapeze*. In Thurber's tale, a college student attempts to "bump off" the dean of his school while having an affair with the wife. He first meets her at the dean's office:

> She was tall and thin and had a white frowning forehead and soft eyes. She wasn't much to look at but she was something to think about. As far as she and I were concerned he wasn't in the room. She leaned over the chair where I was sitting and bit me in the ear. I let her have it right under the heart. It was a good one. It was plenty. She hit the floor like a two-year-old. (121)

During the run of their courtship, he beats her up a number of times, including under a lunch table where he breaks her ankle: "It was still broken when I carried her back to the Dean's office" (122). When he finally lures the dim-witted dean to the top of a water tower to see a nonexistent aurora borealis, he, the girl, and the dean all fall to the ground and are mortally hurt. "I knew it was going over," our narrator confesses, "so I dictated this to a guy from the D.A.'s office, and here it is. And that's all, except I hope it's pretty in Heaven and smells like when the lilacs first come out on May nights in the Parc Monceau in Paris" (126).

In "Poetry" from *One Man's Meat*, E. B. White prefers to question the value of modern poetry, most of which, as far as he is concerned, presents a distorted view of reality and truth. He is not against poetry as an art. Indeed, good poetry, he feels, is "religious in tone" and "scientific in attitude. A true poem contains the seed of wonder; but a bad poem, egg-fashion, stinks" (117). For White, many of the modern poets deliberately create verse that is convoluted and obtuse as a way of parading their being up to date. The more the poem sounds as if it has come from the pen of a madman, the more "modern" it will seem to the reading public. Such intentional obscurity and distasteful artifice all too often reflect the "inability of some writers to express even a simple idea without stirring up the bottom" (117).

> My quarrel with poets . . . is not that they are unclear but that they are too diligent. Diligence in a poet is the same as dishonesty in a book-keeper. There are rafts of bards who are writing too much, too diligently, and too slyly. Few poets are willing to wait out their pregnancy—they prefer to have a premature baby and allow it to incubate after being safely laid in Caslon Old Style. (118)

Consequently, he has his doubts about the sincerity of poets such as Gertrude Stein, whom he still admires in many ways. He is not one to question her experimental form of writing which can, at times, be diverting and exciting. But, he adds, "I am not ready to believe that any writer, except with dogged premeditation, would always work in so elegantly obscure and elliptical a fashion as the author of 'A rose is a rose'—never in a more conventional manner. To be one hundred per cent roundabout one must be pure genius—and nobody is that good" (119).

In "Motivation" from *The New Yorker*, White further adds that the modern writer is often more concerned with financial gain than truth. White recalls a friend who, upon hearing that the National Arts Club was offering a prize for a book that would "reveal the soul of America," busily set himself to work only to abandon it two days later when he found out that the prize was not $30,000, as he mistakenly thought, but $3,000. "True to the soul of America, he gave the thing up immediately" (Dale, 20).

If the "soul" of America is its reverence for money, then surely one of its chief idols has to be the rich. The Depression humorists evidently thought so and reserved some of their finest barbs for this last icon of the past. Don Marquis's Archy has it on good authority from a louse in "random thoughts by archy" that the rich taste no different from bums and that man's sense of superiority, based upon wealth and power, is merely an illusion of arrogance:

i have noticed
that when
chickens quit
quarreling over their
food they often
find that there is
enough for all of them
i wonder if
it might not
be the same way
with the
human race (224)

Similar sentiments are echoed in Nash's "The Terrible People," where the rich are also portrayed as "stealthy / About the pleasures of being wealthy." By doing so, they are able to evade solicitors for charities and a guilty conscience: "You cannot conceive of an occasion / Which will find them without some suitable evasion. / Yes indeed, with arguments they are very fecund; / Their first point is that money isn't everything, and that they have no / money anyhow is their second" (Smith and Eberstadt, 25).

Thus, with the idle rich safely sequestered in their mansions, the literati at summer workshops, the intellectuals in their ivory towers, and the politicians in Washington, D.C., the average man could do little more than mumble over his position and inability to change it. The icons of the past remained the leaders of the present and would continue to shape the future both good and bad. Mumbling, according to H. L. Mencken, was fast becoming a national pastime, "oddly enough . . . not mentioned in the Bill of Rights or the Constitution of the United States" (DuBasky, 28). For Mencken, there was only one true American icon—General Sherman. But then, he was dead, and, besides, even when he was alive, everyone thought he was crazy.

CHAPTER 5

The Anesthetized Giants— Workers and Farmers

One of the most startling paradoxes to arise from the Great Depression was how the lives of so many could be altered and destroyed by the carelessness or greed of a few, and nowhere was this paradox more evident than in the general plight of thousands of factory workers and small farmers who universally found their lives tragically altered by the events of the 1930s. The ability of American labor to produce large quantities of quality-made goods and the tenacity of the American farmer to produce bumper crops during difficult weather conditions by using the most modern and efficient equipment had been well documented and applauded during the previous decade. But now, for reasons few could understand, this ability lay dormant, like some anesthetized giant Gulliver brought down and bound helpless by invisible wires emanating from Wall Street.

The potential of American labor was well appreciated by the Roosevelt administration who realized that such an untapped resource of energy could be harnessed for good as well as evil objectives. Political agendas could channel such abilities into constructive measures that would benefit all mankind or lead it to its destruction. Roosevelt had no intention of letting the unsettling events of prewar Germany become a foreshadowing of America's future, and when advised by one of his children that if he failed he might lose the next election, he responded that if he failed there would be no next election.

As governor of New York State, he had previously overseen the completion of the George Washington Bridge on October 24, 1931, and foresaw a future where government would supplement industry as a vital influence on American labor. Thus were introduced during the early years of his administration a slew of public works projects under the aegis of a veritable alphabet soup of initialed agencies such as the CWA, WPA, and the CCC.

Initiated in 1933, the Civil Works Program, later dubbed the CWA, appropriated 400 million workers for an emergency employment program to be implemented by individual states, and as the then secretary of state, Harry Hopkins, pointedly noted, "If a state does not transfer people from its relief rolls, there will be no government work in that area" (Horan, 108). It was the administration's objective to boost the morale of labor and not merely offer a stopgap measure for the economic crisis. In Roosevelt's own words, "the mere fact of giving real wages to four million Americans [would do more] to relieve the suffering and lift the morale of the nation than anything undertaken before" (108). Its impact would probably be felt more on how it changed the quality of life for all Americans through projects that would ultimately build and improve over 250,000 miles of highways, construct 30,000 schools, 3,700 playgrounds for children, and 1,000 airports for travelers. It would fight the citrus canker in Texas, the gypsy moth in New England, the sweet potato weevil in the Deep South, and earn the praise of Governor Landon of Kansas as one of the "most constructive policies" in the history of America (Leuchtenbury, 32).

Close upon its heels would soon follow even more aggressive and famous programs benefiting labor, such as the WPA and the Civilian Conservation Corps (CCC). From its inception in 1935 to its demise in 1942, the Work Projects Administration would spend close to $10 billion, employing members of 8 million families and directly affecting the lives of 30 million Americans. Indirectly, it would influence the entire nation. Concerts and shows would be sponsored by the Federal Music Project and Federal Theater Project, while researchers collected the musical folklore of the nation and preserved it on tape for the Library of Congress, where it is still available for review. Writers' projects collected anecdotal folklore and recorded the living history of a nation in turmoil while laying the foundation for a good part of American social history during the years following World War II. But its primary influence would be seen and still is seen on the face of the land through the construction of countless buildings, dams, parks, and the restoration of historical buildings slated for demolition. Even Mt. Hood Timberline Lodge in Oregon, featured in the Stanley Kubrick film *The Shining*, owes its existence to this farsighted program.

The intentions of the CCC were even more far-reaching with the objectives being, as Roosevelt put it, to conserve equally the natural and human resources as "sound investments" for the future of the country (Horan, 107). Aimed primarily at aiding the displaced youth of the nation, it set about training them for skilled jobs, as well as instilling in them a sense of purpose and a love for the land. Employing over two and a half million men, it fed wildlife, counted game, battled the Dutch Elm disease, cleaned beaches and camping grounds, built fish ponds, and fought forest fires with forty-seven CCC men loosing their lives in this last activity. Of all the trees planted in America up to that time, one half had been done by CCC youth.

Despite these and other projects sponsored by the federal government, American labor did not always strike a responsive chord. In fact, labor unrest grew increasingly during the thirties with some strikes becoming particularly bitter and violent, such as the one at the Ford plant in Michigan and another at the San Francisco docks. For many workers, governmental programs did not necessarily spell long-term recovery, and the growth of labor unions as a way of achieving an element of job security for the future escalated markedly. When John L. Lewis launched an organized drive in the coal fields of the Appalachians, membership in the United Mine Workers rose from 150,000 to 500,000 in one year. Even the WPA was not immune from labor unrest.

Part of the trouble within the WPA stemmed from the Workers' Alliance, a communist-dominated organization, which promoted hunger strikes, sit-down strikes, picketing, and demonstrations before state legislatures. When the Roosevelt administration misjudged the economic recovery of 1937 and cut back on some projects, serious strikes broke out in large American cities with women office workers handcuffing themselves to their desks and construction workers engaging in fierce battles with the police. As the police commissioner of New York City observed after one brutal confrontation with strikers: "I wonder if the Cossacks ever received as many busted heads, black eyes, cuts and bruises, and torn uniforms as my men have" (Horan, 233).

Such strikes and violent protests, falling close upon the heels of expensive government subsidies, undoubtedly had a chilling effect on the public's opinion regarding labor. The response of the business community was well documented with considerable means applied to suppress strikes and incarcerate labor organizers. For the average man on the street, the prevailing view was even more mixed. Newspaper accounts could simultaneously sympathize with the plight of the workers while advocating stronger measures to curb the growing violence within the labor movement. Even the

Roosevelt administration would find itself baffled at the end of the thirties with the criticism from organized labor directed more at the White House than at its traditional foe—big business. Some began to wonder if the labor movement had exceeded the bounds of propriety and had become a bit spoiled by the spending programs of previous years.

Such mixed sentiments appeared frequently in the writings of the Depression humorists. Sympathetic strains were not uncommon, but they were also tempered by an undercurrent of dissatisfaction with the current situation. Benchley, for one, is of this philosophy. In *From Bed to Worse*, a hint of frustration flavors the humor found in one piece, previously noted in an earlier chapter, called "A Few Figures for Unproductive Labor." In it, he questions all the fuss that has been generated about seeing to the needs of "productive" labor. Why not, he questions, are there any federal programs intended to alleviate the suffering of "nonproductive" labor such as writers like himself? "I think that if I had it all to do over again (and it looks now as if it wouldn't be a bad idea), I would go in more for manual labor. In times of economic crisis like this, it is the manual laborer who gets the pick of the statistics" (220). Why is it, he continues, that all programs for economic recovery concentrate on the number of men it will take to do a *physical* task, such as construct dams, tan hides, or open oysters? "Hide-tanners, dam-builders, and oyster-openers are going to be sitting pretty in the Golden Age. But no one has a plan for those of us who just copy figures from one book to another, or draw borders for photographic layouts, or poke at the letter 'x' on typewriters all day. No new order is arranged for us" (220). In his usual blunt manner, H. L. Mencken echoes these sentiments in one of his numerous letters to friends: "The position of labor is characteristically selfish and anti-social. The labor leaders still think of their followers," he maintains, "as members of a privileged class, with rights superior to those of all other persons" (DuBasky, 253).

The "anti-social" aspect of American labor that Mencken mentions seems to have been a major source of complaint for the Depression humorists. Maybe it has always been a complaint for those who frequently find themselves at the mercy of craftsmen who possess selective skills in an increasingly demanding market. What individual, past or present, has not found him- or herself often reduced to utter helplessness in the presence of those who can fix a broken appliance or start a dead car? Benchley finds tailors particularly intimidating, as he notes in "Old Suits for New" in *From Bed to Worse*.

He panics whenever he is faced with the prospect of buying a new suit because tailors always find secreted in the inner pockets of his old suit a label indicating its purchase in some out-of-the-way, rural backwater region, such as Augusta, Maine, from the "Pine Tree Outfitters." "Now tailors," he continues, "hate old blue suits." Even if they are purchased from them originally, they dislike them, and, even worse, if they have another tailor's name in them, "it is all they can do to bring themselves to speak to you." "From then on," he concludes, "I have a hard time convincing [them] that I am not in the market for dungarees" (211).

Equally intimidating for Benchley are workers who have to come into his home and disrupt the daily rhythm of his life. There can be "no more upsetting announcement than: 'The expressmen are here for the trunks.' Better never to go away for the Summer than face the arrival of the expressmen," he claims, in "Ominous Announcements" from *My Ten Years in a Quandary*. For starters, he continues, they always complain the trunks are too heavy, although "they must run across some pretty heavy trunks in their day's work, and, after all, it *is* their work and they knew what it was going to be like when they went into it " (309). Plumbers are also frightening, arriving at the most inconvenient hours with all their instruments and blowtorches "like a fiend from hell. The water must be shut off, pipes must be hammered and banged, and above all, strangers will be poking their heads out of doors where you are accustomed to seeing only familiar faces" (310–11). Benchley concludes that one like himself, who craves the "Old Order of Things," might retreat to the cellar for peace, only to hear from the top of the stairs of the arrival of the man to fix the hot water heater!

Similar complaints regarding skilled workers and those in the service industries surface in the writings of almost all the Depression humorists. The undercurrents of frustration were indeed running quite deep. Like Benchley, S. J. Perelman finds fault with insolent workers in "Counter-Revolution" wherein he presents a scenario of a "typical" encounter between a clerk and a humble customer in a large department store. Each inquiry from the customer prompts a sarcastic answer from the clerk, who evidently has had little training in public relations. When the customer asks if a pair of shorts have a "banjo seat," the clerk responds: "Banjo seat! Banjo seat! Why don't you wear a banjo and be done with it?" When the customer further asks if some shorts will shrink, the clerk again responds in kind: "Look—Boulder dam shrank six inches last year. You want me to underwrite a pair of lousy ninety-eight-cent shorts against it?" (Namlerep, 120).

Because of similar dreadful encounters with doormen and waiters, Thurber claims he will never wear an overcoat again in "The Gentleman is Cold" from *The Middle-Aged Man on the Flying Trapeze*. The porter of his apartment building, a heavy-set and somewhat muscular man, has the unnerving habit of tossing people around while he "helps" them into their overcoats. Besides being a "tosser," he is also a "coat-tugger, belonging to that school of coat-tuggers who reach up under your overcoat after they have helped you on with it and jerk the back of your suit jacket so savagely that the collar of the jacket is pulled away from its proper set around the shoulders and makes you feel loutish and miserable. There is nothing to do about this except give the man a dime" (3). Waiters, too, he finds to be generally overbearing, condescending, and unsympathetic in such matters, having perfected the art of humiliating the American customer. One terrifying experience with an officious hat-check boy not only leaves Thurber coatless but stripped of his dinner jacket as well, "standing in the crowded and well-dressed lounge in my shirt-sleeves, with a section of my suspenders plainly visible through the armhole of my waistcoat" (5). Such encounters have made him swear off wearing topcoats even in the coldest of weather. The embarrassment they cause matches even the time his suitcase flopped open on Madison Avenue while he was running for a train at Grand Central!

For E. B. White, however, none of the above matches the insolence and arrogance of New York City's sanitation workers. Standing alone, almost in a class by themselves, the City's garbagemen have single-handedly redefined the meaning of careless independence—as he notes in a 1930 column from *The New Yorker*:

> There is no one in all New York we envy more than the garbageman. Not even a fireman gets so much fun out of life. The jolly, jolly garbageman goes banging down the street without a thought for anyone. He clatters his cans as he listeth; he scatters ashes on the winds with never a thought that the windblown ash problem was settled in 1899 when the little old one-horse dump carts had covers put on them. He is shrewd in measuring his pace, and goes down the block bit by bit, innocently keeping just to the windward of you. He drives like a ward boss through red lights and green, and backs his truck over the crossing with more privilege than a baby carriage on Fifth Avenue. He is masterful as a pirate and chock-full of gusto. (Dale, 195)

Watching them, White concludes, one almost expects them to burst out in song as though in some light operetta. And, indeed, why not? "They have the town by the tail and they know it" (195).

For Clarence Day, problems arise with telephone operators as is evident in one scene involving Father from *Life with Father*. When the telephone is finally allowed into the Day household, Mother adapts herself quite nicely to the new technology, but with Father it is a different matter. Whenever he makes a call, he becomes angry with "central," accusing her of being deaf or stupid or not attending to her duties in a suitable manner. "If she said a number was busy, he'd protest: 'I can't sit here waiting all day. Busy? Busy be damned!' " (164).

In light of the above, however, Ogden Nash points out in one of his poems, "Pipe Dreams," that the "problems" with workers might be attributable more to society's reluctance at having become increasingly dependent on an infrastructure requiring specialist expertise. Nash's complaint is not with the plumbers who have to frequently come and mend the pipes in his "waterless cottage" but instead with the fact he has to call them in the first place. Such activities deprive him of enjoying the summer and stocking up on beautiful memories except, of course, "all my beautiful memories of the plumber." The best thing to do, he concludes, is to be a plumber, because then one can have "really beautiful beauties to remember." That is their advantage over the average man: "They don't have to think about plumbers, so they can concentrate on the view" (Smith and Eberstadt, 159).

It is the growing expertise and specialist knowledge of the various skilled professions that is particularly rancorous for H. L. Mencken who sees behind their fancy tools and confusing shoptalk a ploy to fleece an unsuspecting public of its hard-earned money. Yesterday's "plumber" and "mechanic" are now technical specialists who dread a label any less august after their names on the business card. "Today they hold their heads very high, meet in solemn annual conventions [and] wear distinguished buttons," he laments. Soon, they will demand the privileges accorded those with "learned degrees from the universities" (DuBosey, 242).

Such "pretentiousness," however, can never mask the fact that a laborer is still a laborer, as far as some of the Depression humorists are concerned, and it remains with S. J. Perelman, as usual, to register one of the most sarcastic barbs at American labor in his work "Striking from Hunger." In it, he pokes fun at the incompetence and bungling of the various train employees on a particularly unpleasant ride out West, but reserves his main salvo for the conductor who has been riding the rails so long that even he admits to smelling like a train—"and sure enough, two brakemen waved their lanterns at him that night and tried to tempt him down a siding in Kansas City" (Namlerep, 81–82).

Perelman's comments, like those of his fellow humorists, are reflections of a frustration not unique to the Depression years, for America since the twentieth century had held an ambivalent attitude toward labor. Conflicting with the country's traditional belief in the sanctity of labor and the nobility of work and rugged individualism—a belief as old as the American Revolution and on which was based the modern nation's self-assurance of its continuing prosperity—was the ever increasing fear of communism and radical infiltration of the labor movement. As was noted earlier, disruptions and strikes within the very heart of the WPA were bound to cause an element of suspicion in most Americans about the intentions of American labor. Nevertheless, for many, including the more radically inclined Don Marquis, labor has *no* intentions, radical or otherwise. In fact, it has grown fat and lazy on the misguided benevolence and charity of a paternal government.

Of particular concern for Don Marquis and others is the increasing entrenchment of a "welfare mentality" among the working classes—a mentality unheard of before the 1930s when social programs began to take effect. Archy applauds many of the improvements during the Roosevelt years, but not all have been made without cost. In "archy on this and that," he criticizes the new age as one where:

> a lot of people
> would get back to work now
> but they cant afford to take the time off
> from keeping the relief agencies going
> for if they shut up
> that would throw a lot of specialists
> out of jobs
> i heard one of these bozos
> talking to a buddy the other day and made
> a little song out of his sentiments
> as follows
> the dignity of labor
> is a phrase i like to see
> imposing on my neighbor
> but i cant impose on me
> i had rather dilly dally
> rest and loaf and idle
> i would rather far get pally
> with a pretzel and a seidel
> of beer (444)

For Ogden Nash in "More About People," laziness just might become the new American pastime representing a whole new moral order entrenched against the "priggishness" of those who believe in hard work: "It seems to be very irking / To people at work to see other people not working, / So they tell you that work is wonderful medicine, / Just look at Firestone and Ford and Edison, / And they lecture you till they're out of breath or something, / And then if you don't succumb they starve you to death or something" (Smith and Eberstadt, 7). Or in short, as he notes in "Introspective Reflection," "I would live all my life in nonchalance and insouciance / Were it not for making a living, which is rather a nouciance" (5).

In light of the observations of Marquis and Nash, the American laborer is more a product of his time than a manipulator of the future. Indeed, like most of the characters found in the writings of the Depression humorists, he is a victim of situations and circumstances surrounding the decade, as well as a prevailing opinion, still in effect today, that a person's worth is determined more by the size of his bank account than a dedication to industry and an honest day's work. "If you are rich you don't have to think twice about buying a judge or a horse," claims Nash in "Lines Indited with all the Depravity of Poverty." One can breeze through life without the preoccupations of affordable housing, taxes, and living expenses. One never has "to say When, / And you can sleep every morning until nine or ten." All of which explains why he would "like very, very much to be very, very rich" (5).

Laboring under such misguided standards, endemic by the thirties, the working man becomes defensive about his status in society and insolent toward others with larger paychecks. For the Depression humorists, the victim may even become his greatest victimizer, ironically denigrating his own worthwhile skills simply because the rewards for using them are less than he thinks they should be.

Woollcott focuses on this dilemma in "The Little Fox Terrier" from *The Century of Progress* by noting that it is a common enough experience to sit next to a "boorish bully of a financier" at church, listening to a "servile bootlicker in the pulpit," only to discover in the taxi-driver on the way home "a fastidious and sovereign gentleman. We all need such occasional reminders that we ourselves impart to our jobs the only honor and dignity they can have. Hourly the rickshaw boys at the Century of Progress give evidence that there is no such thing as menial work. There is only the menial spirit" (141–42). This, he feels, is something the "planners of our national economy" might contemplate with profit. Don Marquis's Archy certainly has done so in "archy turns highbrow for a minute" when he informs his boss that after digesting a few books in the library he has come to the conclusion "that antoninus the emperor / and epictetus the slave / arrived at the same / philosophy of life / that there is neither mastery / nor slavery / except as it exists / in the attitude of the soul / toward the world" (190–91).

Thus, it becomes a simple matter for the working classes to make themselves the victims of the rich. In Nash's "Let Me Buy This One," the working poor are criticized for frequently catering to those they consider to be their "betters," the rich: "I have never yet been out with a tycoon for an evening in Manhattan's glamorous canyons / When the evening's bills weren't paid by the tycoon's impoverished but / proud companions." So, he concludes, let us counterattack with "sangfroid and phlegm," and pass an amendment that forces them to "spend as much money on us poor as we do on them" (Smith and Eberstadt, 164–65).

The arrogance and cruelty of the privileged over the working classes again surfaces in a short story titled "Horsie" by Dorothy Parker in *Here Lies*. In it, a domestic nurse, Miss Wilmarth, is hired by an upper middle-class family to tend to the needs of the wife who has recently given birth and is recuperating since her return from the hospital. Sequestered in her carefully appointed bedroom with a profuse arrangement of costly flowers and gifts, the young mother becomes annoyed that the only addition to her bedroom that consistently clashes with its costly decor is the nurse whom she frequently notices bears a pronounced resemblance to a horse:

> Sometimes, when she opened the shiny boxes and carefully grouped cards, there would come a curious expression upon Miss Wilmarth's face. Playing over shorter features, it might almost have been one of wistfulness. Upon Miss Wilmarth, it served to perfect the strange resemblance that she bore through her years; her face was truly complete with that look of friendly melancholy peculiar to the gentle horse. It was not, of course, Miss Wilmarth's fault that she looked like a horse. Indeed, there was nowhere to attach any blame. But the resemblance remained. (130)

Nevertheless, the husband finds Miss Wilmarth to be a constant source of irritation insofar that despite her friendly gestures, efficient ways, and professional manner, her appearance clashes harshly with the intrinsic beauty of his wife and child and his own conception of what a woman should look like. He mockingly observes to his wife that he loves horses; they are noble animals, but "nobody has any business to go around looking like a horse and behaving as if it were all right. You don't catch horses going around looking like people, do you?" (131). As such, he is reflecting the arrogance of the hiring classes which value a person's worth according to the cut of his cloth rather than the content of his character.

At times during dinner, Miss Wilmarth's compassion results in her bursting forth with lighthearted observations, such as how the baby girl will inevitably dominate many a man's heart when she is grown, but these comments are more likely to illicit a frown than a smile from the father who feels as though his private life has been "invaded" by one who should best remain apart from it: "[I]t was unseemly, as rouge would have been unseemly on her long mouth and perfume on her flat bosom" (136). When he voices an objection to his wife having to dine every night with the nurse, she languidly looks up from her bed and responds that he only has her for dinner, whereas *she* has her around all day! The two jokingly refer to her as "seabiscuit" and even invite her to dinner with others present so they too can see how funny she looks.

On the day she is to end her employment, the husband finds himself in a holiday mood, humming repeatedly to himself *"The old gray mare, she ain't what she used to be."* He uncharacteristically buys her some gardenias as a going-away present, primarily due to his joy of getting rid of her. In the end, the husband and wife are surprised she has a home to go to where she tends to an invalid mother and an aged aunt. The thought that such people have homes and parents to look after seems strangely alien to the young couple, but as the wife observes, such glimpses into how the other half lives can be amusing and great fun.

For other Depression humorists, the principal factor behind worker abuse is more specific—the bosses. In Perelman's "Waiting for Santy," an overbearing and flagrantly abusive Santa Claus has precipitated disruption among the ranks of his otherwise obedient elves. In the whirl of activity preceding Christmas, we encounter them spinning lathes and drying lacquer in a sweatshop on North Pole Street, all the while grumbling about starvation wages, toxic fumes, and having to paint "Snow Queen" on Flexible Flyers into the wee hours of the morning just so the boss can ride around in a "red team with reindeers" (Namlerep, 15). A moment later, S. Claus makes an entrance, "a pompous bourgeois of sixty-five who affects a white beard and a false air of benevolence" (17). "Boys," he questions his elves, "do you know what day tomorrow is?" "Christmas!" they shout back in unison. "Correct," he continues: "When you look in your envelopes tonight, you'll find a little present from me—a forty-percent pay cut. And the first one who opens his trap—gets this," as he holds out a tear-gas bomb (18).

Another comment on overbearing bosses surfaces in the writings of the Federal Writers' Project (FWP) in New York City. Entitled "In Defense of Crumbs," it starts off by noting that a powerful symbol of American labor, such as Paul Bunyan, never had to contend with the "crumbs" or big shots of the present day. It seems that a number of years ago, a tyrannical boss was poking his head into a workers' bunkhouse to make sure everyone was at work and not goofing off, when he suddenly heard some small voices call out in unison, "Hello, Brother." It turns out that the voices are those of the "crumbs" or body lice from the workers' infested bunks calling out to the boss, who sees this as an insult to his dignity. When he asks them why they are calling him "Brother," they respond it should be quite clear: "We may be a little different looking on the outside, but we got the same souls, ain't we? We get our living from the same source, don't we? It's the blood of the guys you got working for you. You bleed 'em by day, and we bleed 'em by night . . . that makes you and us blood brothers" (Tidwell, 388). The boss gets angry with the bugs and claims he is going to squash them all because they are sapping his workers of their strength and ability to work even harder. But the lice claim this would be a serious mistake on his part because it is their biting that keeps the workers scratching so much that they rarely have any time to seriously think about their living conditions and mount any protests. Getting rid of them will result in the "slaves" getting organized and demanding improvements—a point the boss obligingly accepts.

Although such attacks on management are understandable in light of the fact that traditionally it had been viewed as the natural enemy of the work-ingman, some of the humorists broke with tradition and introduced to the list of victimizers the very politicians and statisticians who were suppos-edly dedicated to improving his lot. For Mencken, the average politician is just as much an enemy of the working class as he is of the middle class. In a newspaper article of 1937, he sees the ever-rising expenditures and pork-barrel grants among the state legislators as reinforcing their annual habit of digging deeper into the pockets of those who do "useful" work: "Politicians never earn it, and neither do the uplifters. It must always come, in the last analysis, from men who go to work in the morning and labor hard all day. All decent farmers belong to that class, and so do all decent city working-men." (DuBasky, 383). It will do them little good to yell, as has the middle class, he concludes: "Thousands of people who used to work for their liv-ings have been given vested rights in the earnings of those who, perhaps, foolishly so continue" (383).

Echoing the economic planners of the thirties, Clarence Day proposes in wide-eyed sarcasm a Swiftian solution to the nagging and ever-present is-sue of unemployment—edible workers! How happy, he notes in *After All*, an employer would be to hire young workers "whom it really paid him well to keep healthy when business was good, and whom he could lay off when he liked without anyone's suffering" (36). Such displaced workers would rapidly move from the assembly line to the pantry shelf, and whereas before there had been much concern about the increasing figures of unemploy-ment, there now would be general celebrations and feasting on "edible workers . . . sold at a discount" (36).

Sarcasm aside, E. B. White envisions an equally destructive future for the American worker, consumed by machines rather than by men. In "Technological Progress" from *The New Yorker*, he condemns the ever-increasing inroads modern technology is making on our lives and especially on the lives of countless workers who may face the prospect of losing their jobs to robots. Gazing up at a newly automated lighthouse on the East Coast, he ponders its relevance to the future of modern man—"new devices putting men and their families out of work" (Dale, 125). The lighthouse keeper's replacement, an automated gas buoy, becomes, for White, a symbol of the new order of things to come. Science, he claims, "is a hard master and perhaps an evil one, giving us steel for flesh, dole for wages, solving every problem save the essential one: what to do about the pride of a former lighthouse keeper, who doesn't want relief, who wants bread earned by toil, seeing his light shine afar" (126). Of course, White further observes, there are those who claim that science opens up new jobs for displaced workers as well. But he doubts their rosy projections given the fact that many of the new jobs seem to be more like government-sponsored sinecures than "real" jobs. After all, who wants to make his living, as did one displaced engineer, devising a new way of catching and processing flies for frog growers!

Yet despite the problems created by the government bureaucrats, bosses, and growing technology, many of the Depression humorists reaffirm in their writings the persistent resilience of labor to overcome every obstacle that comes its way and maintain its status on the American landscape of the future. Will Rogers is among these writers.

In one of his stories, "The Dog Who Paid Cash," Rogers presents us with a dog that becomes a metaphor for the rugged individualism of the average American worker. Rogers comes across this dog one day in a Western saloon. Homeless and without an owner, after having been bumped off a freight train, the dog surfaces at the saloon, alert and friendly with all the cowboys, and begins performing all sorts of tricks like turning somersaults, rolling over, shaking hands, and sitting up on his hind paws.

> The boys would lay a coin on his nose, and he'd toss it high in the air and catch it in his mouth and pretend to swallow it. But you could bet your life he didn't swallow it—he stuck it on one side of his lip and when he got a lip full of money, he'd dash out the back door and disappear for a few minutes. What he really done was hide his money. As soon as he worked one salon, he would pull out and go to another place. (Tidwell, 386)

The cowboys, Rogers claims, are never able to find the exact spot he hides
his cash; he is too smart for them. He eventually shows up at the local
butcher shop, puts down a coin on the counter, and walks off with a nice cut
of beef or a bone: "[H]e always paid for what he got in the line of grub"
(386). Rogers wonders why he isn't as smart as that old dog, rather than sitting around the saloon all day, drinking down his problems, five hundred
miles from home and without a job. In the end, the dog takes off for brighter
prospects, Rogers concludes, and isn't heard of until a passing railroad man
informs him that the same dog is now making a good living in Trinidad,
Colorado!

The strength and determination of the American worker to bounce back
from adversity and overcome obstacles is again evident in Don Marquis's
favorite cat—Mehitabel. In "do not pity mehitabel," Archy informs his boss
not to worry so much about the resilient cat; she is used to hard times and
finds within the tragedy of the Great Depression the strength to cope:

> start her in
> as a kitten
> and she would
> repeat the same story
> and do not overlook
> the fact that
> mehitabel is really
> proud of herself
> she enjoys
> her own sufferings (214)

Mehitabel's strength lies primarily in her self-confidence—a confidence
stemming from her belief in her noble roots. She is, after all, supposed to be
the reincarnation of Cleopatra and has no need to convince herself of what
she is certain. When Archy asks her if she is going to the "swell cat" show,
she declines, claiming she has as much lineage as any of those swell cats,
"but i never could / see the conventional / society stuff archy / i am a
lady / but i am bohemian / too archy i / live my own life / no bells and
pink / ribbons for me" (217).

Will Rogers's dog, like Don Marquis's cat, reflects attitudes toward
American labor that had been evolving since the 1920s primarily in the
popular folklore of the nation. During those booming years, the power of
American labor took on almost mythic proportions and found itself represented in such larger-than-life characters as Paul Bunyan, who had originally surfaced in the early twenties in the advertisements of a lumber

company. The common motif for Bunyan was that of an improver or per-
fecter of one industry or another, and as such he became a fitting symbol of
American labor. During the thirties, he frequently surfaces as a benevolent
farmer, lumberjack, oil field worker, or in any capacity involving strenuous
physical labor—his strength and agility put to good use and no less dimin-
ished by his gargantuan size.

The WPA writers quickly picked up on his abilities and were soon re-
cording his numerous exploits in their collections of American folklore.
They noted he was popular in Texas folklore as an oil field worker who can
pull out of any adversity:

> Once while he was drilling for oil at Breckenridge, he struck a dry hole.
> Furious, he smashed the derrick with one blow of his fist. Then he saw
> an advertisement for 10,000 post holes wanted by a rancher in the Pan-
> handle where "the wind blows prairie dog holes inside out." So Paul
> hitched a chain to the dry hole, pulled it up and, realizing that the hole
> was too long to handle in entirety, he cut it into proper lengths, shipped
> the pieces to the Panhandle and made a fortune. (Weisberger, 334)

In Oregon, he becomes a one-man Tennessee Valley Authority, building
dams and digging rivers with his big blue ox, Babe. Into Crater Lake he
dumps a pile of blue snow his ox has accidentally knocked off a mountain
range. When the snow melts, it creates the "azure phenomenon" that greatly
amazes later visitors (378–79).

Peopling other tales from American folklore are characters maybe not as
imposing as Paul Bunyan but equally as formidable. Cooks on the ranches
in the Black Hills of South Dakota expect "stray" men who want a good
meal to pitch in a bit for their keep by assisting in some of the kitchen duties,
such as washing dishes piled as high as a man, chopping wood sixteen
inches thick, and fetching water in large buckets from the well, "just 110
steps from the kitchen, mostly downhill both ways" (Tidwell, 318).

Slappy Hooper, the sign painter featured in the folklore of Chicago during the Depression, was duly recorded by the Federal Writers' Project.
Standing over six feet high and weighing in at three hundred pounds, without his bucket and brush, he is a man who is willing to take on any job, including painting the sky! Using some cannons, he fires his skyhooks up into
the heavens, pulls his scaffolding up toward the clouds, and begins his task
without the aid of any modern contrivances such as air compressors, preferring instead his trusty brush.

> His biggest job was for the Union pacific railroad, and stretched from
> one end of the line to the other. The only way you could read it all was
> to get on a through train and look out of the window and up at the sky all
> the time. Everybody got stiff necks, of course, so Slappy had the bright
> idea of getting Sloan's Liniment to pay him for a big sign right at the
> end of the Union pacific sign. (Tidwell, 436)

Nor is their size their only call to fame. Slappy produces quality as well as
quantity. The realism of his smaller canvases is so pronounced, it sometimes
creates an unexpected effect. One billboard advertisement for a local bakery
presents such a realistic representation of a loaf of bread, birds get confused, fly into it, peck at it, and roost on the frame, "trying to figure out what
was the matter until they'd just keel over" (437).

Another poster, this time for a stove company, captures a flaming hearth
so accurately it causes flowers to bloom on the adjacent ground during the
coldest days of winter and passing hobos to set up camp under its benevolent warmth. Responding to complaints from some citizens that the hobos
are becoming a nuisance in the community, the company requests Slappy to
paint the fire even hotter, which he obligingly does. Its effect is immediate.
It drives out the transients, but simultaneously sets an adjoining building on
fire!

Another piece of Chicago Industrial Folklore found within the manu-
scripts of the Federal Writers' Project focuses on Hardscrabblers or those
who work the rock quarries of Hardscrabble County. These men are so
tough, the story notes, they can split huge rocks "just by spitting on them"
(Tidwell, 444). When they set off a blast, the loosened boulders are used by
the workers for an impromptu game of catch—without any gloves, and
when faced with constipation, blasting powder is the favorite laxative!
These men whip their unruly children with barbed wire, which doesn't hurt
the kids too much, and often come into town riding atop snarling panthers
and carrying whips made of three 6-foot rattlesnakes knotted together!

One story has it that a Hardscrabbler comes into town looking for a pair
of shoes, size fifteen, broad. He finds a pair, but has to modify them to his
liking by driving a box of roofing nails through the soles and heels. "That's
the way I like it," he tells the startled salesman. "It gives you a good grip and
all you do when your foot itches is to wiggle it around a little" (445). Next he
goes to the barber for a haircut and a shave, but all the barber's tools fail until
he employs some tinshears for the hair and a blowtorch for the beard. After
this, the quarryman heads for the Blue Moon Saloon and asks for the meanest liquor on tap, but when he tastes what the bartender offers, the strongest
brand of forty-rod in the county, the Hardscrabbler spits it out onto the

countertop, removing its lacquered varnish, and shouts out he would as soon have a "pinky, sticky ice cream soda with a cherry on it" (445). The nervous bartender then asks him what he has in mind: "Gimme a prussic acid cocktail with a little sulfuric for a chaser . . . and see that you don't go diluting it with no carbolic, neither. What are you, anyway? One of them temperance cranks? You must think I'm a plumb teetotaler!" he shouts back. The bartender collects the various ingredients from a local chemist and serves up the drink which puts the quarryman in a better spirit as he passes the time spitting onto the hardwood floor and burning holes through to the ground underneath. For dinner he has a can of tomatoes—without bothering to open the can—which alarms the bartender, who inquires if such a diet will affect the digestion. "Not long," claims the quarryman. "I soon digest the can from around the tomatoes. It's easy. A doorknob is harder, but I can do it easy as pie when I set my head to it" (446).

As the story progresses, the bartender becomes increasingly apprehensive that this quarryman might have intentions of moving into the town permanently, but he soon finds out that the fellow has no desire to "set up shop" in a town that can't even serve a decent drink. No, he is heading elsewhere. Back to Hardscrabble County, the bartender questions: "No," says his customer, not Hardscrabble County; he was thrown out of there. Was it because of a fight, the bartender queries: "A fight? Are you plumb stark, staring loony, man? Who ever heard of a man getting into trouble over fighting in Hardscrabble County rock quarries?" Well then why did he have to leave, the bartender pursues: " 'Well,' said the quarryman, looking like a sheep-killing dog. 'They chased me out because they said I was a sissy' " (446).

Unlike our "sissy," however, labor's influence is not limited to power without direction. In another story from the annals of the FWP, the servants of society are, in actuality, the savants of the present as well as the creators of its future. Such is the case of Hank, the friendly bartender in "Hank's Bar Specials." Hank, as we find out in the beginning of our tale, is no ordinary bartender. Mixing a Tom Collins or making a perfect dry Martini is child's play for Hank. His specialty is sizing up the special needs of each and every customer who comes his way and creating the right "medicine" for the situation:

> He'd run his eye over the bottles on the back bar, take a little of this and a little of that, hold it up to the light, sniff it, taste it, and then add a little something else. And whatever it was it was always right. Hank got to curing so many human ills that he got the doctors down on him and they threatened to have him pinched for practicing medicine without a li-

cense. So Hank, being a good union man, gave up curing people's ills and turned to other fields. (Tidwell, 432)

Another field he turns to is to making the fame and fortune of some of his customers. One day a dejected Italian appears at the bar, unhappy he doesn't have a good singing voice so he could make lots of money in the opera. Hank fixes him up with a special concoction and soon thereafter reads in the papers how his former patron is now the famous Caruso! Wild Bill Hickok can't shoot straight until one of Hank's drinks makes him a famous Indian fighter. A third patron who is plagued by a passive, timid nature takes a drink at Hank's bar and becomes a man willing to confront the entire U.S. Marine Corps in battle, while another who is noted for his pugilistic ways is turned into an angelic pacifist. Thus, in his humble way, Hank, like some backwater Wizard of Oz, continues along his merry way, doing his part in changing the face of the nation, effecting reforms and changing destinies far quicker than any government-sponsored program.

Hank's real fame stems primarily from his influence on the outcome of a train race from Chicago to Kansas City. It seems Hank gives the fireman for one line a bottle of liquid courage, which he downs just before the start of the race, throwing the empty into the firebox. The effect on the fireman is predictable, but the remaining drops in the empty bottle so fire up the engine that the train takes off at a feverish clip. The competition pulls into the Kansas City station forty-five minutes ahead of schedule, but where is the fireman's train, the dispatcher wonders, calling up to see if they have broken down. "Broke down, Hell," comes the answer, "we just got her stopped in Colorado!" (434).

The competitiveness of American labor is featured in another story from the archives of Chicago Industrial Folklore. In it, a professional stunt diver for a traveling road show tells us about his experiences on the road and the competition he has faced, primarily from Eddie La Breen, The Human Seal, who boasts he can "dive higher into shallower water than any man alive" (Tidwell, 446).

Our narrator, Billie the Dolphin, "spectacular and death-defying high diver extraordinary," but now permanently on crutches, is moving along nicely with his life on the rural circuit until his rival's outfit sets up a tent ten blocks away during one exposition. They immediately start competing with each other to make the highest dive into increasingly shallow pools of water. The ladders are raised from 100 to 200 to 300 feet, while the depth of their pools decreases steadily until they are down to 3 inches. Eddie claims that Billie has no chance of ever beating him in a high dive. "Why," he boasts to his rival, "when I was a kid of ten or so I could dive off a silo onto the dew in the grass, bellybuster, and never even grunt when I lit" (447). Eddie's boast gives our narrator an idea. He soaks a heavy bathmat and dives from a height of 300 feet onto that! "First time I hit that bath mat," he claims, "it sort of knocked me dizzy. You know how it is when you have the breath knocked out of you and all you do is croak like a frog," but he does beat his rival who isn't "man enough to admit it or take it like a man" (447). Some time later, our narrator continues, Eddie reveals exactly how "rotten to the core and treacherous from the word go" he can be (447). While performing the bath-mat stunt up in Wisconsin, Billie severely hurts himself when unbeknownst to him, someone secretly wrings out his bathmat before the jump! "I heard somebody say later that a man answering to the description of Eddie La Breen had been seen lurking around the show grounds that evening. And if he didn't do it, who did?" (448).

The competitive, fighting instinct evident in Billie and Eddie is at the root of what Don Marquis sees as the rebellious, radical nature of the American labor movement. Cats, unable to find jobs, are forming, according to Mehitabel in one poem, "soviet societies" that hang out around Washington Mews in lower Manhattan and advocate the nationalization of all fish markets (264). In "a radical flea," Archy stumbles across a flea on his boss's Boston Bull Terrier who claims that the fleas of the nation are turning to communism in a big way. If there is any justice in the country, he claims, the government should give them Russian Wolf Hounds to feast on.

Even Archy gets caught up with the prevailing spirit when in "the return of archy" he tells his boss:

> i have been organizing the insects
> the ants the worms the wasps
> the bees the cockroaches
> the mosquitoes
> for a revolt against mankind
> i have declared war
> upon humanity
> i even i shall fling
> the mighty atom
> that splits a planet asunder
> i ride the microbe
> that crashes down olympus
> where have i been you ask me where
> i am jove and from my seat
> on the edge of a bowl of beef stew

i launch the thunderous
molecule
that smites a cosmos into bits (188)

Archy's protestations may be sincere but nevertheless strike a mock-heroic chord, pathetic in its ineffectualness. Even Archy understands the limits of his abilities and asks his boss to better ask "what i have been drinking / exclamation point" (189). The ability of the working class to effectively alter its destiny remains limited in the outcome. Archy's outburst mirrors a rousing speech in Union Square on Labor Day—galvanizing the audience temporarily, but hollow in substance. The anesthetized giant continues to sleep, dreaming of a better future, but occasionally resorting to "grumbling," which, according to Mencken, was the only practical form of protest left for the workingman because it did not use insulting language, was not a form of assault and battery, and was not definitively impudent or disobedient (DuBasky, 28).

For the American farmer, the thirties sparked a different kind of disaster. The unemployed city worker or factory worker had a greater number of avenues for escape. Mobility from one job to another, although not pleasant, could be effected if the jobs were there, and the requirements were similar. With some retraining, often sponsored by the WPA, the average worker might be able to make ends meet during the lean years without the total disruption of his family's lifestyle. Each day he could return to the familiar neighborhood, and his children could stay in school. This was often not the case for the small, American farmer who had few—if any—avenues of escape.

Despite the government's numerous attempts to stem the alarming number of small farm failures, countless farmers not only lost their land but everything on it, including their homes, furniture, and equipment. Entire counties in rural Arkansas, Oklahoma, and Texas became dust-blown deserts of shattered dreams, and for many in these blighted regions, the only avenue of escape was a belief that in California a new life could begin, free from the vicissitudes of a failing economy—a dream that many firmly believed in but few would achieve. Ironically, the prevailing attitude throughout the land and principally in the cities was that the rural landscape offered a possible retreat from urban ills.

In actuality, if there was a difference between the two cultures, it was in the astonishing pockets of poverty one encountered in the hinterland. Along with the nation's growing mobility since the advent of the automobile, and the increasing popularity of newsreels at the theater, it was virtually impossible for anyone in any city to remain blind to the thousands of rural Americans who had been reduced to living in tin shacks in the shadow of the Ozarks or ramshackle clapboard huts along the Mississippi. Such images of America were bound to take a firm hold on the American imagination and shake it vigorously, for we were still a nation that had traditionally accepted the American farmer and his environment as the foundation of all our ideals—political as well as cultural. It was a belief nurtured since the Revolution and championed by such leaders as Jefferson and Washington who saw in rural America the clearest exponent of democratic values. The failure of rural America presaged more than an economic downturn; it was a harbinger of the eventual collapse of American culture in its entirety and all of its dreams for a better future. Thus, in the writings of the Depression humorists as well as in the general folklore of the thirties, a trend appears reaffirming values which had been, it was felt, quickly eroding away since 1929.

Writers for the WPA, came back from their excursions into remote sections of the country with reports that the American spirit or, at least, Yankee hardheadedness, was alive and well in towns such as Naples, Maine, and Litchfield, Connecticut. In "The Political Flagpoles of Naples, Maine," the author notes that expressions of strong political feeling may have disappeared in certain parts of the country, but in Naples, "politics is still of paramount importance" (36).

> The people of Naples take their politics so seriously that until a few years ago the town was openly divided, with two entrances to the public buildings, one for the Democrats and the other for the Republicans. In these buildings the seating plan was so arranged that each party had its own half of the room. This sharp party line was drawn even in the schoolroom, with the children of Republican parents seated on one side of the room and the children of Democratic parents on the other; the climax came when it became necessary to assign two teachers to each room to satisfy the rabid feelings of the parents. (36)

Things may have quieted down a bit recently in Naples, but the author notes that the town green is still sporting two flagpoles—one for the Democrats and one for the Republicans!

In "A Heated Argument in Litchfield, Connecticut," a controversy erupts over whether to use a church stove during the Sabbath. The elder church folk are convinced that the road to salvation is better traveled without catering to the whims of the flesh, but others of a different persuasion see no harm in taking the chill out of a Sabbath morning. One such morning, the prostove faction clusters around the stove before a sermon, rubbing their palms contentedly together. This, of course, elicits a severe reaction from the antistove faction that gathers at the other end of the church, perspiring profusely and mopping their brows in great distress. "One indignant lady," our WPA writer notes, "fainted from the heat and had to be carried to the open air," whereupon a pro-stove "warrior" boldly walked over to the cast-iron object of controversy and placed his bare hand on the stone cold lid—it had never been lit! (36).

The fighting spirit of America's country people again surfaces, this time in the South in "The Fighten'est Feller in the Holler." Our narrator claims that he once asked Windy Bill Hatfield, "the best talker in the entire Holler," if he had ever known some genuinely bad fellows in his day. "Wal now, lemme see," Windy drawls. He once met the James brothers, and members of the Dalton gang came through a number of times, as did Cherokee Bill, Henry Starr, and a fellow named Doolin, who "kilt all them folks over t' Southwest City," but these gentlemen were merely hardworking bank robbers and not really "scrappy." That distinction fell more to Abner Yancy, a local boy, also know as "Little Ab." According to the narrator, Little Ab was quite popular with the locals, always on the lookout for a good fight but never in jail for disturbing the peace because his opponents never pressed charges against a compatriot who was merely doing what comes natural. Ab's last fight, unfortunately, was with two armed men; their guns were loaded but his wasn't—a point, our narrator reflects, that left Ab at something of a disadvantage! Still, the town comes through for their local boy, giving him a "high-tone" funeral and burying him out in the cemetery under the "biggest grave-rock in th' hull dang country." " 'Twas only right," Windy concludes, " 'cause Ab was one o' th' best-liked fellers ever lived in th' Holler" (Tidwell, 62).

Such pluck and daring, albeit foolhardy at times, became for many an anonymous rural storyteller a symbol of regional pride and an indication that the pioneer spirit and need for independence had not died. Those who wished to change regional lifestyles and alter traditions, as did the federal officials and their famous Tennessee Valley Authority, were sometimes surprised by the resistance they encountered from the very people they wanted to help. Regional pride was quite strong during the Roosevelt years, and, even if it was sometimes paranoid, for many in depressed regions, it was all that remained. Such sentiments appear in *Folklore of Romantic Arkansas*, published in 1931. From it comes a short piece, "Change the Name of Arkansas? Hell, No!" in which the citizens of the state are worked into a frenzy by the allegations that the federal government is proposing a name change for the state. As one local official speaks out: "Gentlemen, you may tear down the honored pictures from the halls of the United States Senate, desecrate the graves of George Washington and Abraham Lincoln, haul down the Stars and Stripes, curse the Goddess of Liberty, and knock down the tomb of U.S. Grant, but your crime would in no wise compare in enormity with what you propose to do when you would change the name of Arkansas! Change the name of Arkansas—hell-fire, no!" (Tidwell, 63).

Such sentiments were occasionally echoed by the Depression humorists as well. For E. B. White, however, the problem is not so much with the federal government's wish to change the lives of country folk for the "better," but its insatiable need to dictate lifestyles to those it barely knows. Is not such intervention constitutionally repugnant and inherently a violation of the civil rights of American citizens and their right to determine their own manner of living? What cause, he notes in *The New Yorker*, does the Department of the Interior have in dictating whether the inhabitants of the Ozarks should have running water if they choose not to, or, the obverse, should *not* have it even if they want it? Notes from the Department claiming that the characteristics and habits of such mountain folk "must be preserved, along with other natural features of the region," such as wildfowl and exotic plants as endangered species, and that no attempts should be made to significantly modernize and thereby "destroy" the national frontier, seem to be at odds with official policies attempting to eradicate poverty and relieve the plight of the underprivileged third of the nation—"ill-housed, ill-clad, and ill-nourished" (Dale, 217). A nation so determined in its policies that it has become willing to sacrifice its past ideals in favor of new ones that deprive the countryman of his independence is, for White, definitely on the wrong track.

Will Rogers, the primary spokesman for the American farmer during the Depression years, also questions governmental intentions and their outcomes. In one piece from 1934, he hopes the government won't force the farmer to irrigate more land so he can raise more things than he can sell, resulting in his having to "plow up more rows, and kill more pigs to keep 'em from becoming hogs." What Henry Wallace, the secretary of agriculture, is trying to do, Rogers claims, is "to teach farmers acreage control, and the hogs birth control, and one is just as hard to make understand as the other" (Sterling and Sterling, 241).

But for Rogers, the biggest threat facing rural America is not the government but bankers and Wall Street. Investors are increasing in number on the rural scene, and the days of the independent small farmer are becoming more and more limited. In fact, the most famous farmer Rogers knows isn't even a farmer anymore, having recently retired as a "big wheat man up in Montana," moved to Pasadena, and become an advisor to foreign and domestic governments on how to grow plentiful amounts of wheat.

As a dinner guest at the Rogers household, he educates his host about one of the wonders of the modern age—the combine or "binder" as it is known in the profession. A combine is a very intricate machine, Rogers notes, which makes only one pass over a field but in that one pass is able to perform multiple functions. First it tills the ground, digging up all the roots and herbs and grinding them into an herbal medicine. Following this comes a plow that makes a furrow, the seed planter, and another plow that closes up the furrow. Soon after these comes the fertilizer and then the sickle that cuts the grain, all of which is carried along a "little platform into the threshing machine where it's threshed, then out and into sacks, and into the big grain elevator that is fastened onto the thing" (187).

The American farmer may be in the middle of this entire operation, but, Rogers observes, at the front of it sits a banker, with the rear being taken up by "a stock market board, where a bunch of men that don't own the farm, the wheat, or the combine, buy it back and forth from each other. That is, if you have threshed a thousand bushels, why, they sell each other a million bushels of this thousand bushels which was exactly threshed, then they announce to the farmer that on account of supply and demand, the wheat is only worth 25 cents. That's what you call a combine" (187). While on a recent trip as an agricultural advisor in Russia, Rogers's guest makes it quite clear to Stalin that he doesn't believe much in the communist way of life, but an unperturbed Stalin shakes his hand warmly and tells him "We will get on fine, we at least understand each other. It's wheat we want to agree on, and not politics or religion" (187). The new age of industrial farming has arrived—an age without political or ideological boundaries.

It was the general consensus during the thirties that farmers and other rural inhabitants had their own peculiar ways of getting all things done successfully, and, as far as most were concerned, who was to argue with success? The FWP, at any rate, delighted in documenting the "unusual practices" of country people with "The Tenacious Clam of Eddington, Maine" being one curious example.

A common custom among the inhabitants of such coastal communities as Eddington is to dig a hole in the cellar during the spring, fill it with moist sand, and use it as a storing bin for keeping clams alive until the fall. Our story has it that one old retired sea captain is even able to get double-duty out of his clam pit, using the oversized bivalves as rat catchers! As the solemn WPA writer concludes, the old gentleman frequently goes into his cellar only to find a rat struggling against a clam that has "closed its shell in a tenacious grip on the rat's tail" (Weisberger, 33).

faced angrier herds on many a ranch out West. Launching out with the crew of the *Tossup*, he waits until the nets haul in a particularly big catch with one of the meanest, heaviest hoss-mackerels in the middle of it all, thrashing up the white water as if a "hurricane stoppered up under them net-buoys." The two thousand–pound fish breaks free of the net and seems to be making it to freedom in the open water when Bowleg pushes aside the captain and crew and dives in after it, boots and all. The crew thinks he's destined for suicide when Bowleg surfaces, astride the fish, now nicknamed Slickbritches, as though it were some wild bull on a ranch, "whipping astern with his hat, and hollering like the yoho-bird of every dead sailor come home from hell" (1). Flabbergasted, the narrator's admiration swells for this farmer of the sea:

I don't know where he larned it, but somehow that cowboy has took a grip on the foretops'l fin, and no matter how bad Slickbritches broaches to, he can't shake him loose. They go scudding a wide circle of the harbor, with the big hoss-mackerel getting madder every minute. He dives to starboard, he lashes to larboard, he all but pitchpoles head-over. But somehow—and may the divil spit me over hell's hottest hearth if I can explain it—Bowleg hangs on, with his knees bearing in close amidships, riding easy as grandmar in the Sunday-parlor rocker. (612)

Slickbritches tries to shake Bowleg by jumping over the bow of the *Tossup*, but this fails to deter the cowboy who soon has the fish under his control, and is heading into shore where the whole town is cheering over landing notoriety as being the place where the biggest fish in history was caught. But just as Bowleg is about to land the fish, he jumps off and lets it go. As he wades ashore, a now furious town descends on him, certain that he is gone completely mad and should be incarcerated on the spot! Bowleg calms them down a bit when he explains his apparent loss of reason: "That's one old windbroke waterbug!" he laments, wiping a tear off his cheek. "I tell you, folks, there ain't nawthing that'll break a cowhand's heart like trying to find a critter—two legged or four—with the rough all rode off him" (613).

Although country folk could boast the prodigious exploits of those like "Bull" Runnels, but this didn't deter them from realizing their fantasies in another manner as is evident in a wonderful story captured by the Tennessee Project titled "A Real Hunk of Dreaming." The central character is a big, strapping fellow named "Bull" Runnels who has always been regarded by his friends and neighbors as somewhat

---

Tall-tale stories about farmers and their rural exploits circulated freely in much of the humorous folklore of the Depression era and often imitated the tone and bombast of the best Paul Bunyan stories dealing with American labor. However, as one writer for the WPA notes in "Farming the Up-Forty in Wayne County, West Virginia," some of the strangest exploits are indeed factual. What seems to be exaggeration is merely a modest "extension" of the truth. In the above piece, the writer informs us that hillside cultivation is no easy matter, "and hilltop farming is not much better." Although the natural difficulties that beset the typical West Virginia hill farmer have become the topic of much humor and exaggeration in American folklore, he continues, stories of clifftop farms in Wayne County, "where the fields are reached by ladders and the mule and plow are hoisted by block and tackle up the cliff, is no myth." However, a "slight" exaggeration might be perceived, he concludes, in the story about a motorist who, while driving along a narrow valley road, is abruptly stopped by a great cloud of dust and general commotion up ahead. Getting out to investigate, he comes across an old weather-beaten hill farmer, emerging from the dust, "rubbing his elbow and beating the dust from the denim jeans with a tattered hat." When the astonished motorist inquires as to what happened, the farmer looks up and in a "tone of plaintive disgust" replies: "That's the third time I've fell outen that danged cornfield this mornin', and I've still got seven rows to grub" (Weisberger, 167).

Around Parkertown, Ohio, another WPA writer notes in "A Prodigious Exploit in Parkertown, Ohio," they "grow tall corn and tell tall stories." The locals, he observes, frequently like to talk about the adventures of one of their local heroes, Lemuel Hunt, who had "twinkling blue eyes and a fringe of whiskers from ear to ear." The locals claim that the story of his having jumped over the Ohio River is not true—it was the Monongahela! It seems that while heading home after a day of hunting and loaded down with a stag and a sack of geese, he came to the river which was flooding and overflowing its banks. Undeterred, he decided to jump across it, but halfway over realized he wasn't going to be able to make it, and in midair, "turned around and returned to his starting point." But except for this "youthful failure," the locals hasten to point out, his life was regularly "characterized by prodigies in hunting, fighting, shooting, and farming" (Weisberger, 95).

Other "prodigies" of farming surface in different regions of America as well. Down South, black farmers boast of their exploits in "Dat Land Wasn't So Rich." In this tale by Zora Neale Hurston, a group of black farmers trade stories about crop productivity. One claims that his father's land was one of the most fertile for miles around primarily due to an abundant use of mosquito dust, "de finest fertilizer in de world." It seems his daddy once raised a pumpkin so large that they tunneled five miles up and down and ten miles across without ever finding how far it went. While his father was busy erecting a scaffold so as to get at more of the meat without too much trouble, he dropped his hammer and asked his son to go fetch it. "Ah went down in de pumpkin," the lad narrates, "and begin to hunt dat hammer":

> Ah was foolin' 'round in there all day when I met a man and he asked me what Ah was lookin' for. Ah tole him my ole man had done dropped his hammer and sent me to find it for him. De man tole me Ah might as well give it up for a lost cause, he had been lookin' for a double mule-team and a wagon that had got lost in there for three weeks and he hadn't found no trace of 'em yet. (Tidwell, 297)

His friends, however, are not so impressed, claiming that their ancestral farms had borne equally spectacular crops. A fellow by the name of Will House claims his old man planted cucumbers, just dropping the seeds at random on the ground, and before he could get out of the way, he had ripe cucumbers in his pockets. Another, Ulmer, claims his father once drove a marker stake at the end of a cornrow only to find four ears growing on the stake the next morning!

The richest land seems to be owned by Joe Wiley. His father once buried a dead mule out in the pasture, and the next morning it "done sprouted li'l jackasses." Not to be outdone, he continues:

> [O]ne year we was kinda late puttin' in our crops. Everybody else had corn a foot high when papa said, "Well, chillun, Ah reckon we better plant some corn." So I was droppin' and my brother was hillin' up behind me. We had done planted 'bout a dozen rows when Ah looked back and seen de corn comin' up. Ah didn't want it to grow too fast 'cause it would make all fodder and no roastin' ears so Ah hollered to my brother to sit down on some of it to stunt de growth. So he did, and de next day he dropped me back a note—says: "passed thru Heben yesterday at twelve o'clock sellin' roastin' ears to de angels." (298)

The other fellows remain silent after this, evidently giving tacit approval to his claim of having the richest farm around.

But such talk would be "small potatoes" compared with some of the crops produced by a farmer named Old Jim up in the Snake River Valley of Idaho, that is, if we are to accept without question the observations of a writer for the FWP in *Idaho Lore* of 1939. This farmer once grew pumpkins

but soon gave it up because they grew so large he couldn't g[...]ket. Next he ventured into potatoes but had problems here a[...]that a few years back, the writer notes, he was approache[...]from a nearby CCC camp who wanted to purchase a hu[...]spuds. "Only a hundred pounds?" the farmer questioned, [...]of his head. "No, I can't do it. I wouldn't cut a spud in two[...]well, 298).

The stories about Old Jim of Idaho compare well wit[...]Bowleg Bill, the seagoing cowboy from Wyoming who[...]a fishing town along the Cape Cod shore. The narrator, [...]cals, notes in the story, "Why Bowleg Bill Let the Big[...]that while Bowleg's reputation as one of the wildest [...]up the sport of fishing may have fascinated the new[...]first, didn't cut "much slack among the boys that go[...]hoss-mackerel." Hoss-mackerel is the local term fo[...]off Cape Cod, our narrator points out to Bowleg ear[...]particularly mean-tempered fish that grow to size[...]pounds. Their "run" is particularly in the summe[...]have a "long streak of hell in each of 'em" (Tid[...]

Such talk doesn't deter the former cowpoke, w[...]some of these "critters" that cause such a fus[...]work, it is, ridin' herd on 'em?" he asks our na[...]you got to know how to gaff 'em in. Hoss-mac[...]green hand." This intrigues Bowleg Bill, who[...]go out in one of the fishing boats and catch the[...]own inimitable way—western style. Anythi[...]tells the narrator, to require the use of a rop[...]used only for the wildest and heaviest of an[...]snortin' bull with half a ton of devilment t[...]sound that ominous. "I have yet to meet up[...]rator, "two-legged or four . . . which I cou[...]With this said, a bet is set up between the[...]able to bring in not only the meanest an[...]do it bare-handed, and if he fails, he tel[...]silver dollars and marry yore meanest[...]

The next day the whole town gathe[...]go out and specifically to see Bowle[...]challenge has been interpreted as so[...]don't take kindly to "off-Cape lunati[...]business. None of this succeeds in d[...]

The fis[...]even th[...]all tire[...]its impe[...]was cau[...]it go! A[...]he has g[...]leg calm[...]"That po[...]cheek, "[...]so quick [...]at first m[...]Not al[...]Bowleg B[...]other man[...]Writers' P[...]The cen[...]who has al[...]

simple, or "bored for the simples" as the natives call it, on account of his occasional lapses into odd behavior. When he was a boy, the town caught him frequently climbing trees and craning his neck in all directions from the highest limbs so as to get a better look at the weather. "You can see a heap more of it up there," he would tell the passerby. Later as a young man, he often surprised his friends by trying to carry on conversations with barnyard fowl. "Now, chickens is clever," he would tell his amused friends, "if you get to know them good. I figger they can talk like anybody else, only we can't make it out. I got a theery if I just set around the coop a-listening long enough I'll get to where I can understand them. Now, that would be a reel novelty!" (Tidwell, 472). He fails at this venture and soon turns his mind to something else—dreaming.

It seems that Bull has never had a dream in his life, and he is worried he is missing out on something. His friends often tell him about their fantastic dreams and how much fun they can be. One informs Bull that one can have an "eating" dream where a "big fat waiter [is] always ready to heap the grub on your plate! Ice cream and pie and stripe candy—the more you eat, the more they feed you when you are dreaming." Another friend claims that even better than that are "money" dreams: "Why, man, you find it in piles! Yes sir, big stacks of bright shiny dollars! You can just rake it in a wagon, and haul it away." A third friend, however, claims that "girl" dreams are the best, where "all the pretty gals love you and you hug them all and buss them good. Stuff like that." All this talk fascinates Bull, but it seems that no matter how hard he tries, he is never able to muster up any good dreams. Instead, as he tells his friends, all that ever happens is that his eyes close and "*pop*!—I'm a goner. Next thing I know it's time to go to work again. Nothing happens but plain nothing in between" (472).

His friends suggest that maybe his digestion is too good and that he has to consume lots of exotic, spicy food before he hits the sack. This is the only way to insure having a solid dream. But regardless of the pigs' knuckles, "chittlins," and sauerkraut with plenty of vinegar he consumes, he remains stuck in the status quo until his friends decide that the best solution is to *manufacture* a dream for him one night.

They head off to Sneed's drugstore to fetch something they can administer to Bull as a "dream medicine" and settle on "Doc" Sneed's suggestion that a bottle of baby soother might work fine—something that will induce a tranquilized, dreamlike state in Bull without completely putting him out. With Bull in this condition, his friends can stage a "dream" that he will think has actually happened when he completely regains consciousness. As one of them happily observes:

Then we'll really fix him up, boys! Nothing that'll really damage him, of course. Nope, just a regular little old initiation like we give at the lodge. He'll be so dope-headed with that soothing syrup he won't hardly know what's happening. We'll lay it to him to a fare-you-well, then take him home. In the morning he'll be sore behind and scared in the head. I'm willing to bet good money he won't want no more dreams. And what's more, he'll quit this everlasting talk about it. (474)

They all agree that the idea is a "ripper" and set about planning it with only one concern in mind: No one must ever let Bull know what actually happened to him. He gets "tempered up easy," as one of the conspirators observes, "and when that happens he'll crack bones like kindling wood" (475).

Bull eagerly accepts the "medicine" he gets from his friends on their assurance that he will have a "real hunk of dreaming" *that* night, and he downs the bottle before going to bed. Unbeknownst to his friends, the syrup fails to effectively knock him out, so he is lying in bed, restless and wide-eyed, when they appear at his bedroom window, dressed in sheets and ready to perform the "dream." Startled by their sudden appearance, he assumes this must be the beginning of the dream he was promised but doesn't like the prologue. "I ain't studying to dream about old white nothings like you!" he shouts out, frightening them away, "It's eating dreams and gal and money dreams I'm after" (476). With this said, he bounds out of bed and heads into town in his nightshirt, sleepwalking he figures, determined to fulfill his expectations.

His first stop is Tom's Dandy Eats where he startles the owner with a demand for a whole series of four-course dinners, claiming it's the first stage of his dream and he doesn't expect to have to pay the tab because, as his friends have told him, everything is supposed to be free. Tom obligingly piles on the food, having heard of the joke and assuming the young man's friends will pick up the bill. After downing four helpings of fried potatoes, a plate of brains and eggs, cabbage and turnip greens, some batter cakes with molasses and soda biscuits, corn pone, lamb fries, and coffee, he heads off to "Doc" Sneed's drugstore where he proceeds to raid the cash register in his pursuit of his promised "money" dream. "Doc" knows he can't intervene because Bull might tear the drugstore apart in a frenzy if thwarted, so he can only stand back and watch, "madder than Tucker the day his dog died" (477).

Finally, to complete the "pretty gal" part of his dream, he pays a visit to Birdie Nugent who is at home at the time with her beau who is none other than one of Bull's best friends, Slim. Bouncing in through the parlor window, with half a bottle of sweet hair oil on his bushy head, Bull startles the pair. His friend ducks for cover behind the couch, and Birdie stands up, "pale as death, and her knees about to jack-knife under her." "Here I am, little hossfly!" he cries out, and starts kissing her. But this last "dream" is rudely interrupted when Slim musters up the courage to knock him out cold with a fireplace poker (477).

The next day, Bull awakens in his own bed, having been carried home by his friends, and rushes off to tell them just how great the "medicine" worked. " 'Boys,' says he, 'it done the trick! That medicine give me a sure enough reel hunk of dreaming, now! I had a gal dream the sweetest ever . . . made me fifteen dollars and seventy-five cents in my money dream, and I won't never forget the eating dream. I'm satisfied now, though, don't want to dream no more ever, now. It gives you too big a headache when you wake up.' " Headache notwithstanding, it seems that Bull's friends are going to suffer more from this "dream" having to pay off "Doc" Sneed and Tom's Dandy Eats. As Slim observes, "I ain't so sure about *who* ought to be bored for the simples now!" (478).

For many in the Depression audience, Bull Runnels's dreams were symbols of an idyllic existence that only a rural America could offer. A hearty country meal free of the chemical additives and synthetic flavorings of canned goods, friendly townspeople who let you raid their cash registers without immediately calling the police, and wholesome farm girls who don't slap strangers who "buss" them—all are variations on a common theme running throughout American culture and literature since the days of Samuel Clemens. During the thirties, it would take on an added significance in the modern culture with popular humorists, such as Will Rogers, frequently espousing the simple pleasures of rural living and a need for all Americans to reorient themselves to these values that had long since been forgotten in the industrialized cities.

Rogers's response to a criticism that he mispronounced the word "ate" as " 'et" in which he claimed that there were many people who "ate" who never " 'et," clarifies his position on the virtues of country fare—a position elaborated further in "Home Cooking" from 1931. In it, he nurses a stomach irritated by city cooking, reminiscing about the meals he used to get back home at his sister's house. The tables were and still are heaped with the bounty of the field. No shortages of "beans cooked with plenty of real fat meat" or baked ham, cured by his brother-in-law. Then there is the corn bread—not city bread, not the kind of bread Rogers's father used to call "wasp nest" and cast off as not fit for human consumption—but corn pone, "made with nothing but meal, and hot water and salt."

Then the cream gravy. You know, there is an awful lot of folks that don't know much about eating gravy? Why, not to be raised on gravy would be like never going swimming in the creek. They got their own cows and real cream. Ham gravy is just about the last word in gravies. Course, good beefsteak gravy is good. You know, we fry our beefsteak. It's cut in thin pieces, and say, let me tell you something. Did you know all this eating raw, bloody rare meat, like they order in these big hotels, and that city people like, well, that's just them. That ain't western folks. Ranch cooks and farm women fry steak thin and hard. That old raw junk goes for the high collars in the cities, they are kinder cannibalistic, anyhow. (Sterling and Sterling, 184)

His sister-in-law, Rogers continues, is also a good cook, even though she is not a native country girl having been raised in Los Angeles. Years of country living have turned her into one "real rancher's wife, and a good one" (185). Like her neighbors, she cultivates a large, private garden to offset the tough winters, and her table is so bountiful that Rogers is hard pressed to do little more than shake hands and eat when he visits.

All of the above is in stark contrast to the living conditions Rogers has to endure at his present address in sunny Pasadena, California, where it is "awful hard to get good vegetables and fruits" because the state has a law against importing anything better than it produces (185). The actual meal that put him under with a good case of jaundice was a diet of *canned* oysters and *canned* tomatoes at a restaurant in El Paso. If the microbes were "laying" for him, he concludes, they certainly *got* him!

Still, the fundamental difference between urban and rural America, according to Rogers, lies not in an individual's eating preferences, but instead in his or her "orientation" toward life, a point he makes clear to one of his well-educated city friends in "This Philosophy Racket" from 1931.

It is not Rogers's intention to belittle the achievements of those who prefer to live in the city or of those whose education has been garnered more from the books of academe than the experiences of farm living. But he does find something seriously lacking in the fiber of a nation that has lost touch with the land and has forsaken the primitive for the sophisticated. When asked by a close friend, a philosophical savant, as to what keeps him going, what is the "motive force" of his inspiration and energy, and that his answer will be sent to some of the most famous men in the world such as Hoover, Einstein, and Gandhi, Rogers is momentarily silenced by a proposal so preposterous that if it had been asked by anyone but his friend, he would have cast it off as a lot of "hooey" and disposed of it in the trash bin.

The fact that eminent scholars, such as his friend who has pondered over many a textbook of philosophy but, like Faust, has not found satisfaction, must ask a "simple" man like Rogers about the meaning of life indicates that something is wrong with the "Philosophy Racket." Maybe America has to listen more to its rural philosophers like farmer Bill Hanley, another friend, whose knowledge has come "from a prairie, and not from under a lamp."

> An educated man just teaches the things that he has been taught, and it's the same that everyone else has been taught that has read and studied the same books he has. But if these old fellows know anything, it comes direct to them by experience, and not by the way of someone else. If I had Hanley's knowledge, I wouldn't give it for even Secretary of State Hughes' and Columbia University's Nicholas Murray Butler's, combined—and I like 'em both personally, and think they are great men. But I would know I knew something, if I knew what one of these cattlemen knew; and if I was as smart as Hughes or Butler, I would still be in doubt, because I would be educated so high that I would know that I only had a smattering of what I did have. (193)

Like Thoreau, Rogers criticizes progress at the expense of traditional values—values still found in rural America but not in its cities where man's dependency on others has eroded his independence and sapped his fortitude. Those living close to the land, including primitive races and the Indians, he feels, are more "civilized" and contented in that they depend less on each other and take less from each other. The urbanite, conversely, cannot live a day without depending on everybody and, as such, lives in a world without independence or liberty. The urban standards of happiness have invaded the country but have brought little peace of mind or a better way to live:

> Fords and bathtubs have moved us and cleaned us, but we was just as ignorant when we got there. We know lots of things we used to didn't know but we don't know any way to prevent 'em from happening. Confucius perspired out more knowledge than the U.S. Senate has vocalized in the last 50 years. (193)

Far better, he concludes, is it to live like a farmer, feet planted firmly on the ground, with rational expectations in an unpredictable world rather than pursuing the chimerical illusions of urban dwellers—"then you won't start out that life with a disappointment. Live your life so whenever you lose, you are ahead" (194).

For Rogers and others close to the land, the city dweller's arrogant confidence defensively masks his subconscious fear of being perpetually lost in

America—a fear absent in rural America and nicely summed up in a short story published by the Texas Folk-Lore Society in 1937. In it, a city slicker finds himself lost while driving through lonely, deserted country roads. For a long time, he follows the windings, hoping that every bend in the road or crest of a hill will bring him in sight of some civilization where he can get directions. Not until it is almost dark does he come across a young fellow chopping cotton. He calls out to the boy who calls back but continues wielding his hoe with little time for polite conversation. "Where does this road go to?" the city man asks. "Hain't never seed it go nowhars. Hit allus stays right whar hit is," comes the reply. Frustrated, the city fellow asks how far may it be to the next town, but again gets a noncommittal answer: "Don't know; never measured it." Totally exasperated, the driver loses his temper, telling the field hand he is without a doubt the biggest fool ever to walk the earth. With this said, the country boy stops his work and, facing the city man squarely, responds with contempt that *he* knows he knows nothing and that he is a fool: "But I ain't lost!" (Tidwell, 33).

Such cockiness from a field hand would have ruffled the feathers of H. L. Mencken, who finds in all the "down-home" drawling an element of insincerity if not outright imposture. For him, the farmers, like labor in general, have been abusing the national trust long enough. "How much they have got out of the public treasury since the war no one seems to know," he complains as early as 1933. All the money they did get has been wasted, he continues, but "they still believe that the way to get rich is to steal money from the rest of us, and to that end their agents in Washington prepare the usual crop of bills" (DuBasky, 19).

For Mencken, rural living is anything but ideal. Having suffered terribly from allergies all his life, he turns a jaundiced eye to the pleasures of living in the country and even questions why farmers persist in pursuing an occupation that never seems to be without a crisis at hand, either economic or environmental. They'd all be better off, he notes in another piece, forsaking a life always on the verge of bankruptcy and instead adopt one punching time clocks, knocking off work at five in the afternoon, and accumulating wardrobes, betting on the races, home brewing, and playing miniature golf like the rest of the population living in the cities.

Ironically, Mencken's skepticism with the prevailing view of many, both in the country and in the city, that a rural lifestyle offered a far better form of existence and a stable lifestyle was sometimes matched by those he would least likely see as among his avid supporters—the farmers, many of whom, as future decades would show, found the allure of materialism too great to be ignored. Country living was tranquil but, at times, it bordered on the comatose. There was nothing much one could do for entertainment in the country, and, after the great dust storms devastated the lower Midwest, there was not much one could do but leave the farm altogether. No one by the late thirties could deny that the American farmer was a pessimist at heart; anyone who had endured what he had had to endure during the decade would be a pessimist as well and express sentiments similar to those of a character in a piece of Illinois folklore captured by the FWP, fittingly titled "The Pioneer Pessimist."

In it, a young man tells his weather-beaten pioneer father that a new rail line is projected to pass by their local town. The old man stares back in disbelief. Why would anyone want to pass a railroad line through this God-forsaken place, he tells his son. "Why, they won't even survey the line," he declares. After the line is surveyed, the son again approaches his father, who now claims they will never build a grade or lay a tie. But these, too, are accomplished, along with the stringing of the rails—all of which fails to impress the pessimist who adamantly declares to his son that, nevertheless, the train will *never* run through the town. When the day does come and a train runs through the town, the son approaches his father for the last time with the news, but the unwavering reply of the pessimist remains, "Well, it may go through, *but it'll never come back*" (Tidwell, 317).

In the years that followed the Depression, many with similar sentiments would abandon their farms for the attractions of the city. Some would be enticed by the lucrative pay offered by wartime industries. Others would leave to serve on the battlefronts of Europe and in Asia, despite draft exemptions for farm workers. Few would return to a land that the Depression had forever uprooted and changed, until, that is, a shrewd promoter converted hundreds of acres of what was once Long Island potato farms into a new retreat for a new generation and named it Levittown.

Postscript

By the end of the thirties, it became increasingly clear for all Americans and especially the literary humorists that the Depression was soon to retire from its prominent position in the headlines, which now were filled with the events of a world on the brink of war. Those who had devoted their lines to the evolution of American values and temperament now found their witticisms directed at foreign powers bent upon world domination. E. B. White and others had different grist for the mill, and that grist was the fascists.

However, the lingering effects of the Depression on the American consciousness would continue to persist well into later decades. A younger generation that had just returned from the battlefields of Europe and the Pacific had no inclination to return as well to a stagnant economy that had plagued their parents and grandparents before. For the new generation, the key word was prosperity. For them, the growth of the suburban dream was a given and not an illusion created by an overly optimistic press, and the government willingly acquiesced to their demands for affordable housing, filled with a plethora of labor-saving appliances, as well as nicely trimmed parks and streets and modern up-to-date schools. Such dreams were not entirely borne out of distant foxholes, but had their genesis as well in the fears of the thirties. It had become inconceivable that any nation capable of practically single-handedly defeating the greatest armies since Attila the Hun could not now provide a decent lifestyle for all its citizens.

If prosperity had to be the destiny of the nation, many would and did ask during the dark years of McCarthyism why that prosperity, or at least the ideals it represented, occasionally eluded the average American. Why were there occasional recessions despite the apparently prosperous economy? Why were large segments of the American population, especially African and rural Americans, still living at or below the poverty level? Why, despite all the advantages of material success, were many school districts beset with the problems of juvenile delinquency? So certain had we become of our destiny that the only answer lay with foreign infiltration.

The movie industry capitalized on such fears, albeit in a subliminal way, and churned out many a melodrama involving some threat or other to the security of the United States or the world, equally synonymous for most Americans during the fifties. Soon-to-be film classics, such as *The Thing*, *Invasion of the Body Snatchers*, or *Not of This Earth*, would flicker on the projection screen the fears of a nation still trying to recover from the Great Depression. But this new generation did not hear the reassuring voice of a president warning them that the only thing they had to fear was fear itself. The voice now heard was the voice of Senator Joseph McCarthy, and he assured the nation that conversely, there was *indeed* a lot to fear, and that fear lay primarily with a communist invasion into the very bosom of sacred American institutions, such as the university, Capitol Hill, and especially Hollywood.

Many of America's principal writers, including the humorists who had penned their observations during the thirties, were now called in to question the implications of those observations, as well as their political affiliations. During this dark decade in American history, where everything was now turned upside down and revealed in a different context, the ghosts of the Depression again surfaced. Those who had felt a need to criticize American institutions as a means to rehabilitate our national consciousness and project alternate avenues for our escape from the Great Depression now found their sentiments and themselves under attack for being un-American in approach and ideal. The Depression had been a time of vast reorientations in terms of governmental policies, the family unit, racial agendas, and the like. Whereas in the past one had felt free to speak one's mind, now one was expected to say nothing at all. To be critical was to be un-American, if not subversive. So it was that the radical approaches and observations of the writers of the thirties were to be eschewed, tucked away in musty libraries, and ignored forever.

It is no wonder then that the biographers of American literary history have, even to this day, tended to ignore the best that was produced during that decade, to bypass their writings in virtually every modern anthology of American literature, and to downplay their importance in the shaping of our national heritage. Benchley, Perelman, Parker, Woollcott, and Nash have been all but forgotten in the American literary panorama, and if not for the occasional excerpt from survivors such as Thurber or White, would be as quiet as the dust that settles on their graves. Hopefully, their time will come, and in their writings will be seen again not only the reflections of a forgotten era but a foundation on which a country's future can be built.

————— . "The Secret Life of Walter Mitty," in *The Thurber Carnival*. Ed. James Thurber. New York: Harper Brothers, 1945; 47–51.

Tidwell, James (Ed). *A Treasury of American Folklore*. New York: Crown, 1956.

Wallach, Mark. *Christopher Morley*. Boston: Twayne, 1976.

Weisberger, Bernard (Ed). *The WPA Guide to America: The Best of the 1930's America as Seen by the Federal Writers' Project*. New York: Pantheon, 1985.

West, Nathanael. *Miss Lonelyhearts and the Day of the Locust*. 1933; reprint New York: New Directions, 1962.

White, E. B. *One Man's Meat*. New York: Harper, 1938.

Woollcott, Alexander. *While Rome Burns* in *The Portable Woollcott*. Ed. Joseph Hennessey. 1946; reprint Westport, CT: Greenwood, 1972; 41–366.

Wohl, Anthony (Ed). *The Victorian Family: Structure and Stresses*. New York: St. Martins, 1978.

Index

About the Author

ROBERT A. GATES is Associate Professor of English at St. John's University. His previous books include *The New York Vision: Interpretations of New York City in the American Novel* (1987) and *Eighteenth and Nineteenth Century American Drama* (1985).